THE ART & SKILL OF DEALING WITH PEOPLE

Brandon Toropov

MJF BOOKS

NEW YORK

Published by MJF Books
Fine Communications
322 Eighth Avenue
New York, NY 10001

Art & Skill of Dealing with People
Library of Congress Catalog Card Number 98-68231
ISBN 1-56731-310-8

This edition published by arrangement with Prentice Hall Direct, a division of
Prentice-Hall, Inc.

Production Editor: Zsuzsa Neff
Formatting/Interior Design: Dee Coroneos

Manufactured in the United States of America on acid-free paper

MJF Books and the MJF colophon are trademarks of Fine Creative Media, Inc.

VB   10   9   8   7   6   5   4

Acknowledgments

My grateful thanks go to Bert Holtje, Leslie Tragert, and my wife, Mary Toropov, for their ongoing support and assistance while this book was being written. In addition, no list of debts would be complete without acknowledging the trust, honesty, generosity, and encouragement of Glenn KnicKrehm, without whom this book, and so many others, would never have come into existence.

Dedication

To Mary, again.

How This Book Will Help You

Every day, it seems, we are asked to do more with less.

In today's leaner organizations, budgets are small, staffs are overloaded, and time is short. The managers who stand out from the pack seem to possess a special knack for getting results, with relative ease, from others in the organization. These people often show a remarkable ability to get people at various levels to look in the same direction and to focus on a common goal. Somehow, this type of manager delivers results even in the face of tight schedules and scarce resources. On the other hand, many others struggle constantly with peers, superiors, and subordinates, pleading, cajoling, and haggling, and even taking on a good deal of work that wasn't meant for them. Typically, their jobs expose them to excessive stress, and their departments have trouble meeting their goals.

Some managers get great results from their interactions with others. What do these managers know that other managers don't?

In today's business environment, the seemingly elusive ability to elicit the cooperation of others in short order is essential to your organization's—and your career's—success. Mastering that knack for enlisting the support of others is the topic of this book.

Interaction with other people is both an art and a skill, and you can develop it with practice.

Dealing effectively with others in a business setting is an art:

➤ Because it often requires a certain degree of creativity

➤ Because inspired improvisation will occasionally play a role in successful outcomes

---

Dealing effectively with others in a business setting is a skill:

➤ Because it arises out of craft, knowledge, and aptitudes that are developed over time

➤ Because you can, with a little practice, learn how to appeal to certain basic principles that will usually help you get the results you want

However effortless or inborn the ability to deal with others may seem on the surface, it is a talent you can master.

FOUR INITIAL MINDSETS

In the first part of this book, you will learn how to improve your listening skills—and how to deal with the *four distinct initial mindsets* from which people on the job tend to operate. You'll also find out about some of the major human motivators we tend to focus on through our own particular dominant mindset. You'll then learn how to apply your familiarity with these principles to:

➤ Get more done through your subordinates—and increase their level of job satisfaction

➤ Deal with your peers more effectively

➤ Interact with your superiors more constructively—and enhance your own career prospects by proving that you know how to make things happen for them

In the later parts of the book, you'll also learn some of the best ways to handle interactions with clients and customers, members of the media, and outside vendors. Finally, you'll learn about some of the most effective methods for handling conflict in the workplace, interacting harmoniously with groups, and using the skills outlined in this book to develop your own long-term leadership abilities.

You'll get the most out of what follows if you read Chapters One and Two thoroughly before proceeding to any other part of the book. I suggest that you read the book from beginning to end, but if you decide to focus on a particular chapter of interest to you, please be aware that the first two chapters contain important information you may need in order to implement the ideas outlined elsewhere.

SECOND NATURE

Once you review—and practice—the ideas in *The Art and Skill of Dealing with People,* you'll quickly begin to recognize ways in which you can improve your ability to interact with others during your workday, and you'll find that incorporating the solutions offered here will become second nature.

Dealing effectively with people—even difficult people—doesn't have to be a matter of making nerve-shredding concessions, or attending night-mare-inducing meetings when you can no longer postpone them, or enduring a seemingly endless series of high-stress confrontations. If you take the time to learn who you're dealing with and what's important to them, interacting with others can be a professional challenge you can meet, a matter of pointing the passions and predispositions of others in the right direction. After a while, you'll find that you've become quite accomplished at discreetly targeting people's energies toward mutually agreeable goals. You'll also find that something totally unexpected has happened. You'll find that you actually *enjoy* translating the pent-up aggressions and dissatisfactions of others into positive outcomes.

How's *that* for a surprise?

Contents

CHAPTER 1

MAKING MAJOR HUMAN MOTIVATORS WORK FOR YOU / 1

CHAPTER 2

LISTENING AT ALL LEVELS / 39

CHAPTER 3

DEALING WITH SUBORDINATES / 53

CHAPTER

DEALING WITH PEERS / 135

CHAPTER 5

DEALING WITH SUPERIORS / 171

CHAPTER 6

DEALING WITH CLIENTS AND CUSTOMERS / 209

CHAPTER 7

DEALING WITH THE MEDIA AND THE GENERAL PUBLIC / 229

CHAPTER 8

DEALING WITH OUTSIDE VENDORS / 251

CHAPTER 9

MANAGING CONFLICT / 267

CHAPTER 10

WINNING THE RESULTS YOU NEED FROM GROUPS / 279

CHAPTER 11

NURTURING YOURSELF—AND MASTERING LONG-TERM LEADERSHIP SKILLS / 291

Making
Major Human Motivators
Work for You

"I just wish he could understand where I'm coming from."
"It's like she's on another planet when I try to talk things over with her."
"He's got no idea what we're trying to get done here.
He might as well not even show up in the morning."

Did you ever feel as though you and a co-worker were speaking in completely different languages? Is there a colleague who always seems to "throw you a curveball" whenever the two of you must assess a situation together? Can you think of a member of your family or a professional acquaintance with whom even simple social interaction is difficult because each of you seems to look at the world in a way that seems to exclude the other?

It's easy for us to assume that the reasons for such frustrating exchanges is rooted in the other person's failure to see circumstances "accurately" or in his or her lack of "flexibility" when it comes to discussing and resolving important problems. But are matters really that stark?

When it comes to getting work accomplished with others, each of us has certain broadly defined priorities and predispositions. This is not to say that we will always approach problems in exactly the same way or that we will never view an issue differently over time. But we do bring a certain favored way of doing things to the situations in which we find ourselves.

Each of us, in other words, has a set of priorities, an unwritten but fundamental "to-do" list that tends to be the first one we appeal to when it's time to get something done. Sometimes those lists of priorities make sense

1

to other people; sometimes they don't. Sometimes *other* people's lists of priorities seem baffling to us. Why can't they focus on what's really important?

FOUR FRAMES OF REFERENCE

Based on observations of formal and informal interactions in real-world workplaces over a number of years, and on reading as much as I could find concerning workplace communication, I've concluded that there are four major *initial* frames of reference that people typically bring to bear in their dealings with others.

These are four basic styles of working that, taken together, describe the first instincts of the vast majority of people we come in contact with every day. The various followers of these four styles take radically different approaches to the task of getting things done.

I hesitate to call these four frames of reference "personality types" because personality is, by definition, an intensely subjective matter. Most psychology books that focus on "personality types" generally break the basic types down into a bewildering array of subcategories. (As well they should!) The tools we use for evaluating a task or sudden crisis, however, seem to me to be more likely to fall into a few distinct patterns. This book will focus less on defining another person's *identity* than a psychology textbook and more on learning the best ways to deal with others who may (or may not) respond to a situation in roughly the same way we would.

Let me be clear on this point! Two people who share exactly the same initial frame of reference can have radically *different* personalities. Even so, I've found that dealing with each of them effectively is a matter of appealing to certain key concerns they share on a fundamental level, despite their possible differences in temperament.

OBJECTIVES, PRIORITIES, AND PREDISPOSITIONS

This book is concerned with helping you *manage* the objectives, priorities, and predispositions of others. It will tell you about the styles of communication that are likely to arise from members of each of the four groups. It will also offer some strategies for overcoming the inevitable roadblocks your own predisposition may give rise to when you meet someone else's.

Becoming familiar with the four-part model can help you interact more effectively with others in the workplace (and in other settings as well, for that matter). Once you review the material in this chapter closely, you'll probably be in an excellent position to assess the viewpoints and needs of others more accurately than ever before. And you'll probably be well on the way to learning how to transform the negative messages and intentions others direct toward you into positive interactions—whether the people you're dealing with are subordinates, peers, superiors, clients, customers, members of the media, outside vendors, or anyone else.

WE'VE ALL GOT OPINIONS ABOUT HOW TO GET THINGS DONE

The four frames of reference are based on two priority scales. Most of us don't fall exactly in the middle of these two scales; we have a preference (and sometimes a very strong one!) about the way we should approach a task.

When it comes to first instincts, most of us prefer, *to some degree,* either to:

➤ Do things ourselves

or

➤ Get things done through others

When it comes to first instincts, most of us prefer, *to some degree,* to:

➤ Forget about the clock if we possibly can and check for every likely error or potential problem in a project

or

➤ Accomplish as much as we can within the time constraints imposed by a preassigned deadline—whether it's this afternoon or six months from now

PRIORITY SCALE:
Doing It Myself vs. Doing It Through Others

Jane and Rita, partners in a growing business, have a major presentation to prepare. Jane, who will be giving the presentation, quickly rattles off lists of things she wishes to cover during the talk. Rita jots them all down, adds a few important observations of her own, and helps to massage the staccato ideas Jane offers into a coherent outline.

At the same time, Rita is mentally reviewing the important questions of *what* needs to be assembled for the presentation and *how* the company's staff will work effectively to assemble the information, tables, and support materials Jane will need for her speech. Later in the day, Jane will work on her delivery, skipping over blank spots in the presentation until Rita can supply the facts and figures the staff will develop. Clearly, Jane and Rita have very different ways of doing things.

The division of labor between the two top people has emerged over time as the best between these two. Each knows there are limitations in her approach. For instance, in her dealings with the staff, Jane realizes she often has difficulty getting across key ideas or vital pieces of information, but she hasn't really developed a communication style that overcomes this problem. She may remark offhandedly to a junior team member, for instance, that there's "no hurry" in assembling a report. She means by this that she does not need the report by the close of business today, but by the close of business *tomorrow*. Jane's expected deadline, however clear it may be to her, remains unspoken. When the junior team member is called on the carpet for failing to provide Jane with what she needed, the atmosphere becomes strained. Jane knows how *she* would have handled the situation; why wouldn't everyone else have responded in the same way?

Such misunderstandings are much less common with Rita; she is far likelier to quantify what she needs, when she needs it, and, for that matter, what it should look like when she deals with others. These are all key pieces of information, but they are usually omitted by Jane, who tends to assume that others in the company will think the matter through using her approach, reach the same conclusions, and deliver the same results she would. By the same token, however, when Rita is placed in a situation in which she must make a difficult decision on her own, without Jane's guidance or the help of other key people in the organization, she has a tendency to "freeze up." The prospect of acting independently in an important area is profoundly frightening to Rita. She's likely to ask herself questions like these:

- What will happen if I miss something?

- Suppose one of my key assumptions is incorrect?

- Suppose one of my colleagues has some experience in this area that I should be taking advantage of?

Jane, on the other hand, is likely to ask herself questions like these:

- Why can't people understand things the first time around?

- Why do we have to spend so much time in meetings?

- What's wrong with acting on a hunch every once in a while?

Jane's first-instinct mindset, even when she delegates tasks to others, is best described as a "doing-it-myself" mindset. Rita's first-instinct mindset, even when she approaches projects independently, is best described as a "doing-it-through-others" mindset. *These two mindsets mark the two ends of the "who-does-it" priority scale.*

As far as these basic mindsets are concerned, neither Jane nor Rita is "right" in her approach to her work and neither is "wrong"—any more than an individual's eye color or taste in television shows can be said to be right or wrong.

Each mindset profoundly shapes the way its owner interacts with others, and each is capable of being employed effectively (and ineffectively!). For their company to work at peak efficiency, Jane and Rita have found that *both* of their outlooks are essential.

In Jane and Rita's case, their "opposing" mindsets have been a source of tension from time to time. Their differing world views have also emerged as the pillars of a trusting, mutually dependent relationship. Jane has come to depend on Rita's ability to communicate important initiatives and details to others in the organization; Rita has learned to rely on Jane's ability to size up situations quickly and to develop bold goals and initiatives that might not arise from a more consensus-driven style.

THE "WHO-DOES-IT" PRIORITY SCALE

First Priority: First Priority:

Doing It Myself ◄─────────────────────► Doing It Through Others

---

PRIORITY SCALE:

Getting It Out the Door vs. Getting It Error Free

Paul and Michael work at a large software company. Paul is in marketing; Michael is in engineering.

At team meetings about the release of a major new product, Paul focuses on the fact that retailers have been given three different dates for the release of a new software product. Three times, he points out, the retailers have watched the date come and go, with no product to put on the shelves. How, Paul asks, are relationships to be maintained with key vendors if the company's word ends up counting for nothing? And how is he to minimize the damage at key accounts when he himself has no idea when the software will actually ship?

Michael, who is heading up the program's bug-elimination effort, does not dispute this account of things, but he argues in turn that shipping the product in accordance with any one of the announced dates would have been disastrous, even though doing so might have seemed the easiest thing in the world. Michael paints a grim picture of the consequences that would have followed: Although the software looks impressive, thorough testing keeps turning up errors, and some of them are potentially serious. Michael admits having missed the deadlines, but he points out that he has probably saved the company millions of dollars in customer-service headaches by doing so. How can it possibly benefit the company, he asks, to ship product that no doubt still has grave defects waiting to be discovered?

Paul's career has been based, to a large degree, on making and, so far as humanly possible, keeping time-related commitments. Paul prides himself on his ability to deliver on schedules he has promised to his customers—or at least come as close as he possibly can to that goal.

Michael's career, by contrast, has been marked by pursuing a conviction that *something* is wrong with the product he is developing. If only he or one of his team members can track down exactly what that something is, he'll have a good shot at averting a potential disaster. More often than not, Michael is right: There is a flaw lurking somewhere. And more often than not, he and his team fix the problem.

It's not that Paul is blind to issues of quality or that Michael has no understanding of what a deadline means. Each is eager to ship the best possible product; neither is hoping to disappoint customers. Although during tense meetings such as the one described here the two usually find themselves guarding different "corners," each knows that the other is performing an invaluable function. Paul and Michael simply have profoundly different emphases when it comes to evaluating a situation.

For Paul, it's tempting to ask questions like these:

- What good will a technically perfect product be—if, indeed, such a product can actually be developed—if the company's competitors bring out a rival release ahead of time and steal away customers?

- Is there a strategic cost associated with spending so much time developing a piece of software that the generation of computers for which it was written is no longer state-of-the-art? Does the company then return to the drawing board—and begin *another* round of product development that incorporates new features, each of which must be just as exhaustively checked for errors? How would the cycle ever end?

- Are all errors really of the same potential magnitude? Is it worth holding up a multi-million dollar release for *any* error?

For Michael, it's tempting to ask questions like these:

- How meaningful will keeping retailers happy seem when the company is swamped by calls from angry customers demanding to know why their software refuses to function properly?

- Why can't "hard-dollar" costs (including the cost of lost sales) be associated with the customer-service function as readily as "hard-dollar" revenue estimates are associated with the marketing function?

- Why does talk about quality and product excellence fade into the background when it's most essential—during the time when errors can still be addressed?

Paul's first-instinct mindset is best described as a "get-it-out-the-door" mindset, even when, as often occurs, he is helping to resolve an important quality-control issue. Michael's first-instinct mindset is best described as a "get-it-error-free" mindset, even when, as often occurs, he is offering advice on the most efficient means of completing a task. *These two mindsets mark the two ends of the "how-do-we-do-it" priority scale.* *

Just as Jane and Rita did, Paul and Michael each offer important perspectives when it comes to decision making, problem resolution, and long-term planning. Each has a tendency to see things in a particular way; each is a valuable member of the team.

Neither Paul nor Michael is "right" in his approach to his work. Both mindsets are valid ways of perceiving and reacting to one's situation. Neither Paul nor Michael has a monopoly on accuracy when it comes to resolving problems, and both approaches are essential to making sense of the issues their business faces.

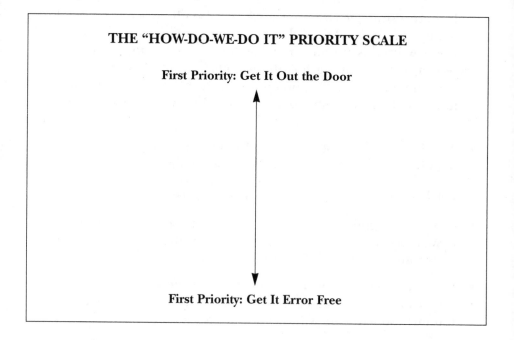

THE "HOW-DO-WE-DO IT" PRIORITY SCALE

First Priority: Get It Out the Door

First Priority: Get It Error Free

---

*Dr. Rick Brinkman and Dr. Rick Kirschner discuss a similar continuum of predispositions, the "perfectionism" and "getting it done" viewpoints. They cover this topic in their fine book *Dealing With People You Can't Stand,* McGraw-Hill, 1994.

FRAMES OF REFERENCE

Do these two poles sound familiar? Most businesspeople I talk to can recall dozens, if not hundreds, of discussions that have revolved around issues similar to those Jane and Rita faced, and just as many that are highly reminiscent of the varying viewpoints expressed by Paul and Michael.

As I noted earlier, most of us tend to operate, not exclusively but nevertheless primarily, within one or the other of the mindsets on these two scales. It is a rare person who has absolutely no initial preference about whether or not a typical task is best undertaken on one's own or through arranging work with others. And it is a rare person who does not view a new project as either a deadline-oriented commitment (in which one does the best one can within a specific time frame) or an error-eradication-oriented commitment (in which one strives to achieve the lowest possible incidence of error).

This is not to say that our initial predispositions in these areas make us automatons! During the course of a given day, we may find it appropriate to adopt, for a time, a viewpoint that is not our first instinct. That ability is a sign of flexibility, and flexibility is an important factor for the successful resolution of problems. Indeed, as we will soon learn, when it comes to dealing with others, flexibility with regard to initial predispositions is essential.

It's a good bet that the people we find most frustrating on a day-to-day basis are those who make little or no effort to view matters from any vantage point other than the easiest one (from their point of view, at any rate) on a particular scale. By the same token, if *we* show little or no flexibility and make a habit of clinging tenaciously to the far end of one of the two poles described for virtually every discussion of strategy or resource allocation, we are likely to find a good many discussions ending in deadlock and disappointment.

When people insist on tackling massive projects entirely on their own, even though assistance is available . . . or insist on "delegating" even the most inconsequential tasks to others or recklessly cut corners to meet a deadline or take a mandate to "improve quality" as an invitation to painstakingly review every comma, regardless of schedule or resource issues—in short, when people follow their predispositions to the bitter end and have no interest in issues of balance or in alternate viewpoints—then there are problems. As each of the two fictional cases illustrates, balance is everything when it comes to working effectively with others.

TWO SCALES, FOUR SQUARES

All four points on the two priority scales can be incorporated within a "four-square" model. Each corner of the large square identifies a smaller square corresponding to one of four basic predisposition sets. These four sets match the first-instinct tendencies of the vast majority of people who are trying to *get something accomplished* on the job or in virtually any other setting.

Get It Out the Door

Lone Ranger	Cheerleader
Sharpshooter	Professor

Get It Done Myself (left)   **Get It Done Through Others** (right)

Get It Error-Free

FOUR WAYS OF APPROACHING THINGS

For many people, the four groups outlined above look familiar almost immediately. For others, the categories take a little getting used to. Here are four thumbnail sketches; we'll go into more detail later.

Can you think of someone who always says (or might as well always say) . . .

"I Can Spot Disaster on the Horizon!"

Pro: Will often catch potentially catastrophic errors. Con: May drive people crazy with "nit-picking." The Sharpshooter lives to track down mistakes . . . and usually considers that end worthy for its own sake.

Perhaps you can think of someone you work with who manages to turn the tasks that come her way into a relentless search for quality, and who effectively performs this work more or less on her own. She's the one who will take well-earned delight in having found a discrepancy or inconsistency in that pile of important documents she was given to review. That's the lower left-hand corner of the square, the Sharpshooter.

Think of the *Sharpshooter* as the attorney who stays up late at night reviewing a legal document for every possible problem—or as the engineer who can spot dozens of possible flaws and cite their exact causes.

Can you think of someone who always says (or might as well always say) . . .

"I Can Make Big Things Happen All By Myself!"

Pro: Has been known to move mountains. Con: Often overcommits or makes unrealistic predictions. The Lone Ranger lives to work miracles . . . and craves individual credit for having done so.

If the Sharpshooter lives to find flaws and put things on hold, the Lone Ranger lives to bring new projects into existence. Did you think of someone who's happiest when she's closeted in a corner, hacking away at a time-sensitive project? She's probably one of the people who, from school days onward, always seemed to "get her best work done under pressure." She may wait until the last minute to attack a project (though not all Lone Rangers do so), and she is likely to find it easier to undertake something herself than to explain how to do it to someone else. That's the upper left-hand corner of the square, the Lone Ranger.

Think of the *Lone Ranger* as the "one-person band" who delights in developing new ideas and approaches more or less independently: the prolific artist, say, or the multitalented team member who knows enough to get by in a great many different subjects, and, although she may not be an expert in any one field, nevertheless delights in putting that knowledge to practical use.

Can you think of someone who always says (or might as well always say) . . .

"I Can Put All the Puzzle Pieces Together!"

Pro: Has a way of turning chaotic groups into well-oiled machines. Con: May get distracted with endless minutia. The Professor lives to anticipate and overcome problems . . . and keep the operation running smoothly.

Perhaps you recalled someone who works well with teams, and whose ongoing focus is on seamless, trouble-free operation. This is the team member who gets most excited when quantifying the department's results, or establishing "tolerances" for particular performance levels. She may take a special joy in setting up—and closely monitoring—systems and procedures that have been implemented to help others work more efficiently and with less conflict. She's just as concerned about flaws as the Sharpshooter, but she's focused more on implementing workable *systems* than on spotting potential *problems*. The lower right-hand corner of the square describes this group.

Think of the *Professor* as the team member who brings order out of confusion: the supervisor who helps others make sense of a challenging piece of computer software, or the office manager who helps to make sure that people are working harmoniously. . . and aren't duplicating one another's efforts or engaging in sabotage.

Can you think of someone who always says (or might as well always say) . . .

"I Can Get Almost Anybody Excited About Almost Anything!"

Pro: Makes people feel great. Con: May be perceived as someone who "talks a good game" or is willing to "say whatever people want to hear." The Cheerleader lives to interact with others . . . and often excels at getting others engaged in the latest adventure.

Perhaps you found yourself thinking of a "team-first" co-worker whose specialty is inspiring both himself and others when it comes to meeting a preassigned deadline. He's the "people person" who continually finds new ways to make the department's current goal exciting, who posts signs highlighting the "days-till-deadline" status all over the office. Not all Cheerleaders are inherently optimistic, but they do, by definition, enjoy talking things over with others. These are the people in the upper right-hand corner of the square, the Cheerleaders,

Think of the *Cheerleader* as the individual who excels at "working the room": the executive who radiates enthusiasm, the entrepreneur who knows what bankers or customers want to hear, the salesman who delights in face-to-face presentations, or the politician who lives to stir the crowd to action.

SOUND FAMILIAR?

You may already have a good idea of which group best describes your own outlook. (For the record, I'm a confirmed Lone Ranger. I tend to get restless when I deal with long procedural discussions and wide-ranging attempts to "gather input" and I have also been known to chafe at the bit when trying to explain a complex procedure to someone else. As a general rule, I'm most comfortable thinking about a current project and working within the context of a specific time-frame.

Once again, please bear in mind that we're talking about working *styles and priorities,* not "personality types" as such. The question is, what key concerns do people focus on most easily and most readily? The answers, I believe, are to be found in the four-square model outlined here.

Typically, each of the four groups has something important to contribute to any given initiative. In fact, you may conclude that no critical initiative should be considered complete until one valued team member from each group has had the chance to review it thoroughly.

The perfect initiative may well be one that the Lone Ranger develops from scratch, the Sharpshooter troubleshoots and redirects, the Professor plans internally and helps to execute, and the Cheerleader inspires everyone to complete on time.

THE FOUR MINDSETS IN DEPTH

What, specifically, can you expect to encounter when dealing with representatives of each of the four categories? Here's a detailed look at some of the most prominent traits of the members of all four groups.

➤ **Lone Rangers** are self-directed, goal-oriented, and generally quite persistent. They take deadlines very seriously indeed. They occasionally overcommit, but only because they have great faith in their own abilities.

Lone Rangers tend to be able to summon tremendous inner resources as deadlines approach. It's worth noting that they do not always *hit* the sometimes imposing deadlines they set for themselves . . . but they always seem to approach the work to be done from a deadline orientation. They sometimes make the mistake of believing that the others they come in contact with are as capable of sustained bursts of highly productive work as they are. This error leads to one of the classic challenges faced by Lone Rangers who try to move into a managerial role. When, during "crunch time," team members do not perform at the levels the Lone Ranger associates with his or her own work at such times, the manager assumes (usually wrongly) that his or her charges are slacking off.

Successful Lone Rangers in the managerial ranks typically overcome this problem by either surrounding themselves with *other* Lone Rangers, or by making the extremely difficult transition necessary to alter their expectations about the work of others. Lone Rangers typically focus with *extreme intensity* on one project at a time; once they commit to working on a project, it's as if the rest of the universe has ceased to exist. Early in their careers, the long-term planning skills of the Lone Ranger often need work, although they are certainly capable of improvement in this area—or, indeed, in any area they associate strongly with a personal challenge.

> **Sharpshooters** are just as self-directed and persistent as Lone Rangers; their primary focus, however, is on bringing their technical knowledge (which can be staggering) to bear to a particular assignment, and finding the "holes" in a particular system.

For Sharpshooters, finding flaws (and, to a lesser degree, developing potential solutions for those flaws) is a lifelong obsession. They search doggedly for the inconsistencies they assume are present, and when they find the inconsistencies, they feel a flush of triumph. Sharpshooters typically excel at troubleshooting and design-related tasks; they may make excellent engineers, consultants, or attorneys.

Their pronouncements, while usually superbly reasoned, can sometimes come across as harsh and tactless. Some Sharpshooters, namely those who have no taste for interpersonal conflict, have learned the advantage of indirect communication styles when sharing their evaluations with colleagues. (They might ask, for instance, whether a particular paragraph of a contract has been reviewed closely, rather than isolate the sentence they feel contains an error. They will not, however, take "No, it hasn't," as the final word on the matter.) Other Sharpshooters rely very heavily indeed on the written word, a medium that allows them to support their conclusions without fear of interruption, and one that they may come to prefer above all others when it comes to communicating with others.

As a general rule, Sharpshooters are comfortable making decisions on their own when they feel they have gathered all the necessary facts. For Sharpshooters, the worst sin is overlooking a critical detail. Because they excel at unearthing such details, they expect others to spot logical flaws or errors in reasoning as quickly as they do.

As valuable as their observations can be to an undertaking's success, Sharpshooters often point their "something-must-be-wrong-here-and-I'm-going-to-find-out-what-it-is" focus in the wrong directions. When attending industry trade shows, for instance, they have been known to drive sales managers to distraction by expounding at length to potential customers on why the company's product *isn't* an exact fit for them.

➢ **Professors** share with Sharpshooters a penchant for technical detail. In their world, however, the focus is on developing policies, procedures, and systems that keep *everyone* focused on high-quality activity.

Professors love to measure, quantify, and justify. They conduct trial experiments, and they measure the outcomes that result against predetermined criteria. To be sure, Sharpshooters may engage in such activities from time to time, but when the Professor probes, tests, and demands data, she does so *in order to help others resolve errors in their own work,* preferably before the errors arise in the first place. Professors often show a profound concern for helping others to avoid mistakes; sometimes this concern is misread by the people the Professor is seeking to help.

In addition to testing and reviewing, many Professors take a special joy in establishing and/or implementing systems that will be of benefit to others.

Although they typically rely heavily on technology and established organizational procedures, Professors are far less likely to call attention to their own technical expertise than Sharpshooters. They live to create harmonious, effective interactions among their colleagues. Properly encouraged, they are likely to become superb problem-solvers, and not simply by attaching blinking neon signs to the mistakes of others in the hope of blustering them into correcting a problem themselves. (This is a tactic employed by a few of the more troublesome Sharpshooters.)

Unlike Sharpshooters, Professors make a point of involving others in key decisions. If anything, Professors run the risk of asking for *too much* in the way of charts, graphs, and trial runs. They have also been known to have difficulty embracing initiatives that they believe will adversely affect an important constituency. Professors have been known to throw roadblocks in front of important new initiatives in a seemingly endless quest for "new data."

> ➤ **Cheerleaders** share with Professors a reluctance to alienate others. They are generally optimistic and gregarious; they operate with a time-sensitive, goal-oriented focus.

The upbeat enthusiasm Cheerleaders radiate for their chosen goal has a fortunate habit of rubbing off on others. (The Lone Ranger's brand of enthusiasm, by contrast, is often more than a little intimidating.) Cheerleaders *do* want to avoid major errors and help others to work efficiently and harmoniously, of course, but they typically emphasize the specifics of a particular, imminent, goal rather than the intelligent design of systems and procedures. Cheerleaders generally love to talk to other people.

When a Cheerleader is presented with a daunting problem or challenge, his reaction is typically to cite his team's past accomplishments in a similar area. Often, a Cheerleader will happily go out on a limb for his group; he is likely to display an inherent trust in their abilities and level of commitment, and he will, if the situation requires, take heat for those with whom he works.

Not surprisingly, Cheerleaders are often quite popular with others. They may make excellent managers, and they may also inspire truly remarkable degrees of loyalty and dedication among their charges. However, they may run the risk of "assuming the best in people" even when a major performance problem or information gap is staring them in the face. A few Cheerleaders, their name notwithstanding, make the managerial transition all too successfully, and overcompensate for their initial instincts by learning to hold their subordinates to extremely high and often unrealistic standards.

As managers, Cheerleaders typically have difficulty learning to discipline or replace team members. And while firing someone is no one's idea of a good time, for the Cheerleader it is a little like disowning a member of the family.

EVERYBODY'S RIGHT, NOBODY'S RIGHT

Each of the four predisposition groups is valuable; each can provide an important viewpoint for any matter under discussion. Each is capable of perceiving things that those in one of the other three groups *cannot* typically provide.

Although a given organization may feature a predominance of one kind of team member at various points in the organization (thanks in part to the fact that people tend to hire others who share their outlook on things), there's a good argument to be made that a truly balanced, informed approach to problem-solving will call on the skills of all four predisposition groups.

A word of warning: Please remember that the four predisposition groups outlined above represent *initial instinctive responses,* not unwavering principles governing every possible interaction in which we may find ourselves. We are discussing the ways we are *likeliest* to think about approaching a given task, not about standards that can be counted on to dominate each instance of communication with a friend or colleague.

After all, every individual is unique, and dealing with people in all their diversity requires, as I have said, flexibility and no small degree of creativity. Some people seem to fit the patterns I've just laid down more or less perfectly, because they rely on their first instinctive responses very heavily indeed, and they rarely make an effort to approach things another way. Other people follow their initial, instinctive responses at some times, but not at others. But the vast majority of people *do have initial, instinctive responses* that fall into the outline above, and that serve them well *most* of the time. If you know what those responses are (and what your own instinctive response is likely to be), you'll be in a much better position to interact harmoniously with others.

"THE SWORD THAT KILLS US IS THE SWORD THAT SAVES US"

If you recognize your own predisposition group immediately (and that's not unlikely), you may feel not only a sense of recognition, but also a certain pride. "That," you may find yourself thinking, "is the style that *works.*"

This attitude is often reflected in such statements as these:

- "If we can't keep an eye out for minor errors as well as major ones, we're in deep trouble." (Outlook: Sharpshooter.)

- "People who need a lot of hand holding, or who can't tear into a project right away, are usually highly inefficient." (Outlook: Lone Ranger.)

- "There's no way the organization can run well if people are unwilling to follow the procedures that have been set up." (Outlook: Professor.)

- "People who won't take the time to sit down and talk through problems are in denial." (Outlook: Cheerleader.)

Your mindset is yours. Embrace it. Use it. Get the most out of it, because it has benefits to offer you and the organization you represent. But make an effort not to judge the rest of the world by it.

That mindset may work for you, in certain situations, and in certain contexts. (Then again, from time to time, it may not.) But the only real style that works in *all* settings involves being able to view things, as appropriate, as *each of the four groups would*, if only for a brief period.

All four methods of approaching a situation can be used constructively, and all four can, by the same token, be pushed to an unhealthy extreme. There is a Zen Buddhist saying that points out that "the sword that kills the man is the sword that saves the man." This means that the various qualities we find in ourselves—the persistence in the face of obstacles, say, that marks the work of Sharpshooters and Lone Rangers—are neither good nor bad in the abstract. They exist on their own terms, and must be treated with respect, rather than subjected to snap judgments.

Let me offer an example that puts my own group under the microscope. We Lone Rangers (at any rate, a sizable portion of us) share a particular kind of persistence that may take the form of stubbornness or even the refusal to admit an error that is obvious to others . . . and perhaps, secretly, to us as well. In certain settings, this is a distinct disadvantage. It leaves us open to the possibility of working without the right information, and it may even cause resentment among the people who have to interact with us. Our single-mindedness may come across as arrogance or an unwillingness to change a position under any circumstances.

And yet that same persistence may also allow us to work wonders. It may take the form of a single-minded commitment to an objective, or the ability to withstand hardship or unexpected setbacks. It may help us to achieve, more or less on our own, goals that are key to the organization's future. Sometimes, our inability or unwillingness to step aside from a particular way of doing things may serve to inspire those around us.

It may be convenient, in limited sets of circumstances, to view the first set of examples of our own persistence as "productive" and the second set of examples as "unproductive." These are accurate enough assessments when viewed in their proper context, but attaching "right" and "wrong" labels to what is essentially a single trait, as though those labels applied to each and every situation in which we might show persistence, is misguided.

For the often bull-headed Lone Ranger, there are times to stand one's ground, and times to admit defeat. Identifying and acting appropriately during the latter cases may be a bit of a learning experience. Sometimes we recognize them without difficulty. Sometimes we don't. Similar advantages and disadvantages accompany virtually every trait of every person you encounter every day.

The trick—or, to be more accurate, the art—of dealing effectively with others is to get their traits working productively, in a manner that is beneficial both to you and to the person with whom you're dealing. All of us are inclined to accomplish *something,* and usually we are inclined to do so in a particular way. The question is, is what we're after constructive, and are the ways we're going about getting what we want likely to work out well for everyone involved? Often, very small adjustments can help to point "bad attitudes" in the "right" direction. This book will help you help others to make those adjustments.

Of course, this is a talent that is acquired over time, not in a flash of inspiration. It requires not only practice, but also a certain healthy knowledge of the common problems and opportunities faced by members of each group as they deal with one another day by day.

WHERE DO YOU FIT IN?

Even if you feel strongly that you fit into a particular corner of the square, it's worthwhile to review your own typical response patterns carefully before you move ahead in this book.

Tempting though it may be to conclude that your first instinct is best reflected by the Lone Ranger, the Sharpshooter, the Professor, or the Cheerleader mindset, you should stop for a moment and analyze yourself. There are two reasons for this.

For one thing, we often don't see ourselves with perfect clarity, and reviewing the specifics of your situation may help you to settle your personal style more accurately. It will come as no surprise to learn that knowing, with some certainty, which of the four mindsets you fall into is essential if you hope to manage your interactions with others in the most effective way.

The second reason is just as straightforward. You are interested not only in *your own* instinctive first responses to situations, but also in the instinctive first responses of *those people you must deal with every day.* By focusing for a moment now on the specifics of the two priority scales that underlie the four-square model, you'll get a better idea of how best to classify the actions of others.

An investment of just a little of your time will help you reap major benefits when it comes to familiarizing yourself with the potential (and potential blind spots) of members of all four groups. Before long, you'll know for certain which of the four groups best describes your style. You'll probably also be able to identify members of each of the four instinctive-reaction groups almost immediately. That means you'll probably be in a good position to correct some of the most common communication problems you have with others.

Take a moment before proceeding any further in this book. Using a separate sheet of paper, answer each of the following questions honestly. Don't answer according to how you think you "should" respond; there are no right answers to the following quiz. There are only answers that accurately reflect the way you look at things!

If you are unsure of which of the two answers to select, or if you feel that neither is a completely accurate representation of the way you'd approach the problem outlined, pick the answer that most nearly reflects your own outlook.

Have you got a piece of paper and a pencil ready? Start in!

TEST ONE

1. When you tackle household chores, do you:

   a. work at various jobs until the house looks to you as though it's been thoroughly cleaned; or

   b. make a list (mentally or on paper, formal or informal) of tasks that seem appropriate, complete them, and then move on to something else besides housekeeping?

2. When you need to find an item in a book and you do not know what page the information you want appears on, do you *first:*

   a. consult the index (or table of contents); or

   b. leaf through the body of the book, scanning for headlines that seem appropriate to the question at hand?

3. You have parked in a metered parking space in the city; you are a few minutes late for a very brief, but important, meeting with a vendor at

which you will pick up a formal bid for a major project. You have no change for the meter. Do you:

a. rush across into a nearby store to get change for the meter before going to your appointment; or

b. proceed directly to your brief appointment, then return as quickly as possible to your car?

4. A friend in another city calls up one evening to ask your advice on a major career move she's contemplating, a move that is likely to have lifelong impact. She informs you that your opinion means so much to her that she will probably weigh it more than that of anyone else to whom she speaks. You're under no time pressure; this is the first you've heard of her plans. Do you:

a. listen to her outline her plans, then tell her that you'd like to think things over before offering advice on so important a topic; or

b. during that conversation, offer the best parallels from your own experience (or the experience of others with whom you're familiar), then offer a brief conjecture about what you might do if you were in your friend's situation?

5. You are responsible for purchasing a new phone system for your firm. The model you are leaning toward has all the features you want, and it does not exceed the budget figure you have been given to work with. Four of the company's five department heads have seen the model you are considering; each is satisfied with your selection. The fifth, however, is on vacation this week, as is the head of the company. The fifth department head is a veteran member of the firm whose people will use the phone system heavily. None of the members of his department are available to discuss the matter with you this week. If you issue a nonrevokable purchase order for the system within 48 hours, the company will save 40% on installation fees. Assuming that you have been granted authority by the head of the company to "make the best decision you can" in this matter, do you:

a. wait until the fifth department head returns to offer input, and forego the discount on the installation fee; or

b. authorize the purchase?

6. When you arrive at the supermarket one Sunday afternoon, you realize that you've left your lengthy grocery list at home. Assuming that there is no significant time pressure, do you:

   a. try to recreate (or return home to retrieve) the list before you begin shopping; or

   b. begin shopping, hoping that the products you see in the aisle will help stimulate your memory as to what was on the list?

7. You've just purchased a new piece of computer graphic-design software. After installing it on your computer's hard drive, do you:

   a. review the manual for instructions on getting started; or

   b. see what happens when you call the new program up and issue a few commands?

8. You're having quality-control problems with a key vendor, but do not wish to terminate the relationship. Do you:

   a. summarize the problems as you see them in a detailed memorandum, mail them to the vendor with several samples of the defective product you've received, and ask for a detailed, point-by-point review of the issues you've raised; or

   b. call the vendor directly so you can discuss the quality problems?

9. You and your spouse (or roommate) have discussed changing long-distance telephone services. A salesperson calls your home one evening while your house mate is away. The salesperson is offering a new long-distance telephone service that sounds like a significantly better deal than your current company offers you. You ask a few questions, then ask for a written information packet, or a call back when your house mate is home, so that the two of you can evaluate the service the salesperson is proposing. The salesperson says, "I'd be happy to send you some information on what we have to offer. Now I know you need to review what I'm going to send along, but I'm just wondering: Based on what you've heard so far, if you had to make a decision right now on our service—and I know you don't—but if you *did* need to make a decision based on what I've told you so far about what we have to offer, what would it be?" Do you:

   a. tell the salesperson you're not in a position to answer that question at this point; or

b. honestly assess the merits of the service he's described, tell the salesperson what your decision would be if you had to make it now, and remind him that no decision will be final until you discuss the matter with your house mate?

10. At the end of a cab ride, the driver, with whom you have been conversing pleasantly for some time, informs you that he has no change for a five-dollar bill. You believe him, and are quite confident that there is no attempt to take advantage of you. The fare is five dollars and eighty cents. You have only two five-dollar bills. Assuming you have arrived at your intended destination five minutes before an important meeting, do you:

a. try to talk the driver into accepting a personal check, even though he has informed you that he never accepts such payment; or

b. either overtip him or underpay him?

11. You're moving from a small apartment to a larger one. As you pack your possessions into boxes, do you:

a. classify each item as it goes into the box, assigning each box a specific category and/or number, so that you can decide where best to place items of a certain type when you unpack according to the new floor plan; or

b. place all the items in a particular broad functional area into boxes that you label with very broad names—such as "living room things"—or no names at all?

12. You're a self-taught artist who has never worked professionally. A friend notices one of the drawings you have sketched in your spare time and asks whether you'd consider submitting some of your work to an acquaintance of hers in the advertising industry. She thinks that if you do so, there is the possibility of some freelance work coming your way in the future. Your friend does not know exactly what types of drawings her friend is currently looking for. Do you:

a. ask your friend to learn more about the projects the contact in the advertising industry typically works on, so that you can better target the drawings you pass along to her needs; or

b. pass along copies of three drawings about which both you and your friend are extremely enthusiastic, because you are confident they show the ability to master a number of styles, and represent the very best work you are capable of doing?

13. Why did you last change the oil in your car? Choose the statement below that best reflects your answer. (If you do not have a car, or do not have responsibility for changing the oil in it, please answer this question based on the last car for which you *did* have this responsibility, or based on the approach you would probably take with your own car.)

   a. "There is a regular schedule I follow for changing the oil based on the specific mileage readings on the odometer." (Or: " . . . on regular visits to service outlets.") (Or: ". . . on reminders I write for myself on the calendar.")

   b. "It seemed to have been a while since I last changed the oil." (Or: "Someone or something reminded me about how important it was to change the oil periodically.") (Or: "The car's information system signaled that the car needed oil.")

14. You have mislaid the cards that accompanied the gifts you received at your birthday party. Twenty-five friends attended the party. You got quite a few gifts, all of them of the "inexpensive-but-thoughtful" variety. Now it's time for you to write out thank-you cards. Although you know *who* was at the party, in about half-a-dozen cases, you can't be sure about what each person gave you. Do you:

   a. call up a close friend and attempt, through a process of elimination, to determine which friend gave which gift in each and every case, so you can write a note to each giver that specifies the gift he or she gave; or

   b. write thank-you notes that specifically mention the gift when you clearly recall what it was, but write generalized thank-you notes for the six or so guests whose presents you can't remember?

15. You are eating out at a nice restaurant with four friends. No one is planning to order an extremely expensive entree, but there are price variations among the items people plan to order. On general principle, would you rather:

   a. ask for separate checks (or in some other way determine what each person should pay for an order) so that a person who selects a less expensive item does not end up paying the same amount as a person who orders a more expensive item; or

    b. assume the difference among the orders is not all that significant in the long run, since you will all probably eat out again together in the near future, and split the check five ways?

16. Your CD player can be programmed to select songs from a number of discs at random, or to play a predetermined selection of songs in a particular order. You are throwing a party tonight, and you have loaded five of your favorite CDs into the machine. Assuming you are under no significant time pressure, will you:

    a. select a large number of favorite songs that will play, in the order you select them, until you change the settings on the CD player; or

    b. allow the machine to choose songs at random from the CDs, all of which feature music you like a great deal?

17. A new friend of yours who happens to be a vegetarian is coming over for dinner. You are not a vegetarian. Do you:

    a. call your friend beforehand and review the specifics of what you're planning to cook and how you're planning to cook it; or

    b. plan an entree that does not include meat and prepare it as you normally would?

18. Which of the following statements best reflects the way you handle the task of writing Christmas or holiday-season cards? (If you do not send holiday cards, or do not generally have responsibility for doing so, please answer this question based on the last time you did have this responsibility, or based on the approach you would probably take if you were assigned the job of sending holiday greeting cards to your company's clients, vendors, and associates.)

    a. "I make a list of the specific people who should receive holiday cards, then buy a supply of cards that is sufficient for the task—or perhaps slightly in excess of the number I've arrived at."

    b. "I purchase what seems to me, based on past experience and my own instincts, to be an adequate supply of cards, then develop a list that allocates the available cards."

19. You have been asked to bring coffee, doughnuts, and sweetrolls for an early-morning meeting of managers. Do you:

    a. conduct a brief canvassing effort of the various managers the afternoon before the meeting to find out what kinds of coffee, doughnuts, and sweetrolls they prefer; or

b. stop in at the doughnut shop early the next morning, making sure to get a variety of items (i.e., both decaffeinated and nondecaffeinated coffee, sugar and cream on the side, and "grab bag" selections of doughnuts and sweetrolls) that are likely to satisfy everyone?

20. While taking a walk in the park, you find someone's knapsack. It contains a wallet with information that leads you to believe the owner, whose name is Julia Gail, lives at a particular nearby apartment building. However, you cannot determine what the owner's apartment number is, and there are several hundred units in the building in question. No names are listed on the outside of the building. Assuming that you have to choose between one of the two options below, do you:

a. call each of the five "J. Gail" listings that appear, with no address information, in the local phone directory; or

b. buzz the superintendent of the building, explain the situation to him, and give him the knapsack?

TEST TWO

1. Picture yourself as you were at eight years of age. Which of the options below would you have been *more likely* to choose as a leisure activity, if both were available at the same time?

a. Reading a favorite comic book.

b. Playing Old Maid.

2. A sudden product-related crisis has arisen at work, and it has fallen to you to approve a course of action to respond to it. Which of the two statements below *most nearly* describes the approach you would be likely to take?

a. "I would hold a series of brief, one-on-one meetings with everyone who might be in a position to provide key facts. Then I would gather a small group of high-level colleagues, people with whom I could share my observations and check them for accuracy, and from whom I could get feedback on the benefits and drawbacks of the various courses of action I was considering. If one of the colleagues offered a course of action that varied radically from the options on the table, I would hear that person out before making a final decision."

b. "I would get the best available summary of the current state of affairs that I could, then I would gather together a group of trusted colleagues, share that summary with them, and ask each of them in turn for their assessments of the situation we faced. After discussing the situation thoroughly in this way, I would ask colleagues (or groups of colleagues) to develop recommendations on the best way to proceed from where we stand now. To insure that we did not overlook any important perspectives, I would consider asking groups that represent opposing points of view to develop their own sets of recommendations independently, and I might even ask each group to evaluate the specific suggestions of the group(s) with which they disagree. "

3. A coworker asks you to prepare an important speech. You spend several days doing so. Assuming that you must choose between one of the options that follow, would you, before you pass along your draft:

a. put it away for one or two days, then review it closely one last time for errors or inconsistencies; or

b. show it to several trusted friends, elicit their comments, and, based on those comments, make substantial changes?

4. You work as one of several editors at a magazine. An overworked coworker asks you to check an upcoming cover story from an outside author. It's the proofreader's week off, and she wants you to check the piece for spelling and grammatical errors. After reviewing the article for only a few minutes, you find, to your horror, that the author's article contains not only typographical errors, but major structural problems and several outright inaccuracies. You conclude that you could conceivably resolve the problems you've uncovered, but you know it will take two or more days of research and review time for you to do so. The publisher of the magazine has recently announced a round of belt-tightening measures, and is in no mood to discuss unbudgeted manuscript rescue work assignments for freelancers. As it happens, the author of the piece has recently been hospitalized after an automobile accident; he will happily review any changes your magazine suggests, but is in no position to rework the article himself. Which of the following approaches *most resembles* the one you would be likely to adopt to deal with this problem?

a. Tell your overworked colleague about the problems you've identi-fied, and let her know that you're willing to spend the time neces-sary to work the manuscript into publishable shape, but that she owes you one.

b. Tell your overworked colleague that there are serious problems with the article, and suggest that you both go to the publisher's office to discuss the options available for either rescheduling or canceling the cover story.

5. A nasty piece of office gossip is circulating about you. It's not true. You have no idea who's spreading the rumor. Which of the following two approaches would most likely reflect your *first instinct* upon hearing the rumor yourself? Even if you might catch yourself halfway through the exchange, select the response that would most accurately reflect your first reaction.

a. Vehemently deny the rumor when it reaches you, and let the per-son who passed it along know that, when you find out who started saying such thoughtless things about you, you won't hesitate to give that person a piece of your mind.

b. Dismiss the rumor, which you consider ridiculous, in an offhand way. Ask the person who's passed the rumor along to you whether he knows why someone would say such a thing. Listen carefully to the answer you get, and try to piece together some kind of motive for the event.

6. You stop into a small bakery to buy a popover. There is one customer ahead of you. Would you be more likely to:

a. Wait your turn at one side of the counter; or

b. Stand two or three feet behind the customer who arrived before you?

7. During office renovations, you have a choice. You may either work in a small, not particularly attractive trailer set to one side of the build-ing, or share a cramped "common" workspace in which three people will share a single computer terminal. The renovations are slated to last for five working days, after which time you will be able to return to your private workstation. Which of the two options would be more attractive to you? (Assume that your job only *requires* you to work on

the computer one-third of the time, and that you could, theoretically, be just as productive in either setting.)

a. The trailer.

b. The "common" workspace.

8. Assume for a moment that a radical reworking of the political system has taken place, and that Senators, members of Congress, and Presidents are no longer elected by direct vote. Instead, they are chosen by a computer lottery, and the citizens who are selected *must* serve as Federal office-holders for a term of one month, and only one month. (Failure to take the oath of office for an appropriate position results in a stiff sentence at a maximum-security prison of at least ten years' duration.) One day, you open your mail to learn that you have been selected by the national computer system, and that you must serve for one month either as President of the United States, or as a member of Congress from the neighborhood where you live. The choice between the two jobs is yours. Which would you select?

a. President of the United States.

b. Member of Congress.

9. During the public question-and-answer sessions that are often incorporated as part of speeches, seminars, discussion groups, and the like, have you ever asked the first question? (*Note:* If the moderator or group leader singled you out and asked you for a comment or question, that doesn't count.)

a. Yes.

b. No.

10. If you had to choose between the two options that follow, which would you rather do?

a. Perform or speak in front of a group on short notice, and without a prepared text, for five minutes.

b. Enter a room occupied by a large number of strangers who are enjoying a party that is in full swing; introduce yourself to, and shake hands with, at least thirty-five of them.

11. If you had to participate in one of the following activities, which would you select? (Assume that you would be assigned a personal trainer who would be willing to work with you in any area you wished, and for as long as you considered appropriate, before you took part in any competitive activities; assume, too, that when it came time to compete, you would be matched against others of approximately the same skill level that you possessed.)

   a. A free-throw shooting contest.

   b. A team rowing competition.

12. You work at an ad agency. After a long-standing debate with a coworker over the best way to target a particular campaign, you read an article in an industry trade magazine that tends to support your view that the correct target audience for the product in question is young women between the ages of eighteen and thirty-four. Which of the following better reflects the message you would probably write on a Post-It note affixed to the article before passing it along for your coworker's review?

   a. "Had a feeling about this. Any reaction?"

   b. "What do you think about their conclusions with regard to the X account?"

13. Which of the following popular television shows did you/do you remember as being more involving? (If you are unfamiliar with the programs, or never particularly liked either: Which do you consider least objectionable, based on what you know or have heard about them?)

   a. *60 Minutes*

   b. *M*A*S*H*

14. You are the manager of a workgroup. Your team has been selected to receive a single company-paid trip to a convention in Honolulu, Hawaii. The company will provide not only airfare and lodging, but also a "living allowance" of $300 per day for five days. Although some company-related duties are required of the person attending, seventy percent of the "work" week the person spends in Hawaii will be open for private leisure and recreation activities. You've been instructed to award the trip to one, and only one, of the team members in your group. There has been considerable speculation about who will be selected to attend the conference; you must make your decision within 48 hours. (Taking the slot yourself, however richly deserved such a "working vacation" might be, is not an option. Neither is declining the trip altogether.) Which of the following approaches most nearly reflects the way you would approach the decision?

a. Develop some kind of contest that awards the trip to the entrant who brings the most creative approach to a pressing business problem you've been wrestling with, with little success, for some weeks. The final decision regarding which entrant comes up with the best solution is to be made either by you, or by a committee within the organization. (*Note:* You should also pick "a" if your first instinct is simply to select the member of the team you feel most deserves the trip.)

b. Develop some kind of contest, either work-related or non-work-related, that would produce a winner based not on your judgment or the judgment of a committee, but on some quantifiable external factor. In other words, develop a contest in which a winner would be selected not by you (or anyone else) having to decide on the merits of a participant's entry, but by, for instance, guessing the correct number of jellybeans in a large jar, or handling the thousandth customer service call of the day.

15. Assume that you have recently become engaged, and have not yet announced your decision to your close friends. As it happens, you and your future spouse are attending a wedding yourselves this weekend. Which of the following options comes closer to reflecting the manner you would find most comfortable for delivering the news?

a. Privately, either during or after the reception, by mentioning it to a single close friend who is also in attendance, and then confirming the details for the three or four other friends close to you and your future spouse who happen to be on hand for the ceremony. You would offer others who came up to congratulate you during the course of the day a brief, polite offer of thanks for their good wishes.

b. Publicly, preferably after one of you has elbowed your way to the front of the group catching the bride's toss of the bouquet, or the groom's toss of the garter.

16. A huge computer problem last month resulted in the irretrievable loss of several thousand customer orders. You have been assigned the task of reviewing exactly what happened, and reporting your findings personally to the president of the company. Over the course of a week, you have done all the necessary research and concluded that a series of employee errors, rather than any hardware or software defects, gave rise to the information loss. (The errors were not the result of your work or the work of anyone in your department.) Which of the two statements below most nearly reflects the way you would begin your presentation to the president?

a. "Based on the research I've conducted, the primary responsibility for the computer failure rests, in my opinion, with . . . ."

b. "The computer failure was the result of a number of costly oversights we hope never to encounter again; the most critical of these oversights, in my opinion, was . . ."

17. Budget cutbacks mandated from the highest levels of the organization, rather than any kind of performance problem, force you to lay off a valued employee of several years' seniority. After passing along the bad news to the employee, how would you be most likely to approach the task of informing the three other members of the team who report to you about this employee's layoff? (Assume there are no company guidelines for you to consult on the matter.)

a. Through a posted written memo, through informal one-on-one meetings, by delegating the task to someone else, or by simply allowing the departing employee to break the news.

b. Through a brief meeting with the three remaining staff members.

18. You are the media liaison for a large consumer products firm. A major public relations crisis related to a product recall has led your firm to craft a detailed, painstakingly assembled press release outlining what your company has done, is doing, and will continue to do with regard to a defective product. The press release has been drafted over a very long weekend, and has been reviewed at the highest levels of the organization. It is your job to distribute the press release to the media during a Monday-afternoon press conference; you are hoping to get your company's message into that evening's news broadcasts. As you prepare the press packets, however, you notice that, through what must have been an error in the latest word-processing stage, what appears to be a confidential paragraph not meant for public review has been incorporated into the copies of the document. (The paragraph features comments from the president of the company to his legal advisors; it also contains several alternate, presumably early, versions of sentences that appear elsewhere in the press release.) Do you:

a. Obtain the disk that contains the most recent edited version of the file, delete the paragraph that seems to have been mistakenly included, and, on your own authority, distribute it to the media; or

b. Revise the document and submit it to the president's office for approval before distributing it to the media, even if that means missing a news cycle?

19. You're leaving work with a colleague, en route to a social engagement across town. You were planning to walk to your destination, but a light rain has blown in, and you and your colleague have no umbrella. You decide to take a cab, but all the cabs that pass by appear to be occupied. Which of the two approaches below is the one you would be most likely to suggest?

a. One of you tries to flag down a cab in the light rain, while the other runs back in the office and calls the cab company to request a pick-up.

b. Both of you return to the building to wait for the cab you plan to call.

20. How do you typically pass your coffee break at work? Choose the statement that better reflects your answer.

a. "I generally spend at least part of it alone, unwinding."

b. "I generally spend it socializing with fellow employees."

NO RIGHT ANSWERS!

Total up your "a" and "b" responses from each test. Remember, this is not the type of test you can flunk (or, for that matter "ace").

TEST ONE

➤ *If you marked more "a" answers than "b" answers on Test One, it's a good bet that your mindset can be best described as "Get It Error-Free."*

As a general rule, you tend to be concerned with evaluating each and every possible problem area as thoroughly as the individual case warrants, and with establishing all the necessary safeguards for dealing effectively with unforeseen situations that may arise. It's important to you to get things right.

When someone suggests that you "address only the major issues" or "do the best you can given the current time or resource constraints," you may feel a deep uneasiness that something vitally important is likely to be missed. It's a good bet that you feel that standards and specifications are developed for a reason, and that you would think twice (at least!) before ignoring clearly stated guidelines in approaching a task.

In most cases, you prefer to look at problems from as many angles as possible before considering them "complete," and even then you may have a healthy respect for reviewing matters after they have been "checked off the list." Odds are that when you start working on a project, you are likely to consider a given approach a success only after it has been rigorously reviewed for possible inconsistencies, overlaps, or inaccuracies. You enjoy the feeling that arises when you find a problem, because finding a problem allows one the opportunity to highlight it before it can cause further trouble.

> ➤ *If you marked more "b" answers than "a" answers on Test One, it's a good bet that your mindset can be best described as "Get It Out the Door."*

As a general rule, you tend to be concerned with completing the task at hand and shutting out diversions while you attempt to do so. When someone suggests that you "keep something on the back burner" or "bear such-and-such in mind as you go along," you may feel a certain frustration or impatience. In most cases, it's easiest for you to see how principles, ideas, and suggestions apply to the matter directly in front of you at the moment. Odds are that when you set your mind on completing a task, you tend to focus on it with a certain intensity, and that as you proceed through the various elements of the task, you enjoy the feeling that arises as you declare each element "complete" or "closed" or "resolved."

TEST TWO

> ➤ *If you marked more "a" answers than "b" answers on Test Two, it's a good bet that your mindset can be best described as "Doing It On Your Own."*

As a general rule, you prefer to work independently and assess situations based on your own instincts and experience. When someone suggests that you "see what other people think" or "elicit some feedback" you may feel a certain sense of impatience, or of concern about losing the advantage that often comes with following a "gut instinct."

Although they may be necessary to attain certain goals, committees or group gatherings are not your preferred method of getting things done. In most cases, you feel that reviewing matters on your own is both the most appropriate and the most efficient way of doing things; this method often seems to you to be considerably more likely to result in a positive outcome than, for instance, trying to explain exactly what needs to be done to someone else.

> ➤ *If you marked more "b" answers than "a" answers on Test Two, it's a good bet that your mindset can be best described as "Doing It Through Others."*

As a general rule, you prefer to work as part of a group and assess situations by gathering as many perspectives from other members as you can. When someone suggests that you "handle the job on your own this time" or "make the best decision you can independently," you may feel a sense of concern that important perspectives may be overlooked.

Although working on your own is sometimes the best available option, you feel most comfortable operating as part of a team in which each member has clearly defined duties, and the input of a variety of people is encouraged before decisions are made. You are usually quite comfortable when it comes to communicating important information to others, especially information that affects their activities as team members.

In most cases, you feel that reviewing matters in concert with others is both the most appropriate and the most efficient way of doing things; this method often seems to you to be considerably more likely to result in a positive outcome than, for instance, trying to adapt to an unfamiliar situation yourself, without making the effort to learn whether someone else with more experience has any input to offer.

Now that you have an idea what your initial instincts are with regard to the two priority squares, you should be able to identify where your own first-instinct mindset falls in the four-square model.

ARE YOU FAMILIAR WITH THE FOUR CORNERS OF THE SQUARE?

Where do you fit in the four-square model? Perhaps you found yourself thinking of present or past acquaintances who fit into each of the three *other* categories besides yours. This is a useful exercise that will help you become more familiar with the four-square model. The model can be an extremely effective tool for predicting the ways in which people are likely to go about getting what they want in a wide variety of situations. In other words, the four groups are worth knowing well.

In the pages that follow, we'll refer to these four fundamental "how-I-see-it" approaches again and again. To get the most from this book, take a moment to become familiar with the four basic mindsets. Please stop reading now and, on a separate sheet of paper, make a list of ten acquaintances—family members, co-workers, or friends.

How does each approach a particular problem? Which of the four groups seems to describe each person best? Were there any with whom you felt you got along particularly smoothly? Particularly poorly?

If, after developing your list of ten people, you find that you have not supplied an example from one or more of the mindset groups, keep going until you have at least one example for each corner of the square.

SO MUCH FOR THE "HOW"—WHAT ABOUT THE "WHY"?

The four-group breakdown we've been examining is helpful in examining *how* people are likely to approach the task of "getting something done" on a day-to-day basis. But what about the driving *motivations* behind our actions?

The psychologist Abraham Maslow developed a system that categorized a number of types of human needs. He identified seven basic varieties. This seven-tiered summary of important human motivators is worth reviewing here before we proceed to the next chapter of the book. It outlines a series of requirements not unlike a pyramid.

Our most essential needs—the physiological requirements—are located at the bottom of the structure. As those are attended to, we are free to seek fulfillment of the needs at the next level. As we approach the top of the pyramid, we are focusing on needs that point less toward physical survival and more toward an ongoing sense of fulfillment.

Every one of us, according to Maslow, acts in accordance with this dynamic hierarchy of needs. If we are not happy with the current status on a particular need level, it's difficult to concern ourselves with needs on higher levels. Obviously, the fuller our understanding of the level of someone else's need, the more accurate our assessment of what is driving that person is likely to be.

Here is a brief summary of Maslow's hierarchy of needs:

Aesthetic Needs: For example, the pursuit of beauty or the development of a satisfying artistic approach

Knowledge/Understanding Needs: For example, the cultivation of deep wisdom or understanding in a particular field or the development of a new system for explaining the world around us

Self-Actualization Needs: For example, a sense of self-fulfillment or of using one's capacities to their fullest

Esteem Needs: For example, respect from peers, sense of mastery or proficiency in work or daily routine, or reputation or eminence in a particular field

Belonging and Love Needs: For example, interactions with spouse or mate, support from others during stressful times, harmonious family relationships, sense of belonging to a group, or close friendships

Safety Needs: For example, protection from violence or chaos, sense of order or stability, absence of fear or anxiety, or sense of order in daily routine

Physiological Needs: For example, food, drink, shelter, sex, sleep, or recovery from injury or illness

If we hope to influence someone in a particular direction, we would be well advised to attach the change in behavior we are seeking to those needs most salient for our listener. For instance, if someone on our staff is consistently having financial troubles and is deeply concerned for the day-to-day welfare of her family, our efforts to appeal to that person's interest in, say, knowledge and understanding issues will probably be in vain. Until her more pressing concerns have been addressed or until we have somehow attached our own aims to her need level, it really doesn't matter what is said (or implied) about how the goal we have in mind for her will help her expand her knowledge and experience. This staff member is going to be preoccupied, whether on a subtle or an obvious level, with her own financial problems.

If we were to tie the same goal to the possibility of her increasing her income by earning a promotion or a substantial raise, however, we could be looking at a very different set of responses!

We must meet people on their own ground if we hope to work well with them—both with regard to their spoken and unspoken needs and with regard to the approach they take in fulfilling those needs.

This book will show you how to adopt, at least for a time, the mindset most likely to help you get good results from your interactions with others. It will also show you how to tie your own objectives to the need levels most likely to resonate with the people you deal with.

Although there are many general pieces of advice in the pages that follow that you will probably find to be of general use in dealing with *all four* groups and people with a *wide variety* of needs, each chapter will incorporate specific ideas for appealing to particular mindsets and need levels. Clearly, knowing who you're dealing with and what they need will serve as an important foundation for implementing the ideas that follow.

WHAT'S NEXT?

Learning to listen well is the first step toward identifying exactly who you're interacting with and what they're really after. In the next chapter, we'll look at some listening techniques.

Listening at All Levels

Listening well to superiors, subordinates, peers, and anyone else you come in contact with is *your secret weapon in dealing with others.* So few people truly listen—or even pretend to listen—that you can instantly set yourself apart from most of the other individuals your conversational partner comes into contact with in the course of a day by merely paying attention to what he or she has to say.

Open, attentive listening is *not* something that should be reserved for meetings with a superior. It's tempting to fall into the trap of thinking that some people are inherently dull. But operating with that working assumption is dangerous.

The better assumption is that everyone, regardless of his or her position in an organization or their rank in society, has an interesting story of *some* kind to tell: an intriguing, unique perspective on events, or an invaluable piece of information you're likely to come across nowhere else. Perhaps the new insight needs a little help from another person, but the fact is that *everyone* has some value as a human being and is worthy of attentive respect.

We may not always have time to offer that respect in the form of an extended conversation, but we should always be ready to let it take other forms.

There's a saying in the East that goes something like this: "Each person you meet knows something you do not."

> ➤ Listening attentively:
>
> > • Exposes you to information you may need
> >
> > • Puts you in a position of strength
> >
> > • Wins allies
> >
> > • Allows an angry or agitated person time to come to his or her senses
> >
> > • Buys you the time you need to find out which of the four initial mindsets your conversational partner is likely to use on first instinct
> >
> > • Buys you the time you need to find out what need level your conversational partner is probably operating from
> >
> > • Is the best response to overbearing people

LISTENING FOR FACTS, LISTENING FOR "SPIN"

Attentive listening has two purposes, only the first of which is generally pursued. We generally listen because we want to obtain information. We hope to learn things that the other person may volunteer to us or offer in response to a question. That's what I call a *content-based listening objective*. There's another kind of listening objective, however, one to which we often don't pay as much attention as we might.

When we listen to find out how our conversational partner looks at the world and to learn what needs drive him or her, we are listening not so much for new facts related to the subject under discussion, but rather to find out more *about the person with whom we're speaking*. I call this type of listening goal a *person-based listening objective*. In terms of our immediate objectives in dealing with someone, person-based listening objectives are just as appropriate and just as important as the fact-based type of listening—and they usually carry far greater implications for the development of long-term relationships.

There are two main questions to answer when it comes to pursuing person-based listening:

➤ Which of the four first-instinct mindsets is this person operating under?

➤ What driving need is motivating this person?

Many of the suggestions in this book will depend on your ability to make "best-guess" responses to each of these questions.

Determining a person's current need, according to Maslow's hierarchy, is, admittedly, an inexact undertaking. It's based largely on inference, your own instincts, and a general familiarity with the hierarchies we discussed in the previous chapter. Finding out which of the four mindsets you're dealing with, however, is a little more straightforward. It doesn't take much practice to learn how a person evaluates the business of "getting things done"—although it does take *some* practice.

Before you can make a confident judgment about your conversational partner's first-instinct mindset, it's imperative that you *listen* to that person—not just for facts, although those are certainly important, but for the "personal spin" he or she puts on whatever issue is under discussion.

Listening *seems* like a simple undertaking, yet so many of us must make a special effort to do it in an open, attentive, nonjudgmental way. Here are some suggestions for specific listening techniques you can easily work into your daily routine.

SIX LISTENING TECHNIQUES TO USE WHETHER OR NOT YOU KNOW YOUR CONVERSATIONAL PARTNER

Let's assume that you don't know exactly which of the four mindset groups your conversational partner falls into. Here are six simple steps you can take during everyday interactions with others that will *get your conversational partner talking*—which is the essential first step when it comes to identifying exactly who you're dealing with. These steps will also give you a better chance of minimizing negative exchanges and getting to the facts of whatever subject is under discusssion.

Although these listening techniques would, in a perfect world, probably be second nature to everyone, even superior communicators overlook them from time to time. Make a conscious effort to work all six in over the course of a specific day, whether or not you consider them part of your current communicating style. Doing so will instill (or strengthen) good listening skills and make your interactions with others more productive.

> ➤ *Before responding to a person's question, comment, or suggestion, rephrase it in your own words to show that you have fully grasped what was said.* Then ask for verification and let the other person take the lead once again in the conversation.

Although it seems a simple enough task, this can be quite difficult, particularly when the other person's message is perceived as a direct or implied criticism. Rightly or wrongly, we often interpret a question such as "When will that report for Mr. Wilson be ready?" as though the query were really something along the lines of "Why on earth haven't you finished the report yet for Wilson?"

When someone poses a question like that to us, the temptation to react defensively to such an implied challenge can be very strong. When we react that way, however, we often provide information the other person isn't looking for . . . or, even worse, we needlessly polarize a situation by offering a counter-challenge of our own, one that may or may not be in keeping with the other person's intent.

Instead, try saying something like this:

> "If I understand what you're asking, you need a date to give
> Mr. Wilson so he'll know when he can expect the report."

By making such a restatement, you accomplish two important goals. You clarify in your own mind exactly what is under discussion, and you let the other person know that you are in fact interested in approaching the issue as he or she has laid it out. (And if you're not quite on target in your interpretation of what the other person has said, you offer the other person a comparatively safe opportunity to clarify the message.)

➤ *Ask truly open-ended questions.*

Queries like "Are there any questions regarding this policy?" are deceptive. They may sound open-ended, but they still require a yes-or-no response from your partner. When they're issued in a curt or brusque manner, especially by a superior, they are generally interpreted as orders—whether or not they are intended as such. ("Now that I've gone to the trouble of discussing things with you, you had better not fail to observe this policy.")

Similar problems accompany any request about whether the person you're talking to "understands" what you've just gone over. After all, which of us is eager to volunteer that we *don't* understand a policy or procedure that has just been laid out for us? Even accomplished engineers, repairmen, and designers fall prey to the trap of nodding their head sagely after being asked whether they grasp something that they weren't paying attention to. If you really mean to encourage discussion, find out what level of proficiency exists or open up new avenues of inquiry by trying questions like these:

"How do you think customers will react to this policy?"

"Is there a problem you think we should discuss now?"

"What can we do on our end to help you implement this?"

"What other kinds of information do you need?"

"So what do you think?"

➤ *When you are tempted to classify something the other person has said as wrong, incorrect, or inaccurate, ask for clarification before doing so.* Then let your conversational partner provide all the necessary details.

Even if your partner doesn't have all the facts straight, if you challenge him directly by abruptly dismissing one of his points, you will probably completely shut down lines of communication. (This is especially true if you deliver your challenge in public.)

When you think you spot a mistake, try to respond with a comment like "I'm having a little trouble with so-and-so. Didn't the report indicate X instead?" Warning: Such a comment must be delivered in a neutral, *nonthreatening* tone. If your comment is perceived as sarcastic, you will encourage your conversational partner to retreat, and you will miss out on any new information that may encourage you to change your own view of the situation.

➤ *During times of stress and conflict, make statements instead of asking questions.*

Stress is a part of business life; how we respond to it determines, among other things, how much information we get. Most of us encounter stressful situations on the job every day, and we often unintentionally encourage others to "shut down" by issuing questions that are perceived as attacks.

Questions are extremely powerful rhetorical devices—and during times of tension, no matter what they look like on the surface, they can all too easily turn into *one* question: "Whose fault is this?" Putting things on that footing is usually a bad idea, because inquisitions don't exactly encourage team productivity. One chief executive I know spent nearly a full week of her own—and her top managers'—time posing pointed questions in an effort to track down the culprit behind a typographical error in a local television advertisement. After she finally found the guilty party, she ended up spending *another* day or two of her managers' time posing *more* heat-seeking missiles disguised as questions . . . all so she could critique the specific language that would go into the employee's (negative) yearly salary review. The seemingly endless tidal waves of questioning served only to demonstrate to her managers, and to the team members who knew what was taking place, that discussing problems outright with the big boss was a nightmare.

When things get tense, don't fire your "question torpedoes" in the first place. Try phrasing the same message in the form of a statement:

> "Then I guess the new materials will have to be prepared by someone else if Michelle is on vacation."

This is far superior to

> "Who authorized Michelle to take her vacation when we need these materials now?"

➤ *Look the other person in the eye; send "keep talking" signals.*

Yes, you're busy; yes, the other person has tasks to attend to; no, you are under no obligation to waste your day with people who love to hear themselves talk. Nevertheless, it is to your advantage when talking with someone to make sure that person knows you value his or her opinion.

Nonthreatening eye contact and appropriate nodding cues will go a long way toward delivering that message. If you fall prey to someone who respects your time less than his own, simply set a time limit ("I can discuss this with you until quarter of two; then I have to get this ready for Sheila."). Then, within the parameters of that time limit, *show that you are open to what the person has to say* by looking him in the eye and silently encouraging him to speak.

➤ *Without asking permission, take notes on what the other person is saying.*

This simple, startlingly effective technique demonstrates to your conversational partner that you are so interested in what's being said that you are willing to go to the trouble of making a permanent record of the conversation. Taking notes is one of the most powerful ways to assume a quiet position of understated control. You can effectively adapt the technique to interactions with peers, subordinates, and superiors alike. (Superiors, in particular, react remarkably well to having their every utterance committed to paper.)

Sales trainer Stephan Schiffman introduced me to this foolproof, yet often overlooked, method for getting your conversational partner to open up. He cites notetaking as one of the most important tools of top-level salespeople. It is that, and it's a lot more. Businesspeople in non-sales settings can benefit from the idea immediately. Taking notes while your conversational partner is speaking may seem a little low-tech, but it carries significant advantages.

- It requires little or no practice.
- It virtually always gets the person talking.
- It gives you something to do during those occasional awkward silences.
- It can point you toward key facts and leave you with hard copy outlining those facts.
- It puts you in the perfect position to suggest what could happen next as a result of the information you've gathered.

WHEN IN DOUBT, FAKE IT

Listening, of course, means more than simply not talking—but sometimes, simply not talking is a pretty good place to start.

It's quite rare to encounter a situation in which you *can't* adapt one of the six ideas just listed to the person you're talking to, yet you may well find yourself at a point in the day when your patience has worn pretty thin. If you have to find out more about your conversational partner, but find yourself in a frame of mind that's unlikely to get good results from one of these six methods, simply *fake it*. Toss your conversational partner the ball, stand back, and see what happens. Don't try to accomplish anything or cross anything off the to-do list. Just be quiet for a moment.

If all else fails, simply ask your conversational partner his or her opinion on an innocuous question, then *stop talking*. (Alternatively, if the person you're talking with doesn't need any encouragement when it comes to offering advice or opinions, let the person talk at you for a while. Don't interrupt.)

Your aim is to get a bead on the person's mindset and needs. That can't happen if *you're* holding forth on the issue of the moment. So don't.

Relinquish any attempt to exercise control of the exchange for, say, sixty seconds. (It *seems* like a long time at first, but it's not.) See what your conversational partner comes up with.

Legendary newsman David Brinkley was once asked about the secret of conducting fascinating interviews with major newsmakers on his Sunday morning talk show. Brinkley responded with words to this effect:

> "I start out by recognizing that anyone who comes on the program *doesn't* do so unprepared. They generally have a message of some kind that they've practiced, a message they want to get across to the public. So rather than challenging them, or trying to keep them from getting their point through, I ask them a question right off the bat that will allow them to get across whatever it is they've practiced. Once I let them deliver their sermonette, they can relax, because they've done their job, and we can move on to other issues."

Brinkley's approach—just let 'em talk *before* you try to get to whatever is on your own agenda—is an excellent one to bear in mind as you try to assemble clues about your conversational partner's makeup.

GATHERING CLUES AS TO YOUR CONVERSATIONAL PARTNER'S INITIAL MINDSET

Once you take the time to listen attentively to your conversational partner, you will begin to notice hints that point you toward an accurate assessment of the person's first-instinct mindset. This won't happen instantly, but it will happen, and with practice, you'll be able to develop a valid profile after a few moments of discussion.

Following are some examples of the types of remarks you should listen for—and the mindsets they probably signify.

➤ If your conversational partner says things like:

> "I can finish it by this Friday—if I can just block out the time to work on it undisturbed."
>
> "It will take me longer to explain it than it will for me to do it."
>
> "She's my kind of employee: A real self-starter, and she can move mountains for you . . . if you just get out of her way."
>
> "You know what they say: If you want something done right, you've got to do it yourself."

"I'm almost done with it. I think I'm going to stay late tonight."

"I can't talk now. It's crunch time here."

"The phone won't stop ringing while I'm on deadline!"

"I need to head to the library to finish this off. It's too noisy around here."

"I don't know why he's having so much trouble wrapping that up. It's a morning's work, tops."

"When do you need it by?"

. . . then you are, in all likelihood, dealing with a **Lone Ranger.**

➤ If your conversational partner says things like:

"I found a problem."

"You're going to need to redesign something for us here."

"What happens if someone uses it like this?"

"This is all distorted. Something's wrong with the manufacturing process."

"There's a typo right here."

"It's off center."

"That clause doesn't cover us if (dire unforeseen event of person's choice) happens."

"The figures don't add up."

"I think there may be a problem with the formula we put in the spreadsheet."

"These don't match."

. . . then you are, in all likelihood, dealing with a **Sharpshooter.**

➤ If your conversational partner says things like:

"I've set up a form that will help us keep track of everything."

"If we just do this for an hour every Tuesday, we won't fall behind."

"Interesting idea. Did the people in Accounting get to take a look at this?"

"Did you log this in yet?"

"Let's pump all these numbers into the spreadsheet and see what it looks like a year or two out."

"The problem is, we didn't get the right people talking to one another."

"Let me put that on my list."

"We need to have a meeting with (departments or individuals of person's choice) to address this."

"You know, we had a problem just like that on my last job. We ended up going with an X-14 widget-sorting system."

"Can I see another analysis that takes (factor of person's choice) into account?"

. . . then you are, in all likelihood, dealing with a **Professor.**

➤ If your conversational partner says things like:

"We can do it."

"My people can work miracles with something like this. You watch."

"Listen, they're exhausted. They're only human."

"You're going to accomplish some great things in this department."

"We've taken on tougher jobs."

"Big project coming up, guys!"

"I know you can pull this off."

"Let's show them where to find the sharpest department in the company."

"I can't tell them that. It will ruin morale in the office."

"It was my fault. I should have told him to watch out for that."

. . . then you are, in all likelihood, dealing with a **Cheerleader.**

MIRRORING

Many of the specific ideas outlined in the subsequent chapters of this book will suggest that you take advantage of a technique known as *mirroring.* That is to say, you'll be encouraged to assume, for a moment, the same concerns typical of the mindset your conversational partner seems to you to be operating under.* You'll also be given an idea of the types of driving needs your conversational partner is probably pursuing, then shown some effective methods for helping the person you're dealing with meet those needs—constructively and in a way that leaves you both feeling better for having connected with one another. Much of the art and skill of dealing with people lies in an ability to frame matters in such a way that they will be likely to become enthusiastic about what you are trying to accomplish.

Mirroring is simply a matter of knowing your partner's first-instinct mindset and making the effort to present your message in a way that complements and does not challenge the predisposition of your partner. Think of the technique as an extremely focused, informed way of summoning the best in your conversational partner.

Many of our unproductive interactions, whether in the workplace or at home, become tense because people send messages that are coded in the "language" of the sender, rather than the recipient. By learning the other person's likely first instinct in interpreting your basic message and altering your message accordingly, you take much of the pressure off the other person, and open the way toward harmonious exchanges.

Mirroring means making the effort to see a problem, issue, or challenge as someone in a particular group would see it and altering the emphasis of one's message accordingly.

Here are some general guidelines on mirroring for use with members of all four groups:

> ➤ *When dealing with a **Lone Ranger**,* frame issues in terms of deadlines— and in terms of your conversational partner's ability to summon persistence and sustained effort to achieve an important goal.

---

* One excellent way to do this, of course, is to emphasize a common trait you may already share with the person in question. As the four-square model demonstrates, each mindset has one element in common with two others. Only one mindset is diametrically opposed to any other, with *no* common priority. If you're a Lone Ranger, for instance, you share a "Get-It-Out-the-Door" approach with the Cheerleader and a "Do-It-On-My-Own" approach with the Sharpshooter.

➤ *When dealing with a* **Sharpshooter,** frame issues in terms of error eradication—and in terms of early resolution of potentially catastrophic problems, thanks to your conversational partner's acknowledged mastery of technical detail.

➤ *When dealing with a* **Professor,** frame issues in terms of systems, procedures, and checklists—and in terms of your conversational partner's ability to implement solutions that work well for groups.

➤ *When dealing with a* **Cheerleader,** frame issues in terms of impending challenges that can be met only by means of pulling together as a team—and in terms of your conversational partner's ability to bring out the best in people.

Those are the four basic framing techniques for mirroring. As you can imagine, they have thousands of possible applications, based on the specifics of the situation at hand. We'll be looking at some of the most important variations later on in the book.

DON'T PARROT!

It's worth noting here that mirroring is *not* the same thing as parroting your conversational partner's style of speaking, figures of speech, gestures, or body language. It is, instead, a continuous process of casting whatever issue is under discussion in terms that will be likely to elicit enthusiasm and buy-in from the other person.

"I REMEMBER, NOT LONG AGO, WHEN YOU SAID . . ."

One last note on the topic of listening is in order before we move on. Regardless of the conclusions you reach concerning your conversational partner's mindset or driving need, you should, if at all possible, make a point of noting one particularly striking remark, joke, or observation your conversational partner makes. (Come on—even truly boring people manage to come up with *something* interesting every once in a while.)

When you get the chance, jot down the person's intriguing remark. Then, when you find yourself face to face with the person once again, you can work the remark into the conversation in a complimentary way:

> "You know, speaking of keeping our quality levels high, I was thinking the other day of what you said about the importance of continuous peer review of our designs. That was right on target, and I've been trying to keep it in mind in my own work ever since."

Quoting your conversational partner's own remarks in this way is a remarkably effective way to win allies—as long as what you say reflects genuine feelings, and doesn't come across as unabashed brown-nosing. It proves to people that you really *are* paying attention to them, unlike most of the preoccupied sorts they come across day by day. And it demonstrates to them that you're quite capable of recognizing true intelligence (namely theirs) when you see it.

WHAT'S NEXT?

In the next chapter, we'll start looking at some of the unique challenges supervisors face in dealing with their subordinates. We'll take a look at some of the best options available when dealing with people who report to you—and we'll review some of the best ways to use the mirroring technique we've just reviewed to make sure the messages you send are productive ones.

Dealing with Subordinates

The ideas on listening that we discussed in Chapter 2 are particularly important to bear in mind when dealing with subordinates. A classic managerial mistake is simply to dictate a series of instructions to a subordinate: "Go to the storeroom, get a thirty-foot-long piece of rope, use it to scale the building, and wait on top of the roof until you hear from me." Sometimes it's a better idea to outline an overall goal and get a little feedback *before* you issue all the orders.

Implementing the listening techniques we just reviewed—including the ideas on note taking—is probably more important when dealing with subordinates than when dealing with virtually anyone else in the organization. Although everyone can use a little improvement when it comes to picking up subtle signals from VIPs, it's unlikely you're going to "tune out" specific instructions from your own boss. (If you do so on a regular basis, you probably won't be working at that organization for very long!) Contacts with peers in the workplace often have their rocky moments, but most of us develop relationships with our colleagues that allow the most important messages to get through. Our interactions with subordinates, however, may present special challenges.

When dealing with subordinates, consciously implementing the listening techniques outlined in Chapter 2 is absolutely essential, because:

➤ We often conduct our discussions with subordinates while we are distracted with something else.

➤ We are more likely to direct inappropriate emotions toward subordinates because of frustrations arising from issues having nothing to do with them.

➤ We frequently believe we already know what a subordinate is going to say and either interrupt the person or fail to pay attention.

➤ We may place subordinates last on our priority list, so they may be subjected to the most severe time constraints when trying to outline complex situations for us.

In addition to enhancing our basic listening skills, there are other steps we can take on an everyday basis to make our interactions with subordinates run more smoothly. Here are ten.

TEN TIPS FOR EFFECTIVE DAY-TO-DAY INTERACTIONS WITH SUBORDINATES

1. *At the beginning of an exchange, let the subordinate deliver the message that is uppermost on his or her mind without interruption.* It is difficult for someone to listen to your message when the person is preoccupied with his or her own. If necessary, you may set appropriate time limits, but maintain an open and attentive demeanor while the person relays the points he or she feels are important. If possible, take notes.

2. *Remember the power of public praise.* Maslow's hierarchy of needs identifies self-esteem as a vitally important requirement. One of the easiest and most effective ways to address this need is to praise someone publicly for a particular element of the job that is being performed well (or even adequately). Effective managers who try this once quickly learn the tremendous power of the technique.

3. *Let 'em vent.* Sometimes subordinates simply need to get things off their chest. Listening to someone sound off about a problem isn't the same thing as *agreeing* with the person's point of view. Let the subordinate release as much energy as possible by speaking. It beats watching them chew up the window blinds, right?

4. *Avoid pronouncements of fact.* You may not get the best results by saying, "This design has all kinds of serious flaws. You're going to have to develop a new draft that corrects that addition error on page twelve and addresses the input/output ratios in much greater detail." Instead, try expressing informed hesitation on key points: "I wish I felt more confident about the input/output ratios. Could you draw up another draft

that addresses them in a little more detail? By the way, I circled a spreadsheet entry on page twelve—there may be a problem there."

5. *Ask yourself whether the person may just have a point before responding to any obstacle the subordinate brings to your attention.* A prominent architect once discovered a major problem relating to the construction and design of a recently completed skyscraper. The building was in danger of collapsing during storms that featured very forceful winds from a certain direction! Fortunately, the architect was able to coordinate the necessary reinforcements in time—all because he had conscientiously followed up a technical query from a college student who was writing a paper on the building's structure. The story is a sobering one for those of us inclined to dismiss anyone wanting to open doors we're busy trying to close.

6. *Unless you're dealing with a chronic insubordination problem, ignore aggressively challenging questions.* Answering a subordinate's questions that attack your authority, level of knowledge, or status as a representative of the organization is a mistake. You will only polarize the situation by responding to the question as posed. Attempt to redirect the subordinate's focus to the matter at hand: "Adam, we're not discussing the rightness or wrongness of the overtime policy now. We're trying to determine what your schedule for the next week looks like." (For advice on dealing effectively with chronic conflict, see Chapter 9.)

7. *Offer sympathy for the subordinate's situation.* Often, a complaining subordinate is simply looking for validation of his or her emotional reaction to a certain situation. Don't be afraid to offer that validation when it's appropriate to do so. By responding with such phrases as "You sound upset," "You're right, that's frustrating," or "I think you've got a right to be worried," you'll be appealing to the person's need for friendship and support, which is third in Maslow's hierarchy.

8. *Ask for advice.* It's cheap, it's risk free, and it makes the other person feel like a million dollars. Your schedule may not allow you to indulge in this during every interaction with every subordinate, but you should nevertheless make a point of asking *everyone* who reports to you for opinions from time to time.

9. *Use the person's first name repeatedly during the exchange.* Don't go overboard; do build a bridge. Names are powerful things. When used in a positive, noninvasive way, they command attention, demonstrate a

level of intimacy and support (Maslow's third need level again), and prove to the other person that you are in fact interested in him or her. *Warning:* Be absolutely sure you've got the name right! Mispronounced or otherwise mangled names get people's hackles up, and a subordinate may well choose to stew about it rather than correct you.

10. *Recognize when the subordinate is fishing for a compliment.* A good many managers miss the opportunity. Sure, you've got a lot of work to do, but how much time will it take to compliment that new hair style the receptionist is showing off? Subordinates place great store by what their superiors think of them. Take the time to remark on how well the employee did in last week's football pool or how beautiful the new baby in the picture is.

PERSPECTIVE CHECKS

Your interactions with the people who report to you represent a critical part of your job. Similarly, your ability to manage these exchanges will have a great deal to do with how effective you are—and how your work will be perceived by others.

Because your work with subordinates may play such a large role in your on-the-job success, and because you are likely to have the time to determine the possible mindset patterns of the people you supervise every day, the ideas in the main section of this chapter feature specific, customized strategies for appealing to Lone Rangers, Sharpshooters, Professors, and Cheerleaders.

Each of these techniques is featured in a "Perspective Check" subsection. Review them closely; they will help you to customize your approach and make mutually positive outcomes more common for you and the people who report to you.

HOW TO EARN THEIR RESPECT

No manager is eager to learn that the people who report to him are saying uncomplimentary things behind his back—or dragging their feet when it comes to important projects—because of problems with personal chemistry. Here are six ideas for earning the respect you deserve from your team members:

➤ *Admit when you're wrong.* Nobody's perfect, but you'd never know it to listen to some managers. Don't be one of them. Supervisors who are incapable of acknowledging error leave themselves open to unflattering parodies and informal out-of-earshot performance assessments. When something goes awry, prove that you know you're human by saying something along the following lines:

> "Well, that certainly got people worked up during the meeting, didn't it? Looks like my Nobel peace prize may go to someone else this year."

> "There it is—my first big screwup of the month. Let's see, now, who picked today's date in the office pool?"

> "Fascinating. Just fascinating how far off I was in that summary I passed along to you folks last week. And it serves to remove any lingering doubts that Einstein was my real father, too."

Feeling really brave? Try *apologizing* for some incident you mishandled at someone else's expense.

➤ *Determine the subordinate's first-instinct mindset and praise some aspect of it openly.* Real-world one-on-one praise based on a specific element of the person's makeup will help to demonstrate that you are "on the same wavelength" as your subordinate. If you're a Lone Ranger supervising a Sharpshooter, emphasize the commonalities you share: "I think you're going to do well here. My impression is that you're someone who really knows how to work well independently, and that's just what I'm looking for." If there are no commonalties between you and your subordinate—if, for instance, you're a Cheerleader supervising a Sharpshooter—praise the aspect of the subordinate's approach that is the most evident to you: "Ellen, you seem to have a real aptitude for troubleshooting. That's great." You'll earn points for your perceptiveness.

➤ *Share something nonwork-related about yourself.* Bosses who focus *only* on work-related issues every minute of the working day have a habit of exhausting their subordinates. Take the time to briefly mention a current hobby, avocation, or vacation plan of yours with your subordinate. Then ask if he or she has a parallel field of interest and ask for details. Try to build nonwork-related topics of conversation with each of the people reporting to you. (But stay away from religion, politics, or personal matters.) Emphasize nonwork-related commonalities of interest you share with particular subordinates. Sports and television programs are good initial candidates for common ground. Make a point of initiating brief conversations in these areas on an ongoing basis. You'll be able to use these discussions to good advantage whenever the atmosphere gets tense and your people need to be able to hold forth on something other than shop talk and unwind for a few moments.

➤ *Tell a joke on yourself every now and then.* There is a great deal of power inherent in self-effacing humor. Top-level leaders in business and politics know that a joke they tell at their own expense doesn't lower them a notch in the eyes of others—it proves they're capable of taking the heat in style. Isolate whatever you feel your team members feel is your weakness as a boss, then show you're big enough to let them laugh about it openly.

Remember all the talk about Ronald Reagan's age when he was president? Remember how he used humor to defuse that potentially difficult issue? Once Reagan quoted a remark of Thomas Jefferson's to the guests at a formal state dinner at the White House, then concluded his story by saying, "And ever since Tom told me that . . . "

Here's another example of the same idea from the Cold War era. Soviet leader Nikita Khrushchev delighted in telling the following joke on himself:

> One night, a Moscow factory worker got roaring drunk and ran through the streets of Red Square shouting, "Khrushchev is an idiot! Khrushchev is an idiot!" Of course, the KGB swooped down on the fellow in an instant and carted him off to a prison cell. The next day he was brought before a judge. After hearing the details of the case, the magistrate sentenced the factory worker to twenty-five years in Siberia. "Twenty-five years?" the worker asked incredulously. "Why such a stiff sentence?" The judge looked down sternly from the bench. "That's five years for defaming a top Party official," he explained, "and twenty years for revealing a state secret."

If you think you've got a perception problem among the people you're supervising, you could do worse than to find a humorous way to prove that you know exactly what people are saying—and that you're capable of laughing as hard as anyone else about it. (But don't go yukking it up in front of the president of the company about your inability to show up on time for work unless you're feeling very confident indeed about the way she'll take it!)

➤ *Treat subordinates as though they were superstars.* In other words, give your subordinate a great reputation to live up to in a particular work area. Don't focus on the negative; give people the benefit of the doubt. During the Pittsburgh Pirates' run of division championships in the early nineties, manager Jim Leyland would visit pitchers on the mound and say things like, "You know, you're one of the best left-handed relievers in the National League. This guy's terrified of you." This tactic is not the same as praising an element of the subordinate's first-instinct mindset; here, you are aiming to praise the specific activity, not the general approach. Focus your praise to a particular, limited area; if you go overboard, you'll quickly lose credibility. What you say might sound something like this:

> "Gina, I think you've got one of the best eyes for text-based design in the department. I want you to take a stab at a new book cover we need to develop."

➤ *When you can, bring your team in on the tough decisions that will affect them.* Say you're facing a difficult resource allocation issue. Your team wants new equipment, and you don't have the budget to give it to them. Pick four or five team members, lay out the guidelines of the problem, and ask them how *they'd* handle the situation based on what's available to you now. There's only one rule to follow: They must develop a formal written proposal that *doesn't* simply conclude that you need a bigger budget. (You know that already.) Following this approach gives your team a sense of involvement, keeps you from being labeled as the bad guy, and stands a pretty good chance of unearthing a creative new approach you can follow. *Warning:* If your team *does* develop such an approach and you ignore it, you do so at your peril! (Trainer Michael Ramundo first mentioned this superior technique to me; it is simplicity itself to outline for subordinates, and it virtually always wins commitment from team members.)

Perspective Check: Earning Their Respect

➤ When trying to win the respect of **Lone Rangers** who report to you, emphasize your appreciation of their independent hard work and goal orientation. Mention examples of their work that impressed you; show that you've been paying attention to the contributions they make. Even though these workers are capable of handling problems on their own most of the time, they enjoy being acknowledged as much as anyone else.

Warning: If you make a commitment to one of these subordinates and then fail to follow through, you will lose points. They set great store on keeping promises—and on being rewarded for attaining important goals.

Do not attempt to micromanage the Lone Ranger! Step back and wait to see what happens by the deadline you have both agreed on.

➢ When trying to win the respect of **Sharpshooters** who report to you, go out of your way to point out instances where their troubleshooting has resulted in tangible positive changes in the way people in your workplace do things. Don't be afraid to construct a hypothetical situation that illustrates something awful that would have happened if a particular mistake hadn't been spotted. These subordinates spin out such catastrophe-aversion scenarios themselves every day. Ask them to review something you know needs careful checking and that probably contains errors. If possible, praise them for every error they identify.

Do not criticize the Sharpshooter for "only focusing on the negative"! Whether or not the assessment appears to you to be valid, issuing it is likely to alienate this person.

➢ When trying to win the respect of **Professors** who report to you, give them something to do that can positively affect others in the organization. Talk about past projects you and the subordinate have *jointly* undertaken that resulted in efficient systems and procedures. These subordinates are likely to react well to group undertakings, especially those that result in solutions for others who had no input on the project. Frame the projects you delegate to these people in terms of group effort, group input, group review, and group achievement.

Avoid, at all costs, pressuring the Professor to "think on her feet" or "make decisions on her own for a change." Such injunctions run counter to the way Professors view the world and can be perceived as personal threats!

➢ When trying to win the respect of **Cheerleaders** who report to you, highlight the subordinate's importance as an example to others in the department or work group.

Before you dismiss this gregarious team member's activities with co-workers as meddlesome or disruptive, put the Cheerleader in charge of something. Ask this subordinate to head up an impromptu group responsible for attaining a modest objective. More often than not, your "troublemaker" will help to focus the others in the group and will turn on the charm in the process. The result? A new solution . . . and a potential leader in the making. (If at all possible, try not to assign two Cheerleaders to the same ad hoc committee. Power struggles may result if you do.) Repeatedly state your confidence in the team member's ability to help others attain a certain goal by a particular time.

Don't be put off by the Cheerleader's possible eagerness to talk about (and with) others. Properly channelled, this habit represents far more than a penchant for "distracting gossip." The Cheerleader's occasional talkativeness can be a tool for achieving important organizational goals.

NINE WAYS TO TAKE CHARGE

Does your team suffer from a morale problem or recurrent productivity gap? Are important deadlines being missed? Have you inherited a crisis situation? If so, you will need to develop strategies for getting your team to focus clearly on the critical issues before them.

During difficult times, you will have to find effective ways to get your team members to look past such distractions as personality differences, personal problems, budget cutbacks, schedule foulups, and heavy workloads. Once you've gotten your team's focus *off* these preoccupations, you can put it *on* something else, but you'll need to take charge of the situation before you can expect them to start moving in the direction you want them to go.

Here are nine strategies that will help you win your team's attention and start shaping them up for the battles to come. Some of them take advantage of a certain theatricality in approach. Using unorthodox techniques to get your team members to snap to isn't something you should resort to every day, but once in a while it's just what you need to get all your subordinates looking at the same thing at the same time.

Don't rely on the ideas that follow for the resolution of everyday disputes or minor obstacles, but don't be afraid to incorporate them when the situation demands that you do so, either. Desperate times call for desperate measures, right?

➤ *Schedule a first-thing-in-the-morning meeting on the topic you need to review. Begin your discussions well before your team members usually begin their other activities.* And be ready and distraction-free yourself at least fifteen minutes before the announced starting time. You will need undisputed focus and attention for the points you are about to outline and the questions you are about to ask. Even fifteen minutes after your team members begin their workday, they are likely to be preoccupied with other matters.

➤ *Start with a bang.* Unveil a visual aid of some kind to make your first, overriding point. (If you don't *have* a single, overriding point that you hope to get across to your team members—some idea that the rest of your meeting supports—go back to the drawing board until you have one!) You might decide to brandish a rubber chicken once all your people arrive as a way of demonstrating that you've learned that a competitor is "chicken" and has missed an opportunity to release a new product that your department is going to unleash first . . . if everyone in the department pulls together. Or you might decide to pass around small photographs of the Beatles in order to illustrate a point about quality control; during the latter phase of their recording career, the Fab Four was known to lay down as many as a hundred takes on a particular song, only to reject the tune as unready for release! The visual aid you use will depend a great deal on the aim you're trying to get people to meet. Whatever you select, your visual aid should be memorable and should express your confidence in your team's ability to make important contributions in a wide variety of areas. In highlighting this confidence, you'll be appealing to Maslow's third-level belonging need.

➤ *Cry wolf—if you see one on the horizon.* If you are trying to rectify a situation that has a real-world possibility of resulting in serious physical injury, catastrophic quality-control lapses, or substantial legal liability for your company, find a third-party source (such as a news clipping) that graphically illustrates how dangerous the problem really is. Sometimes a gripping piece of videotape, a recent story from an industry trade publication, or a tape recording of a victim's story is the best way to get your team to focus on serious problems. Don't do anything in bad taste, but *do* use a trusted independent resource to get your point across—and appeal to Maslow's second-level safety need. If you choose the right third-party message, your own summation of the situation can be comparatively low-key and still win attention and action.

➤ *Focus on a positive point that everyone can agree on before you address controversial topics.* There's no need to get the survival-level adrenaline flowing the moment people walk in the door. Find something praiseworthy in the team's current approach to things before you start talking about problem areas.

➢ *Set a specific, measurable goal that will bring you closer to a resolution of the crisis, then post a chart that regularly updates your team members' progress toward that goal.* Don't be afraid to put an attractive reward at the end of the road, either.

➢ *Express your confidence in the team's ability to attain the goals set forth.* Another appeal to Maslow's third-level need category, and one too often omitted by harried managers.

➢ *Ask truly open-ended questions at the conclusion of the meeting.* Open-ended questions are those that are structured and delivered in such a way as to encourage meaningful input. Asking a question that is structured openly but asked in an intimidating or overbearing way, is not likely to help your cause. See Chapter 2 for all the details on this listening technique.

➢ *If at all possible, keep the meeting's total length to twenty minutes or less.* For better or worse, we live in an age of television-shaped attention spans. Whether or not the topic you're reviewing is of immense importance in the grand scheme of things, whether or not it has manifold technical implications, whether or not there are implementation issues to address, you must nevertheless *keep meetings with subordinates brief.* This general rule has more exceptions the further up the salary scale your team is placed, but it is worth bearing in mind in all settings in which you have a single important message to get across about a serious matter. Handle intricate technical matters on a one-on-one basis after the meeting.

➢ *If you're dealing with a single subordinate, rather than a group, on an issue of immediate importance,* review the Perspective Check that follows.

Perspective Check: Taking Charge

➢ When taking charge with a **Lone Ranger,** make an effort to show your satisfaction with specific past occasions when the person has "moved mountains" for you. Do this *before* you offer criticism on any point. Highlight an imminent deadline and emphasize how your conversational partner is one of the few people in the organization you can count on to meet it satisfactorily.

➢ When taking charge with a **Sharpshooter,** make an effort to show your satisfaction with specific past occasions when the person has identified serious problems for you. Do this *before* you offer criticism on any point. Highlight the criticial errors you know are waiting to be unearthed in the present extremely sensitive situation and emphasize the dire consequences for the organization if they remain undiscovered.

➤ When taking charge with a **Professor,** make an effort to show your satisfaction with specific past occasions when the person has developed systems that eliminated errors and increased group efficiency. Do this *before* you offer criticism on any point. Highlight the need for a new set of procedures for dealing with the difficult situation you both face.

➤ When taking charge with a **Cheerleader,** make an effort to show your satisfaction with specific past occasions when the person has set an example, or helped you get the best from other team members (or out of others, such as employees in other departments, vendors, or customers). Do this *before* you offer criticism on any point. Highlight the help you need in "rallying the troops" in the face of an important deadline.

HOW TO SELL YOUR IDEAS

Getting subordinates to buy into a new initiative or procedure enthusiastically is one of the chief distinguishing characteristics of an effective manager. Here are five easy-to-implement techniques for getting cooperation and support from your team members in new areas:

➤ *Let someone else take credit.* If you can assign the rough outline of your idea to an individual or ad hoc committee for "refinement," you will very often win near-maniacal allegiance for the new way of doing things—and in a hurry. This technique is generally very easy to make work, and it appeals to Maslow's third-need level by inspiring a sense of belonging, both to the organization and to the ad hoc group you assemble. It also carries the potential for significant rewards on levels four (esteem, if the idea is implemented successfully) and five (self-actualization, if the subordinates are personally challenged in a positive way by the assignment). But this technique comes with a catch or two. For one thing, you must usually be willing to let others assume full credit for the innovation or new approach. For another, you must be willing to allow your subordinates to offer input and to take their suggestions seriously. Taken together, those preconditions may seem to be a steep price to pay. A good many effective managers, however—perhaps the majority—have learned from experience that letting others bask in the glory can be the best deal in town.

➤ *Let your subordinates offer modest refinements to the idea.* If you're convinced that the specifics of the initiative you've already got down on paper are right on target, you may be able to win buy-in from your team members by letting them offer cosmetic suggestions. Sometimes the simple act of being consulted on an important new initiative and/or having one's suggestions incorporated in the final version is enough to get your team beaming with pride.

➤ *Offer a reward to the team member who's able to implement the new idea most effectively.* Post the results when the time comes to pass out the goodies. The rewards may be financial, of course, but you can also get great results from offering subordinates sample products you've been given by an important vendor, movie or theater tickets, lottery tickets, time off, or permission to incorporate an unorthodox work schedule on a trial basis. (That last item may be of particular interest to those team members who are currently juggling day-care responsibilities.)

➤ *Offer three ideas for "discussion," two of which are designed to be shot down.* This approach carries two intriguing advantages. First, it allows your team to take part in a "selection process" of sorts, even though the outcome will be fairly easy for you to manipulate. (You, after all, are one of the participants in the "discussion" with your subordinates!) Second, if they enthusiastically embrace some aspect of an option you had thought hardly worth considering, you've got a new approach to consider! In the event that this happens, you can file the results under "unexpected creativity exercise" and see what refinements are worth incorporating in the idea you *do* want to see implemented.

Although this technique must be designed and executed carefully—the "dummy" ideas can't be too outlandish or your subordinates will smell a rat—it can be quite effective, especially if your department is populated by a good many Sharpshooters. If you weight your two "dummy" ideas with enough plausible mistakes for them to identify, they'll very often settle on the stronger idea that you like as the best available alternative. (It sounds absurd, but this method has been known to win over uncounted Sharpshooters, many of whom consider any meeting that hasn't resulted in something being rejected to be an abject intellectual failure.)

The two-bad-one-good technique may be just a *little* disingenuous. Although in the long run it is probably not as effective as the give-them-all-the-credit technique, it is nevertheless appropriate in any number of settings.

➤ *Remember that catchy phrases or rhyming titles often carry the day.* Would "Dennis the Menace" have been a huge hit on the comics pages if it had been called "Fred the Untidy" instead? Would people have lined up to buy the Shoop-Shoop Hula Hoop a few decades back if the product's name had been less fun to say? Who knows? But there's a reason why advertising industry executives and marketing directors stay up all night thinking of the right combinations of words to attach to their products. Memorable names do better in the marketplace than dull ones.

Take a little time to think of what you want to *call* your idea. What three- or four-word slogan do you want attached to it once people discuss it out of your presence? By developing a compelling piece of verbal shorthand that encapsulates the main point for your subordinates, you'll go a long way toward winning support for your initiative.

Perspective Check: Selling Your Ideas

➤ When selling an idea to a **Lone Ranger,** emphasize any component of it that will allow him or her to spend more time alone, unmolested by others, completing a pressing project.

➤ When selling an idea to a **Sharpshooter,** compare it with other ideas that are logically flawed or internally inconsistent.

➤ When selling an idea to a **Professor,** try to isolate some aspect of the idea that he or she can "improve" and implement for others. Focus on the idea's ability to help the Professor help others work more efficiently.

➤ When selling an idea to a **Cheerleader,** tie it to an impending deadline he or she must meet through interactions with others. Highlight the idea's ability to help keep other team members happy, and point out how team members will appreciate the Cheerleader's making their job easier through incorporating the idea into the group's routine.

HOW TO ENCOURAGE CREATIVE NEW APPROACHES

Managers are often given the vague assignment of brainstorming with team members in order to come up with a new product, a fresh marketing plan, or a solution to a pressing problem. But what, exactly, should this brainstorming consist of, and how should it be initiated? Too often, "idea meetings" turn into drawn-out debates on what's wrong with the *current* approach to an issue. That's not the best way to enhance team creativity.

For one thing, because it focuses on existing systems and limitations, this method is unlikely to yield any surprising new insights that transcend current thinking. For another, team members who do come up with new approaches may be unlikely to speak up about them, because the meeting itself demonstrates that one of the main things that happens to ideas, new or old, is that they get picked apart and criticized!

Here are six tips you can use to get your team to open up and start contributing fresh initiatives that may be helpful to your organization. One important rule underlying all of them is that, during the brainstorming phase, *you avoid criticizing or troubleshooting ideas!* If you say you're wide open to input, but then make someone feel small for contributing, you won't get very far.

> ➤ *Change the physical place or manner in which you hold the meeting.* Let's face it. For most of us, meetings aren't exactly events we look forward to, no matter what their stated topic. Changing locations, surroundings, or seating arrangements is an excellent way to get people to look at the "job" of coming up with a new approach as something beyond the normal routine—and therefore more exciting. You might decide to conduct a ten-minute session with everyone standing up or with upbeat music playing in the background. Some managers have been known to take the team out for ice cream when it's time to conduct brainstorming meetings. Whatever path you take, if it looks, sounds, or feels undeniably different, it's likely to change the way people think about the matter at hand. Once you've altered the setting and set up a new, less-than-foreordained mood, consider saying something like this: "We have X minutes today to come up with fifty potential new names for the Model 166. Nothing's out of bounds. Go for it!" Then start writing.

> ➤ *Have a lousy idea contest.* One innovative manager took the daring approach of buying half a dozen scratch-and-win tickets from a local

lottery outlet and awarding them to the people who came up with the six *dumbest* ideas that arose in a half-hour period on a certain topic. (His decisions on alloting the tickets were arbitrary, final, and more than a little whimsical in their own right.) The aim was to get people to stop censoring themselves and start thinking of unconventional solutions. He wrote everything down, and in addition to the six most outlandish ideas, he got some workable ones as well.

➤ *Use an easel.* There's something about recording ideas in a way that everyone can see that makes team members want to contribute. If you simply call out, "Who can think of a way to shorten our average delivery time?" you may be met with stony silence. If you write "Possible ways to shorten our average delivery time" in big red letters across the top of the easel and then supply the first idea yourself, you'll probably hear suggestions from all corners of the room.

➤ *Use associative thinking.* Instead of fixating on the components of the problem, discuss objects or ideas from a completely unrelated category. In trying to design a new telephone, for instance, you might pick— more or less at random—the image of a thunderbolt and then enlist your team's help in cataloging as many of its attributes as you can think of. After five or ten minutes, your list will contain words and phrases like *fast, loud, impossible to ignore, godlike, bright, tempest, jolt, charge, destroy, kite,* and so on. Now use these concepts in connection with the problem or situation you face. Is there any way to design a phone in such a way that it *looks* fast and easy to use? Would a "loud" phone that has a specially amplified ringer be of interest to senior citizens and those with hearing difficulties? What technology could a phone employ that would be absolutely impossible to ignore—might it glow in the dark when it rings?

➤ *Try varying the pace if you don't get the results you want.* Creativity is a highly subjective thing; some people react well to a fast-paced, get-it-all-out-on-the-table-right-now approach, others would prefer to take a little time to absorb all the issues. It's likely that your team consists of people from each group. Be willing to experiment or to divide the group up into subteams to take full advantage of the varying working styles.

➤ *Don't be afraid to take an unorthodox approach when it comes to dealing with creative people one on one.* Sometimes the most creative person in the department is also one of the most difficult to manage. Establishing a trusting working relationship is the key to getting the results you want and maintaining the kind of office environment everyone else will be able to live with. Here are some ways to build that trust.

Find some mutually acceptable way to allow the person to express his or her individuality. Expecting creative people to adopt a conformist approach is a recipe for job dissatisfaction. Make it clear that being a team member does not mean relinquishing one's own identity.

Make an effort to ask regularly for input on a wide variety of problems. Work together to create solutions you both believe in and, when the situation warrants, be prepared to stand together when others in the organization question those solutions.

Bear in mind that creative workers are particularly uneasy about accepting goals that they don't feel they've had any hand in creating. Rather than issuing commands and summarily informing them of deadlines, take the time to meet with them and discuss the challenges and opportunities *they* see on the horizon. Then review the organizational demands you have to meet. Simply by asking for the creative person's views and aspirations, you will go a long way toward winning buy-in toward a mutually defined goal.

Perspective Check: Encouraging Creative New Approaches

➢ When trying to encourage a **Lone Ranger** to take a creative new approach, try to find a way to allow the individual to develop—and receive credit for—a new initiative more or less on his or her own. Lone Rangers may not do their best creative thinking as part of a committee, although the looming requirement to *produce* something of their very own for an upcoming meeting may be exactly what is needed.

➢ When trying to encourage a **Sharpshooter** to take a creative new approach, begin by asking the person to determine what went wrong with another initiative in the same area, and, just as important, how the job could be done better and more efficiently.

➢ When trying to encourage a **Professor** to take a creative new approach, consider asking the person to conduct "feasibility tests" of several possible approaches and to return with a new recommendation, perhaps one based on elements of two or more of those proposals (or on new data arising from the tests). If the testing allows interaction with other people, so much the better.

➤ When trying to encourage a **Cheerleader** to take a creative new approach, find some way to allow the person to act as part of—or, better yet, coordinate—a group effort dedicated to developing a new way of looking at the problem. You may want to ask the Cheerleader to develop a series of questions for others to consider in dealing with the challenge.

HOW TO IMPROVE A SUBORDINATE'S TIME-MANAGEMENT SKILLS

Most of us don't procrastinate when it comes to doing things we *look forward to*. When a subordinate seems perpetually behind schedule, one reason may be that the tasks he or she is being assigned are best suited to members of another first-instinct mindset group.

No two people have exactly the same working style. Getting your subordinates to make the most of their time is usually a matter of learning the work patterns they typically adhere to, then trying to adapt what must be done to that style. Here are six ideas for doing just that:

➤ *Ask yourself: Can you work within a two-deadline system when delegating to this person?* A two-deadline system is a little bit devious, but it keeps everyone happy. Is your subordinate the sort of person who is always a week late with the report, no matter how much (or how little) attention and resources from other people in the organization are made available? Rather than try to pound your subordinate into submission, is it possible for you to develop a formal deadline (the one you tell your subordinate about) and a more pragmatic deadline (one you keep to yourself)?

Such an arrangment may not always be workable. The projects you delegate may have highly visible public benchmarks, obvious to everyone in the department. Similarly, there may be a negative effect on other employees who don't have a mental block about reaching their target dates. (A good many managers have gotten around this problem by building an extra, say, 30 percent into all their time estimates, no matter who they're dealing with. This may make sense if your work can accommodate such a step. Not everyone's can.)

Assuming that you don't face internal problems with other people, however, you may find this approach worth considering. A good many people (many of them Lone Rangers) are *consistently* off in their estimates of how long something will take, and off by about the same percentage of the total time involved each time. Many shrewd, discreet managers have learned to put this information to their own good purposes.

➤ *When in doubt, ask for clarification on the specifics of the project before you accept a commitment for a certain deadline.* Many people are so eager to please that they will commit even to wildly unrealistic deadlines in the belief that this is the best way to keep managers happy. If you have reason to doubt an eager subordinate's grip on reality, don't wait for disaster and then hold the person accountable once the project is in shambles. Address the subordinate's fourth-level Maslow need for esteem in the eyes of others (namely, you) by expressing your appreciation of his or her commitment to the job:

> "It's wonderful to hear that you're willing to work within such a tight schedule, Rosalyn. I really appreciate your willingness to get behind this and make things happen."

Then query the subordinate about the specifics of the project:

> "Just out of curiosity, how long does it usually take you to handle, say, a hundred entries with this software? I'm just looking for a rough estimate."

By prefacing your question with praise for the subordinate's *desire* to meet the deadline, you're in a much better position to evaluate how realistic the deadline is with your follow-up question. Based on what you find out, you may want to set another target—one that will make both you and your subordinate happy.

➤ *Put it in writing.* No one's saying you need to develop a binding, quasi-legal contract with a subordinate who has trouble hitting targets for you. (Trying to do so, by the way, is usually a huge mistake that only polarizes the situation.) But setting up an *informal* written plan that includes mutual goals, mutually recognized obstacles, and mutual acknowledgment of the applicable margins for error can have a strong positive effect with some subordinates. The half hour or so you spend in setting up such a plan can make for stronger lines of communication and pay huge dividends in terms of commitment.

These written arrangements tend to mean most when they are developed *mostly* by your subordinate. As a matter of fact, working to establish guidelines or principles to follow and then stepping back while your subordinate sets up a detailed plan of his or her own is one of the best ways to help the person begin a gradual improvement of time-management skills. Many managers make the mistake of assuming that a subordinate is going to try to mislead them and rely on a written plan or commitment as a means of "holding the person's feet to the fire." Instead, try seeing the situation as an opportunity for success and renewal.

Ask your subordinate to develop new contingencies, based on old experiences and setbacks, and to *learn* to work enough time into the schedule to accommodate such problems. Only by attempting to review past oversights as part of an ongoing learning process can you expect to help your subordinate improve. Your best bet is to undertake this task joyously, without blame or the knitting of brows, and to focus with a good deal of enthusiasm on the subordinate's capacity for personal growth. This is, or should be, a topic of discussion very different from the one the person probably expects: How awful he or she is for having missed a past deadline.

Set the guidelines, offer a few key ideas, then withdraw. Place the emphasis on written targets *the subordinate* takes the lead role in developing, and you may both be surprised at the developments that follow.

➤ *If you can, make time management the primary focus of a quarterly salary review process.* Is it possible for you to monitor the subordinate's time-management skills personally and reward him or her financially for gains in predetermined areas? (These gains could come in areas such as alerting you to unexpected problems when they occur or estimating job functions with increasing levels of accuracy.) If so, you may be able to see significant positive changes.

Some managers adapt this technique by holding the meetings on a quarterly basis but adjusting the *salary* appropriately at the end of the year. That can be quite effective, as well. However you approach the problem, do so without assuming an authoritarian, confrontational mindset, and make an effort to retain a peaceful and harmonious atmosphere in all your interactions with the subordinate. The idea is to let the person know that improvement in this area is important to you and to the organization—important enough for you to establish clear steps for the person to follow and important enough to make future salary decisions contingent, at least in part, on progress in time management. Remember that people tend to get very nervous around salary review time, sometimes even when they are on the receiving end of a *positive* review. Don't use your position as a supervisor as an excuse to rattle the subordinate even more than the circumstances warrant. Make it clear that you are interested in a positive outcome for everyone.

If you play your cards right, you should be able to set up the guidelines for a written plan developed by your subordinate (see above), and then gradually scale back your oversight of the person with the time-management problem. If you can, emphasize your own progress in the face of similar problems earlier in your career. If you make it clear that you are interested in helping the subordinate move forward in his or her career and not in meting out punishments, you will be in a much better position to help bring about a positive change.

➤ *Let the person know you're behind the eight ball.* If you have the right kind of relationship with your subordinate, you may be able to make an occasional appeal to a special set of circumstances that demands greater than usual attentiveness to time-management issues. By moving the focus away from your status as a supervisor and toward your pressing need for support, in the form of dramatic change as the result of an imminent emergency, you may be able to bring about that all-important breakthrough.

Don't overuse this technique; *don't* mislead your subordinate by manufacturing "emergencies" out of whole cloth; *do* consider combining this plan of attack with one of the other ideas in this section.

➤ *Say, "You know, this really isn't the kind of problem I'd expect you to have."* Even if this happens to be wrong, virtually everyone you say it to will accept it at face value. Human beings are usually quite willing to accept even inaccurate compliments.

You aren't out for shameless flattery here. Your aim is to change the way the person thinks about how he or she handles scheduling issues. This simple technique—which is simply a matter in reinforcing the person's best intentions and turning them into positive action—can often work wonders.

Perspective Check: Improving a Subordinate's Time-Management Skills

➤ When working on time-management issues with a **Lone Ranger,** set a mutually agreed-upon target date by which you both hope to see improvement in the person's scheduling skills. Don't simply instruct the subordinate to "delegate appropriately." Many Lone Rangers are notoriously poor delegators; yours may need tactful long-term help in this area.

➤ When working on time-management issues with a **Sharpshooter,** ask the subordinate to make his or her own assessment of the time spent on a particular project over a particular period of time and to identify any undertakings that could be considered unproductive. You'll usually receive a more accurate—and more effective—critique than you could make yourself.

➢ When working on time-management issues with a **Professor,** ask the subordinate to develop, in writing, a new routine or personal schedule for your review and approval.

➢ When working on time-management issues with a **Cheerleader,** point out that the person must serve as an example to others in the organization, and tactfully suggest specific steps that will help the Cheerleader serve as a model of productivity in the department. (If you can, frame the entire discussion around the problems you are having with *other*—unnamed—employees whose time-management skills are lacking and who need someone to look up to in this area.)

HOW TO GET PEOPLE TO PITCH IN DURING "CRUNCH TIME"

Every company has its busy periods—times when subordinates are asked to do a little more to help the company meet important goals. Pleas for support during these periods sometimes fall on deaf ears and sometimes lead to opposition, conflict, and ill feeling within the organization when heavy-handed measures are implemented to ensure compliance with the needs of the time. Is there any way to get through this time without falling into the trap of barking out orders—orders your team members are likely to end up resenting?

Here are four ideas for getting your people to do their part when you need them most.

➢ *Turn it into a party.* If you can, encourage people to take part in the extra work on a "let-your-hair-down" basis. Make it clear that you expect full attention to quality and professionalism—and make it clear that your team members can expect pizza and good music. Such "dress-down" overtime sessions appeal to third-level Maslow belonging needs and often represent great opportunities to build job satisfaction among your subordinates.

You may decide to use the "party" as an opportunity to blow off much-needed steam and to (subtly) remind your subordinates of the importance of using team efforts to overcome obstacles. All the lectures in the world on fostering cohesiveness and facilitating positive group dynamics may not rid you of snide, behind-your-back comments from team members who see any request for additional work time as part of a sinister conspiracy on the part of management to exploit the downtrodden masses. But a company get-together, complete with edibles and good music (try putting "The One After 909" on the tape player) may bring out the best in even the most suspicious of your employees.

➤ *Publicly award those who help you during crunch time with appropriately personalized plaques and/or certificates.* Such inexpensive gestures are long remembered—and will help you win volunteers the next time around. It seems like a silly exercise, but once you try it, you'll swear by it.

Handing out formalized expressions of appreciation allows you to take advantage of the subordinate's (natural) desire to be accepted as a member of the organization. It also helps him or her establish a sense of position and rank within the group and may help to counter the common impression that "no one ever notices when you do something right around here."

➤ *Be sure you're being clear about exactly what you want.* Many managers leap directly into "mandatory overtime mode" after issuing vague or elliptical requests for help. This usually has a pronounced negative effect on morale. Instead of asking:

> "Paul, could you think about whether or not you have time to help out the people in Accounting next Tuesday night?"

. . . try appealing to a fourth-level Maslow need for esteem and respect:

> "Paul, the people in Accounting are in big trouble, and I think you'd be in a good position to show them how to get the most out of the system if you could pitch in and help them. This could also be a plus when it comes to getting the first crack at redesigning that accounts payable project for them, which could be a real feather in your cap. Do you think you could give them a couple of hours on Tuesday night?"

The answer to the first query is likely to be something along the lines of, "Sure, I'll think about it"—with no action following. The answer to the second query will be unmistakeable one way or the other, and it's far more likely to elicit the positive response you're after.

➤ *Reward those who take on the extra work with a modest, predetermined event or award.* You may decide to take your heroes out to dinner or to a ballgame after the rush is over (a pleasant appeal to Maslow's third-level need for belonging). Alternatively, you may opt for a no-budget winner: the group who puts in extra work is granted first dibs at selecting plum assignments when the new schedule is drawn up or gets to select the music played on the department's radio for a week. One manager promised to make breakfast for his team members for a week, at his own expense, after a particularly grueling project. They collected.

Perspective Check: Getting People to Pitch In During Crunch Time

➤ When trying to win help during crunch time from a **Lone Ranger,** consider offering to exchange the time the subordinate will turn in on your project for the opportunity to work alone at home on a project. He or she will almost certainly leap at the chance. Monitor the results of the at-home experiment; if things work out well, you may be able to open up some office space in your department. (Lone Rangers represent the most promising candidates for successful, productive home-based employee arrangements.)

➤ When trying to win help during crunch time from a **Sharpshooter,** try to incorporate some troubleshooting aspect into the work. If you can find a quality-control slot for the Sharpshooter to occupy, and if you can paint a sufficiently dire picture of how dreadfully things will go awry if the Sharpshooter isn't there to keep an eye on things, you may win a volunteer.

➤ When trying to win help during crunch time from a **Professor,** suggest that the person take the opportunity to test out, "on a first-hand basis," a new procedure or system he or she has been lobbying for. (Evaluate the results of this "test" with an open mind!)

➤ When trying to win help during crunch time from a **Cheerleader,** highlight your own deadline—and emphasize how important the Cheerleader's presence will be to others on the team who are trying to meet that deadline. Or make the entirely legitimate argument that the Cheerleader's presence will probably make others more eager to volunteer too.

HOW TO INSTILL A STRONG CUSTOMER FOCUS AMONG STAFF MEMBERS

Getting the members of one's team to "think like a customer" is one of the most popular managerial aims of the day, but it can be an elusive goal. The sad fact is that most of the lectures about the importance of "customer-focused environments" that issue from the top levels of our organizations are usually lacking in specific, ready-to-implement ideas that will help us change unproductive or inappropriate attitudes among the front-line workers who regularly interact with customers.

Here are eight ideas you can use immediately to get your staff members to treat customers with the respect they deserve—and to minimize or eliminate hostile exchanges with the people who use your product or service:

➤ *Reassign Sharpshooters who can't learn to speak the language of the customer.* Some of the tireless error-locating Sharpshooters on your staff have no doubt made a superb transition to the task of making the customer feel great about your organization. For others in this group, the transition may be a little rockier.

For these Sharpshooters, their work represents an unending series of struggles with customers, a series of inquisitions designed to illustrate that the organization was never really at fault, no matter what the customer may have to say about the matter. This approach represents a serious problem for you and your company.

There's no use sugarcoating the matter: Customers hate the treatment they receive at the hands of these representatives of your company. And, truth be told, the Sharpshooters in question probably find themselves a bit worn out at the end of the day, too. Nevertheless, these Sharpshooters assume the same confrontational stance, call after call, problem after problem. For them, the customer is always wrong. This attitude affects others who must deal with the people who come to your company for solutions, and the cumulative effect can be, in a word, catastrophic.

Sharpshooters are strongly predisposed to engage in a relentless brand of error identification that all too often comes across as faultfinding or "emphasizing the negative." As welcome as the Sharpshooter's efforts may be in the engineering room or the debugging department, they can backfire spectacularly when applied to the world of customer service. If you have a Sharpshooter on your team who seems unlikely to be able to put his error-eradication efforts at the *service* of the customer, you owe it to yourself and your company to reassign that person.

There is some other job this particular Sharpshooter should be doing. Whatever it is, you may rest assured that it does not have anything to do with interacting with your organization's customers. Your task is to identify that job—and then convince whoever needs convincing that the transfer must be made. If necessary, assemble verbatim quotations from your Sharpshooter's discussions with customers. If the Sharpshooter truly falls into the "shouldn't-be-working-in-Customer-Service-in-the-first-place" category, that won't be difficult to do.

Once again, not *all* Sharpshooters habitually assume a confrontational attitude with customers. Some excel in the role of problem solver and do a superb job of clearing away obstacles for the customers they come in contact with. Others in this mindset group simply shouldn't be expected to be able to change the way they approach their work. If you can successfully reassign such a person, the entire attitude of your department will almost certainly improve as a direct result of your action.

➤ *Let your team know that you understand that there are jerks out there.* All the customer-first talk from the top is entirely appropriate. But the people on the front line know that putting the high-minded pronouncements into action is tough work that often leads to interactions with extremely difficult people. You'll reduce stress levels and help keep your people from burning out if you subtly send the message that you understand how difficult the job can be—and that you don't expect your people to pretend every customer is an angel. Solve the problems, yes. Make people happy, yes. Pretend people don't get on your nerves, no.

➤ *Encourage your team to use the product or service themselves.* Staff members who give the product or service a solid "test-drive" (or use it as full-fledged customers) have a better chance of viewing problems from the customer's viewpoint.

➤ *Institute a mystery customer program.* Under this system, a bonus is paid to the staff member who gives the best service to an anonymous company representative posing as a customer. The technique can work wonders when it comes to improving front-line service.

➤ *Rotate your staff members' customer-service duties.* If possible, find some way to keep your team members from performing precisely the same duties, week in and week out. You'll increase job satisfaction, improve group cohesion (a third-level Maslow need), and reduce turnover if you rotate the most stressful job responsibilities among the various members of your work group.

➢ *Allow your staff to transfer the most hotheaded customers discreetly.* Here's an unorthodox but time-tested technique from the front-lines of the customer service world. It's a little duplicitous, but it works. When a truly outraged customer calls in and demands imperiously to speak with "the supervisor," authorize your people to transfer the caller over to a fellow staff member. The sly maneuver can work wonders in transforming cranky, get-me-to-the-top callers into calmer, more focused ones. The simple act of getting through to someone else (someone one imagines to be of greater authority) often results in a dramatic improvement in one's outlook. Don't tell your people to lie to the customer; do allow your people to discreetly transfer the call to another team member and see what happens when "Mr. Jones" picks up the line. (Saying "This is John Jones" or "This is Ann Smith" with an authoritative air is as far as your team members should push things when it comes to convincing the customer he or she has in fact reached a Grand Poohbah.)

Those in the know report that the technique just described often does a far better job of calming down furious customers than any amount of pleading or explaining. Allowing your people to employ this idea judiciously will turn stressed-out subordinates into allies . . . and reduce on-the-job frustration for everyone in the department.

➢ *Encourage your people to let the customer vent, rather than interrupting.* Once the customer has the chance to clear his mind and pronounce his judgments, your team member will be in a better position to depersonalize issues, accept responsibility, and outline the steps that will be taken to follow up on the problem.

➢ *Once your staff member has let the customer vent, let the staff member vent—at you, if necessary.* The person being vented at usually needs someone to vent at in turn. Don't fight it. Nod understandingly and wait until your subordinate gets everything out.

Perspective Check: Instilling a Customer Focus

➢ When reviewing customer-related issues with a **Lone Ranger,** encourage the subordinate to review, resolve, or pass along customer problems within a specific predetermined time frame.

➢ When reviewing customer-related issues with a **Sharpshooter,** emphasize the potentially catastrophic consequences of failing to identify and resolve specific customer problems. (And see the notes above on Sharpshooters who shouldn't be working in the customer-service field in the first place.)

➤ When reviewing customer-related issues with a **Professor,** ask the team member to help you develop (and test) specific long-term strategies for fielding and resolving customer problems.

➤ When reviewing customer-related issues with a **Cheerleader,** appeal to the importance of keeping customers in the fold . . . and speak of them as though they were members of the family. Cheerleaders are naturally reluctant to alienate anyone. Turn this passive trait to a positive plan of action by outlining specific steps that will allow your subordinate to help keep your customers happy.

HOW TO INTRODUCE A POTENTIALLY CHALLENGING NEW SYSTEM

There aren't many managers who look forward to the implementation and training period associated with a complex new computer system or organizational procedure. Here are four ways to make life easier for everyone when you have to get people to change the way they do things:

➤ *If at all possible, arrange a guided tour of a department or facility where the system has been implemented successfully.* Organizing a "field trip" to a site where the same system (or a similar system) is up and running can help you reduce tension among your team members about the changes to come. Be sure to allow your subordinates the opportunity to pose appropriate questions and review, first hand, any elements of the new procedure that seem particularly daunting.

➤ *Emphasize the results you want, but show some flexibility when it comes to the means people use to achieve those results.* We live in an age of great technological change. Conducting an exhaustive top-to-bottom training session for a new, complex arrangement may be inappropriate if your team members need only to be able to use a part of the system in question. Let your aim be to get your team to know *enough* about the new way of doing things to accomplish *most* of what needs to be done without supervision—and let them have enough leeway to improvise a little bit in appropriate areas. After all, there's a pretty good chance they'll have to incorporate *another* technological change in the same area before too long! Why demand that your team be able to resolve every problem arising within the system you're introducing now?

In our day, generalists and improvisers tend to be the ones who adapt best to the constant technological changes in the workplace. Encourage this approach; let your team travel the "it-works-for-me" path if they can deliver the results you're after by doing so.

➤ *Don't tell subordinates how to feel about the changes you're implementing.* It's natural to be a little intimidated, at first, by a new way of doing things. Focus on results, rather than attitude, and let your subordinates go through a transition period in dealing with the unfamiliar system.

Many of the people who are most resistant to adopting a new way of doing things around the office became that way because of a supervisor who displayed a certain righteous indignation about the inadequacies of an old way of doing things. (If you'd based *your* entire working life on a particular system, you might be less than thrilled about the idea of turning it upside down, too.) If you've inherited a staff member who has such a history with another manager, you may be able to earn points by making it clear that you aren't out to convert sinners but to help make things a little easier for the people who work for you. Let your skittish subordinate know that you understand that the first time through a new system can be a little intimidating.

➤ *Drive the new car around the block yourself a few times.* You can't expect subordinates to master an imposing system if you yourself seem to be frightened of it. Do whatever it takes to become familiar enough with the new technology or procedure to show off a real-time demonstration of how it works. By getting your own hands dirty—and maybe even showing how to exhibit the necessary poise when things go awry— you'll win points from your subordinates and earn buy-in to the new way of doing things.

Perspective Check: Instituting a Challenging New System

➤ When introducing a **Lone Ranger** to a new system, go over the procedure in person briefly, provide written instructions as appropriate, and then let the subordinate experiment with using the system for the next day or two independently. Mention that you'll be checking back at a certain time to see how your subordinate is doing.

➤ When introducing a **Sharpshooter** to a new system, ask for input on the best ways to improve *your own training methods* for the system. Demonstrate the basics of the system in person, then provide a brief written series of instructions. Pass these along to the Sharpshooter and ask for a critique of what you've written within a certain time period. Are any of your instructions inaccurate? Not only will you receive a solid critique of your instructions, but you'll also have conducted your training of the Sharpshooter—albeit indirectly.

➤ When introducing a **Professor** to a new system, adapt the idea just outlined for the Sharpshooter. Ask for input on how your written instructions will be perceived by the members of a particular group.

➤ When introducing a **Cheerleader** to a new system, explain that the reason you're training the person is so that others will be able to learn from the subordinate's good example. If possible, and if your Cheerleader adapts well to the system, be sure to allow him or her to share insights on using it with other workers.

HOW TO HANDLE A SUBORDINATE WHO IS RESISTANT TO YOUR CURRENT OFFICE TECHNOLOGY

"I'm just not a computer person."

It's all very well for the CEO of your company to say something like this. She can hire an assistant. But when the "computerphobe" is a subordinate (and sometimes one of long standing) whose productivity is lagging because of a refusal to come to terms with your workplace's technological resources, you've got a problem.

Here are five ideas for turning around a subordinate who's having trouble getting the most out of your equipment:

➤ *Introduce the person to an addictive computer game.* Surprise! There are some instances when getting a team member to play games on company time is the surest route to increased productivity. Playing games like Solitaire® or Minesweeper® (both of which come preinstalled on many personal computers these days) can take much of the anxiety out of the experience for novice users. They'll learn in short order that computers don't bite—and that at least *some* applications can be run without inadvertently blowing up the building.

You may want to monitor the subordinate's time closely for a period after introducing him or her to the game. This is a technique that can work all too well! But at least it will help you to get your apprehensive subordinate in front of the screen for other applications.

➤ *Give the subordinate a guided tour of your extensive backup system.* First-time users are often terrifed that they'll make some mistake that will cause irreparable damage or data loss. By reviewing the particulars of your backup system, you may be able to remove the most debilitating fear your team member faces.

➤ *Acknowledge the initial difficulty of getting the system up and running.* There is very little that novice computer users find more frustrating than having an expert tell them how easy something will be. If you are one of those people who finds working with computers and software systems as easy as falling off a log, congratulations! But don't make the mistake of believing that others view the situation exactly as you do. Avoid dismissing the subordinate's concerns with phrases like:

"You'll get the hang of it."

"It's simple. You can't go wrong."

"Even an idiot couldn't mess things up with this software."

These well-intentioned assurances can be quite intimidating for skittish computer users. All they do is confirm the subordinate's suspicions that he or she *is* an idiot when something unfamiliar materializes on the screen.

For some of the people on your team, the simple fact that a task involves a computer makes it frightening. Take that into account in your dealings with subordinates who are trying to catch up with you in the computer-literacy race. It may be easy for *you* to get work done while staring at a computer monitor, but just for the benefit of the others you work with, *pretend* that mastering the basic commands of the system is as daunting a task your subordinates believe it to be. Then offer sincere praise for even the most modest accomplishments. And be extremely careful about the language you use to describe any setbacks the trainee encounters. (See next item.)

➤ *Eliminate the word "mistake" from your vocabulary while in training mode.* It's easy to forget that the words we select while we are training technically skittish team members can have a devastating impact on their ability to master the system in question. The word "mistake" tends to get the adrenaline flowing instantly, often regardless of the context in which we use it. When we introduce the very *idea* of a mistake, we are acknowledging that such a thing is waiting to be made—and who, our trainees wonder, are better candidates to make mistakes than they are?

That's the dynamic for seemingly nonthreatening passing references to "mistakes." When we come out and *tell* people they've made a "mistake," even with a smile on our face and an encouraging twinkle in our eye, our trainees begin plotting escape routes and mapping out defense tactics. They stop listening and start preparing for disaster.

Other difficult, defense-inducing words and phrases include "damage," "loss," "repair," "breakdown," "failure," and (perhaps the king of them all) "system failure." Keep these terms out of your exchanges with people who are convinced they can't come to terms with the computer age. You'll only reinforce their darkest fears.

➤ *Team the subordinate up with a former technophobe who has made a successful transition to the world of computers.* Such workers are often the very best ambassadors available. Don't let their talents—and their humble backgrounds as recently computer-illiterate workers—go to waste.

Perspective Check: Handling Subordinates Who Are Resistant to New Technology

➤ When helping a **Lone Ranger** learn to use your technological resources, draw specific parallels between the task at hand (say, learning how to use the new design software) and previous occasions when the person has "moved mountains" for you (say, laying out a handsome brochure with a waxer and a light table). Compare a particular function of the software with a particular part of the layout project the Lone Ranger is comfortable performing: the "cut" function of the software is like removing part of the image with a layout knife. Emphasize that the ability to master the system will result in greater autonomy and more time to work on pressing projects.

➤ When helping a **Sharpshooter** learn to use your technological resources, highlight the technology's ability to help the subordinate spot problem areas more effectively.

➤ When helping a **Professor** learn to use your technological resources, emphasize the technology's ability to help groups of people work together more harmoniously. If possible, make the Professor responsible for providing the answers to problems others in the work group have about the system. (This is often a powerful motivating factor that will spur the Professor into developing a truly comprehensive knowledge of the system—on his or her own.)

➤ When helping a **Cheerleader** learn to use your technological resources, emphasize how doing so will help the Cheerleader get the very best from his or her interactions with others in the organization. (*Note:* Cheerleaders tend to react particularly well to technological innovations that make communicating with others in the organization easier and faster, such as e-mail. Try starting them out with these applications first.)

HOW TO HANDLE SALESPEOPLE WHO ARE HAVING PERFORMANCE PROBLEMS

Simply encouraging a struggling salesperson to "get back on track" generally isn't enough to stop a slump. Here are four ideas for getting the very best from your salespeople during tough times—and one more to consider for salespeople who may be in the wrong line of work:

➤ *Use radical pattern-disruption techniques when you hear your subordinate talking himself or herself down.* Author Anthony Robbins is a master of this unconventional technique for removing mental obstacles. Robbins has been known to throw some serious curveballs at his seminar and training participants when he spots them engaging in negative thinking. He's tossed water into people's faces, barked out that the meeting has not yet officially begun, and screamed nonsense phrases into the air—all in an effort to stop destructive patterns in their tracks. It works. Stunned silence invariably follows each of Robbins's dramatic displays . . . and stunned silence is infinitely preferable to the mental/verbal "we're doomed" sessions we all indulge in once in a while. When salespeople indulge, they often bring on the type of mindset that leads to missed quotas and probationary warnings. So don't let them indulge. Do something weird.

Note: This idea takes a good deal of chutzpah to pull off, and it may work best if you appeal to it only on rare occassions. During a "poor, pitiful me" monologue from one of your salespeople, you:

- Start reciting a nursery rhyme for no apparent reason.
- Repeat some innocuous phrase over and over again.
- Play a loud rock-music song over and over.
- Calmly break something to bits.
- Clap your hands in unpredictable rhythms until the person stops talking.
- Disengage from the conversation and make an extremely odd phone call—to the White House, say—while the salesperson is sitting across from you.
- Make no verbal or physical response whatsoever for as long as it takes for the subordinate to realize something is amiss.

Engaging (in good humor!) in any one of these ridiculous activities, or one of your own devising, will stop the salesperson's aria cold—and allow you to focus on the positive message you want to get across.

Here are a few guidelines to follow when it comes to pattern disruption:

1. Make sure that whatever you do is completely unpredictable.
2. Make no attempt to explain it until you've gotten the person to break off the negative thought pattern you've identified.
3. Don't get personal.
4. Don't apologize.
5. Don't use pattern disruption as a means of personal intimidation. It will backfire.

The unconventional technique of pattern disruption owes more than a little to Zen masters and the world's most gifted orators. They use pattern disruption for a reason. Getting a little bizarre has the benefit of instantly convincing people to stop playing their familiar self-pitying messages and to focus with fresh attention on the situation at hand. That's a welcome turn of events for all of us. And in the high-pressured world of sales, where attitude really is everything, the opportunity to stop the bombardment of negative self-talk can be a very meaningful gift indeed.

➤ *Change the setting.* Sales is a strange profession. Achievement within it is unusually sensitive to set and setting. The simple act of moving a salesperson to another office or cubicle or altering the office decor has snapped any number of losing streaks. Why? Well, who knows? Does it really matter? One sales manager I know instructed his salespeople to make their calls standing up, rather than sitting down. The department's performance improved noticeably almost immediately.

Give the change-of-scenery (or change of posture!) technique a try. See what happens.

➤ *Find out whether the salesperson's energy and attention are being focused in other directions.* Many persistent sales slumps are merely the outward manifestations of unseen energy-diverting preoccupations having little or nothing to do with sales work per se. Perhaps the salesperson is engaged in an ongoing personal conflict with a colleague or experiencing trouble at home or battling a substance-abuse problem or having difficulty juggling child-care obligations or facing imposing financial obligations. Such issues may represent first- and/or second-level Maslow needs, and they must be addressed tactfully and compassionately before you can expect achievements at other levels.

If you suspect that there are significant questions along these lines for your salesperson to address, try to discuss them in a nonthreatening, noninvasive manner, preferably over lunch in a neutral setting (e.g., a restaurant or café, rather than your office). Show support and respect for the salesperson's privacy at all times, but make it clear that you are concerned about the person's level of performance and you are eager to find a way to help improve the situation.

➤ *Review the basics of prospecting.* More than one salesperson has settled into a sales slump shortly after a deceptively strong, perhaps even unprecedented, period of success in selling. The problem: Old customers fall away, as they have a tendency to do, and there's no new business to turn to! The cycle is understandable; once we do well in sales, we tend to forget about the importance of prospecting.

The best remedy, of course, is to incorporate prospecting as a regular element of one's sales work. If you're dealing with a salesperson for whom this advice is a little late in arriving, your best bet is to work with the person to review the fundamentals of prospecting and cold calling. One of the very best books on the subject is Stephan Schiffman's *Cold*

Calling Techniques (That Really Work!); the program outlined in the book will go a long way toward helping your former star performer get back on the winning track.

> *If all else fails, reassign the person to a nonsales-related job.* Let's face it. Sales is a demanding, potentially ego-shredding way to make a living that incorporates a good deal of rejection and large measures of career uncertainty. Some of us simply aren't cut out for it. Sharpshooters and Professors, in particular, may have difficulty adapting to the role of salesperson. This is not to say that members of these first-instinct mind-set groups *can't* pursue satisfying and lucrative careers in the world of sales. It is fair to acknowledge, though, that the strong error-identification tendencies of Sharpshooters and Professors present certain obstacles that members of the other two groups don't face in this area.

As any number of sales managers can attest, there are some team members who will simply be happier in another line of work. If extensive coaching and long-term performance problems indicate that you've found such a person, you may be doing everyone a favor by finding him or her another area in which to make contributions to the organization. Perhaps there is some administrative or support position within the sales work group where this subordinate could be likelier to excel.

Perspective Check: Helping Salespeople Who Are Having Performance Problems

> When addressing sales-related performance issues with a **Lone Ranger,** set a firm date (say, thirty, sixty, or ninety days in the future) by which you expect to see tangible progress toward a mutually accepted sales goal. Lone Rangers need something to look forward to; they work best when they have unmistakeable targets to shoot for. Don't expect to see results from them if you deal in generalities.

> When addressing sales-related performance issues with a **Sharpshooter,** praise his or her superior technical knowledge of the product and work to find ways to develop new, previously unconsidered solutions for customer problems based on that knowledge. Don't be surprised to learn that you must, from time to time, review the basics of prospecting and interviewing with this salesperson. (See also the note above on issues of

potentially "poor fit" in the world of sales among Sharpshooters and Professors.)

➤ When addressing sales-related performance issues with a **Professor,** praise his or her superior ability to implement complicated systems and procedures for customers, and work to find ways to develop new, previously unconsidered solutions for customer problems based on that ability. Don't be surprised to learn that you must, from time to time, review certain essentials having to do with assertiveness and the willingness to propose controversial solutions with this salesperson. (See also the note above on issues of potentially "poor fit" in the world of sales among Sharpshooters and Professors.)

➤ When addressing sales-related performance issues with a **Cheerleader,** bear in mind that less may well be more when it comes to correcting this group's selling technique. The gregarious, charismatic Cheerleaders represent the best potential mindset for success in the world of sales. If there is a problem, it may be best to take the least dramatic approach for a time and see what happens—or to offer only indirect advice before attempting to overhaul the salesperson's entire way of working. Even Joe DiMaggio had a slump now and then, but the Yankees probably didn't tell him to radically alter his stance at the plate in order to break out of it. If they had, they would probably only have made matters worse!

HOW TO INFORM SALESPEOPLE OF CHANGES IN TERRITORY, COMMISSION STRUCTURE, OR OTHER AREAS

Just about every sales manager has had to undertake such challenging tasks as unveiling new payment scales, reassigning sales territories, or otherwise altering the income potential (and balance of power!) among the salespeople in a department. Here are five ideas for handling such situations with decorum and tact—and keeping your salespeople happy under the new arrangements:

➤ *Embargo the news until you're ready to tell everyone.* It may be tempting to tell a star performer that there may be some changes in the works, but don't do it. You'll set the rumor mill humming, and your people will stop focusing on their work and start focusing on the darkest possible implications of half-understood, misreported "insider information."

Keep the news to yourself until you're ready to let everyone in on the details. If you suspect a leak, schedule a meeting and deliver the news earlier than you'd planned. You may not have all the blanks filled in yet, but by telling your team what you *do* know, you'll let them know that you respect them enough to level with them and give them accurate information. You'll also put to rest some of the darker bits of paranoia before they arise in the first place.

➤ *Go over your main points verbally before you pass out any written handouts detailing the new arrangements.* If you pass out the hard copy first, your people will "tune out" whatever points you're trying to make while they scan the printout for the information that affects them.

➤ *Explain that you'll be monitoring the new arrangement closely, and assure your salespeople that you are eager to receive their input about the new way of doing things.* Then follow through on your promise by accurately relaying the feedback you get from your salespeople to the appropriate decision makers.

➤ *Emphasize the steps you've taken to assure fairness.* If you've gone out of your way to compensate the reps who have lost a favored territory, point out all the relevant details. If you've established separate compensation categories to make up for lost income opportunities, outline how the new system will work—and don't be afraid to go into a little detail about the potential high end of the new payment structure.

➤ *Let people vent.* Salespeople are likely to react emotionally to *any* change in territory or commission structure. Don't try to cut them off when they are expressing their initial feelings about the new state of affairs. Their feelings of anger, confusion, and mistrust exist; don't try to keep them bottled up. As long as the comments avoid personal attacks or insubordination, give the speaker free rein to talk out all the reactions. If you are asked to reverse the decision you are announcing, politely decline the invitation:

> "I can certainly understand your frustration, Diane, but this decision has been made after a good deal of thought, and it has been settled on as the way we're going to go. I want you to feel free to tell me how you think it's working out as we go along, and I hope you'll do that."

Follow through on your promise to listen to the concerns of your salespeople once the new system or structure is implemented!

Perspective Check: Informing Salespeople of Changes in Territory, Commission Structure, or Other Areas

➤ When changing the sales environment of a **Lone Ranger,** highlight the rewards attainable under the new system and ask the salesperson to *work with you* to develop a plan that incorporates specific targets and dates by which those targets should be attained.

➤ When changing the sales environment of a **Sharpshooter,** demonstrate that you hear and understand the concerns he or she has raised about the new system and thank the Sharpshooter for pointing them out. Explain that, because the decision has been finalized, you're not in a position to reverse it, but ask the Sharpshooter to keep a written record of any problems he or she sees with the new system as it is put into effect and to share that record with you.

➤ When changing the sales environment of a **Professor,** try to highlight the new groups of people he or she will have the opportunity to sell to—and implement solutions for. Prepare thumbnail sketches of some of the most promising new prospects.

➤ When changing the sales environment of a **Cheerleader,** point out (in private, after the main meeting at which the changes are announced) that you are counting on him or her to set an example for the other salespeople in the department. Highlight the effect the Cheerleader's reaction to the new system will have on the morale of others in the organization.

HOW TO RESPOND TO A REQUEST FOR A RAISE THAT YOU CAN'T GIVE

Denying a request for more pay isn't a particularly pleasant task, but it beats ducking the question. Failing to give a clear response to this emotionally loaded request is often the first step toward polarization and misunderstanding between supervisor and subordinate.

Here are three suggestions for resolving the issue constructively:

➤ *Regardless of your assessment of the merits of the request, give the questioner the time he or she deserves to discuss the issue.* Asking one's boss for more money isn't easy. It takes time to work up the necessary courage to approach you, and walking in the door and posing the question can be a truly traumatic experience for some employees. When your subordinate makes this request, ask him or her to sit down and outline the main reasons he or she feels a raise is appropriate. Listen carefully to the information you receive.

You may not have the money in the budget, but by hearing the person out, you can at least appeal to a third-level Maslow need: that of belonging and appreciation. Don't make any comments one way or the other on the quality of the person's work. Just listen to the reasons your subordinate supplies, then . . .

➤ *Congratulate the subordinate for having the courage to raise the issue with you directly.* This doesn't cost you anything, and it is a completely appropriate response that your subordinate will no doubt appreciate. Such a remark also has the benefit of occupying the rhetorical "middle ground"—it allows you to say something supportive without either accepting or rejecting the proposed course of action. Very often, the simple act of reinforcing the subordinate, making it clear that you aren't going to blow your top over the decision to raise the issue in the first place, will be enough to make the rest of the meeting proceed smoothly.

➤ *Briefly outline the organizational or budget obstacles you face and identify a "next step" for your subordinate to work toward.* If your options are limited as the result of a company-wide or department-wide salary freeze, say so outright. Explain how long the freeze is likely to last. Express your regret at the current state of affairs.

Even if you can't (or don't want to) offer your subordinate an increase in salary, you can provide a reasoned, intelligent response that points your subordinate toward a meaningful future goal, perhaps one related to tracking the subordinate's contributions for later review. You should do this even if you are currently disinclined to give the employee a positive salary review. Make it clear that you are interested in "hard numbers," objective measures of job performance, not subjective feelings about the work being performed. Where appropriate, you should thank the employee for specific instances of work that was clearly above and beyond the call of duty.

What you say might sound something like this:

> "Joan, as someone who started out as an editorial assistant, I know that the hours can be pretty long and the first salary review can seem to be a long way off. And I think you've raised some important points here today with your summary of the extra work you did on the Dataroll project.

Unfortunately, none of the managers in the company are authorized to grant salary reviews independently. We're all required to wait until the end-of-year salary review process. And to be honest with you, I don't feel I have enough hard information to put together a review at this point, even if I were allowed to. But here's what I want to do. I'd like to be able to incorporate a summary of the work you did on the Dataroll project, in written form, in the employee assessment I set up for you at the end of the year. And I'd like you to continue to keep track of the extra hours you put in and the specific production work you do on the projects you work on. With everything down on paper, I think we'll be in a better position to evaluate the additional contributions you're talking about. I do want to thank you again for all the overtime you put in on that Dataroll project."

Perspective Check: Responding to a Request for a Raise That You Can't Give

➤ When declining a **Lone Ranger's** request for a raise, set a specific mutually agreeable goal for the subordinate to pursue over a particular period of time. If the Lone Ranger performs according to your expectations in the area you have identified, you *must* follow through with an appropriate financial reward. If you are unable to meet the subordinate's salary expectations or if you feel those expectations are unrealistic, it is far preferable for you to inform the Lone Ranger about this tactfully, but directly, as early as you can. Lone Rangers who are denied rewards that they believe they have earned can become quite vindictive and can poison the atmosphere in your department.

➤ When declining a **Sharpshooter's** request for a raise, be very careful about what you say! You're likely to have your words quoted back to you verbatim at the end of the year (or whatever other time frame is appropriate). Consider asking the Sharpshooter to develop his or her own list of *quantifiable* targets for achievement, and be as specific as you can about the financial rewards the subordinate can expect to see connected with the achievement of those targets.

➤ When declining a **Professor's** request for a raise, highlight the importance of putting everyone in the department on an equal footing when it comes to considering requests for salary increases. Outline the existing system for assessing employee pay levels and point out that in postponing the issue for now, you are only following a procedure that has been implemented for everyone's long-term benefit.

➤ When denying a **Cheerleader's** request for a raise, make specific reference to the types of group accomplishments that the subordinate has helped to make possible. Try to set targets for more such achievements—and follow up with appropriate financial rewards if the Cheerleader hits the marks you set.

HOW TO IMPROVE MORALE

Is your team suffering from a sense of purposelessness or a persistent negative attitude? Sometimes this is a sign of a deeper problem, but sometimes a certain malaise among your team members is simply part of the normal cycle of working together. Here are four ideas you can use to help "take a sad song and make it better":

➤ *When your workload allows, assign some of your team members an offsite fact-gathering task.* Change the patterns a little. Let your people head out of the office for a half day to talk directly with customers, retailers, or end users. Ask them to monitor real-world products or service-satisfaction levels. Then let the selected team members report their findings back to the group as a whole (or anyone else in the organization who needs to hear about what they've learned).

Don't play favorites; rotate the assignments among all your team members on an ongoing basis.

➤ *Show team members that you're willing to undertake a certain amount of "guerrilla action" on their behalf.* On paper, your organization is a seamless one-for-all—all-for-one operation. In the real world, it matters whether your department or someone else's gets the first shot at the new unclaimed office furniture. (Trainer Michael Ramundo often makes this compelling point in his management seminars.)

Make an unorthodox move on behalf of your team members when it comes to securing scarce resources for them. Go out on a limb for them. (*Example:* Meet the truck delivering the yet-to-be assigned office furniture at the loading dock. Scrawl your department's name on the outside of the most promising boxes.)

No, you probably shouldn't make a daily habit of such guerrilla behavior. Then again, you shouldn't hesitate every time a resource allocation decision falls into a gray area, either.

Even if your effort to secure the best for your team fails, you can share the details of your attempt. Make it clear that you're willing to perform above and beyond the call of duty for people who do the same for you on a daily basis. By doing so, you'll show them that you hold them in high enough esteem to take a risk or two for them every once in a while—thereby appealing to the fourth Maslow level in the need hierarchy.

➤ *Send the message: "There are such things as minor errors."* Developing a passion for quality is certainly a laudable goal, but you can't expect your team to develop a healthy approach to their work if every (inherently human) lapse results in an inquisition. Meting out penalties for every infraction of the rules should not be allowed to become an aim in itself or a dominating management philosophy. The best managers learn to dispense not only praise for a job well done, but also an all-important "it's not the end of the world" signal for mistakes that don't represent potentially catastrophic outcomes. Let your team know that you understand that everyone makes mistakes, and that minor ones are part of the workday, too. This is *not* the same as lowering your standards! In fact, it may help your organization get a *better* sense of the errors in your workforce because a healthier attitude toward the discussion of minor errors (and what can be learned from them) will make people more likely to talk about problems before they become serious.

Most important for our present purposes, however, is the effect the "no biggie" message has on your subordinates' outlook on work—and indeed on life in general. It encourages them to loosen up.

➤ *Let your people blow off some steam after a particularly stressful period.* Yes, you all show up in the morning so you can get work done. But once in a while—and especially after a furious period of deadline-intensive work—your subordinates deserve to be cut a little slack. Make a *conscious* effort to lighten the load, if only for a short period, after the rush passes. Once they've worked all those miracles for you, allow your team members the opportunity to decompress.

Perspective Check: Improving Morale

➤ When addressing morale issues with a **Lone Ranger,** look twice—or three times—at the person's workload. Lone Rangers are in the high-risk category when it comes to burnout and chronic workaholism. They have also been known to exhibit impressive levels of denial when asked to assess their own tendency toward overcommitment. If necessary, order a vacation.

➤ When addressing morale issues with a **Sharpshooter,** try to point the person toward a specific project that will allow for all the nitpicking your subordinate can dish out. This is generally enough to bring a little sunshine to the person's day.

➤ When addressing morale issues with a **Professor,** acknowledge openly that there are more potential problems related to system application and procedure implementation than the subordinate can possibly hope to track down and resolve on his or her own. Make it clear that you don't expect this team member to resolve every possible problem anyone in the organization may run into.

➤ When addressing morale issues with a **Cheerleader,** cite specific examples of the subordinate's ability to serve as a strong example for others. In private, reinforce the team member's image as a catalyst and role model within the organization.

HOW TO ADDRESS TARDINESS AND ABSENTEEISM PROBLEMS

"Stan's been late four times this week," your boss grumbles one Friday morning. "Do something about it." You agree to take care of the situation— but what can you do?

Relying on an autocratic approach when it comes to dealing with issues of tardiness is likely to lead to conflict and misunderstanding. Before you indulge a temptation to recite the rulebook to the subordinate, consider some alternate approaches that will help you to stop the problem in its tracks. Here are three ideas for resolving tardiness and absenteesim issues in a constructive, nonconfrontational way:

➤ *Do some digging before you assume you're dealing with someone who has no respect for the rules.* If a new employee seems to be following a different set of standards from everyone else, there's a better than even chance you're dealing with a person who is simply used to a different culture or working environment.

Sit the team member down in private and ask how things have been going in the first two weeks (or two months or whatever time the employee has spent at your organization). *Listen* to the answers you receive; address any concerns the subordinate has. As the brief discussion draws to a close, casually mention that the standards for timeliness and on-site presence at your organization are probably a little stricter than some others. Offer a concise summary of your organization's policy on lateness and absenteeism. Thank the team member for his or her efforts thus far. Move on to whatever you have to do next.

This will usually be enough to do the trick. Remember, a certain amount of "culture shock" among new employees—even those who are used to a nonjob environment, such as a college or vocational school—is to be expected in the early going.

➤ *With other employees who aren't new to the workplace, tie your demand for a change in behavior to some positive aspect of the subordinate's work performance.* Make the connection during a private conversation, and emphasize your subordinate's importance to others in the organization as a role model. (This is a fourth-level Maslow esteem appeal that is best suited to Cheerleaders, but it can be quite effective with members of the other groups, as well.)

The aim is to find some way to cast your subordinate in the role of *someone whose example should be followed* before you make a point of telling him or her about following the rules. It's not *always* a workable strategy—some team members who have attendance and tardiness problems also seriously lag in performance, too, and you don't want to send incorrect signals about their level of performance. But with a good number of the people you'll be dealing with, it will not be difficult to find *some* area in which there is the potential for a good example to follow. What you say might sound something like this:

> "Joe, I know it's been a very productive time for you: You just hit your bonus level for the second straight month, and I want you to know I really think that's great. Congratulations—and remember that people who can perform at that level are the people the others in the company really look up to. Oh, and listen, that reminds me: I've had a couple of comments from Mr. Greeley about attendance. He wants me to start working with people to help improve our record as a department. I think I'd have a better chance of getting the message out to everyone if they knew you were giving it your best shot, too. Mr. Greeley wants us to hit an average of only one day lost out of every twenty, and he wants us all behind our desks by nine A.M. sharp. Can you help me get everyone focused on this, and shoot for those targets yourself?"

This approach should yield the results you're after, but if it doesn't, you should feel free to make more and more specific references to the problem—during private one-on-one meetings, of course. (Never dress down a subordinate or anyone else in public!)

If your subordinate's performance does not improve, there is a good chance that more serious issues than simple punctuality need to be addressed. Try to meet in a neutral setting (such as a restaurant) with the subordinate and determine exactly what the problem is.

➤ *Avoid written warnings; use them only as a last resort, when you are willing to terminate the employee over chronic tardiness or absenteeism.* Written warnings tend to polarize the situation and convince the subordinate that you are an enemy. Use written warnings only when you have no other recourse. Do not issue a written warning to an employee with whom you have not conducted an in-depth, on-site interview to try to determine the underlying reasons for the absence or tardiness problem.

Perspective Check: Dealing with Tardiness and Absenteeism

➤ When addressing tardiness and attendance issues with a **Lone Ranger,** set a specific target date for progress. Let the subordinate know exactly what kinds of improvement you expect to see by that time. ("Over the next twenty working days, there really shouldn't be more than two times when you show up for work any later than nine.")

➤ When addressing tardiness and attendance issues with a **Sharpshooter,** consider asking the subordinate to chart, quietly and on paper, the attendance and punctuality of others and to forward the results to you regularly. For *some* Sharpshooters, this will work wonders, but not for all of them. If you cannot expect tact, decorum, and a willingness to follow instructions from your Sharpshooter when it comes to monitoring the attendance and timeliness of others in your work area, you should consider other ways of changing the person's behavior. One of them might be to find some area in which the Sharpshooter's precision and technical skills can be brought to bear on a troubleshooting problem that represents a "plum assignment"—but that requires prompt attendance at regular meetings scheduled for precisely nine o'clock (or whenever the start of your business day).

➤ When addressing tardiness and attendance issues with a **Professor,** consider asking the subordinate to chart, quietly and on paper, the attendance and punctuality of others and to forward the results to you regularly, and privately. This may well result in a painless, instant turnaround.

➤ When addressing tardiness and attendance issues with a **Cheerleader,** highlight the subordinate's importance within the department as a role model.

HOW TO HANDLE A SUBORDINATE'S TRANSFER TO ANOTHER DEPARTMENT

When we tell people of new assignments and new duties, we often forget that a sudden change of workplace circumstances can be a profoundly threatening and destabilizing period in one's career. By treating the subordinate less like a chess piece and more like a business partner, we can make the likelihood of a good long-term "marriage" far better.

Even with tact and diplomacy, you may find that a subordinate is unhappy about an impending transfer to another department. Here are three ideas that will point you toward smooth transitions:

➤ *Agree to help manage the change personally, and on a regular basis, during the early going.* This "concession," which is probably what you would have done anyway, can serve as a guarantee of good faith in helping the subordinate make things work out with an unknown or mistrusted supervisor. *Don't* promise to serve as the referee of any disputes with the new manager—that will only serve as an invitation for trouble—but *do* promise to supply, during the changeover, occasional emotional support to your subordinate and a continued relationship of *some* kind once the person is settled in the new area. You are dealing with an individual who is in all likelihood eager to retain personal ties that have been built up over time while working with you. Although you cannot offer to continue the job of supervising the person in question, you can make it clear that you have an interest in making sure the transition goes smoothly and in maintaining an ongoing connection with this person.

➤ *Keep the time line specific; appeal to it tactfully and firmly.* You won't always have control over the timing of an employee's transfer to a new department, but sometimes you will. By identifying a particular (and preferably fairly close) date, one that both you and the subordinate need to find some way to work with, you will be able to refocus the conversation on *when* the transfer is going to take place, rather than *whether* it will. Sensitively employed, this technique represents a great way to avoid getting sidetracked with peripheral considerations (such as the strategic reasons behind the transfer, which you may not want to discuss). Specifying a target date for the transfer, perhaps at the outset of your discussions with the subordinate, lends a feeling of resolution to the decision. This resolution is something you can couple with emotional support (just mentioned) and appeals to the subordinate's working style as compared with his or her future manager (see following). When there is a specific date to fall back on as a means of discussing the transfer, you can use that date as a starting point in evaluating what needs to be done—and perhaps use a modest shift of that date as a "concession" that will leave your subordinate feeling better about the situation as a whole.

➢ *During a private, one-on-one meeting, highlight a first-instinct tendency of someone else in the department that matches the subordinate's.* "You're going to love working there. Joe's just like you. He really knows how to focus on a deadline." (Or " . . . how to track down problems.") (Or ". . . how to get the best out of people.") (Or " . . . how to get rid of obstacles and let people do the best they're capable of doing.")

Preferably, the tendency should be one the subordinate shares with his or her new supervisor, but a co-worker in the department can provide a good match, as well. If you need to, please review the appropriate material in Chapter 1 on the two priority scales for detailed information on the traits you should highlight about the new person your subordinate will soon be working with. (And take a look at the Perspective Check that follows.)

Perspective Check: Handling a Subordinate's Transfer to Another Department

➢ When discussing an impending transfer with a **Lone Ranger,** highlight the *deadline orientation or appreciation of the ability to work independently* of someone in the new department. (Ideally, that someone should be the Lone Ranger's new supervisor.)

➢ When discussing an impending transfer with a **Sharpshooter,** highlight the *error-locating ability or appreciation of the ability to work independently* of someone in the new department. (Ideally, that someone should be the Sharpshooter's new supervisor.)

➤ When discussing an impending transfer with a **Professor,** highlight the *error-locating ability or appreciation of the ability to work well with others* of someone in the new department. (Ideally, that someone should be the Professor's new supervisor.)

➤ When discussing an impending transfer with a **Cheerleader,** highlight the *deadline orientation or appreciation of the ability to work well with others* of someone in the new department. (Ideally, that someone should be the Cheerleader's new supervisor.)

FOUR WAYS TO RESPOND TO THE WORK-GROUP PROBLEMS YOUR SUBORDINATES RAISE

A subordinate is deeply concerned about a particular problem in the work group. What's the best way to respond? There are, of course, as many answers as there are potential problems in the workplace. Some guiding principles are worth bearing in mind, however, before you hand over the decision to your "gut instinct."

Here are four basic principles to bear in mind as you try to address the dilemma your subordinate has brought to your attention:

➤ *Listening attentively should be your first reaction, whether or not you consider yourself familiar with the matter your subordinate has raised.* Remember that a very little listening goes a long way indeed! Many managers fall into the trap of believing that taking the time to hear a problem out is the same thing as committing to *resolve* that problem. Your subordinates almost certainly know that every decision is not going to go their way, and most of them will respect the demands on your time if you allot a certain amount of it to devote full attention to the problem at hand. Listening skillfully is an essential skill in managing people; offering your undivided attention, even for a brief period, has a wonderful way of allowing people to leave discussions with a feeling of having been treated with dignity. (In most cases, if you set and enforce realistic time guidelines, active listening has the advantage of consuming less time and energy than dodging people or tuning them out. Haven't you found the process of *pretending* to listen to someone to be a profoundly draining experience?)

Take advantage of the big results you can generate with just a little carefully targeted listening. To do so, you may want to review the specific advice on listening techniques that appears in Chapter 2.

➤ *Remember that many of the seemingly drastic problems your subordinates bring to your attention can be resolved if you can make effective responses to unspoken third-, fourth-, or fifth-level Maslow needs.* A good many of the "must-address" issues your team members bring to your desk are subtly (or not-so-subtly) disguised pleas for attention in these areas. If a sober review of the situation leads you to believe that the crisis your team member is agitated about represents more of a cry for attention than a potential disaster for the organization, don't dismiss the person. Try addressing the problem on terms that will speak to the subordinate's issues of concern.

For a problem that seems to relate, directly or indirectly, to a subordinate's desire to feel that he or she is part of the work group (a third-level Maslow need), emphasize a next step that incorporates a group approach to the issue the subordinate has raised with you. Call a (brief!) meeting when you feel it is appropriate to do so; ask other team members for their input on the valid issues this team member has raised.

For a problem that seems to relate, directly or indirectly, to a subordinate's desire to feel that he or she is respected and esteemed within the work group (a fourth-level Maslow need), take the next convenient and appropriate opportunity to praise the subordinate for having raised an important issue with you. Offer all the specifics you can, and promise to follow up on the issue when you have a solution.

For a problem that seems to relate, directly or indirectly, to a subordinate's desire to attain greater job satisfaction or greater competence within a certain field (a fifth-level Maslow need), try to offer your subordinate a new challenge, preferably closely related to the problem he or she has identified, that will present a greater challenge.

➤ *Demonstrating your personal accountability will go a long way toward making your subordinate feel that raising the issue was worthwhile.* If there was a problem or oversight, say so, and say what you intend to do about it. By showing the subordinate that you understand when there are legitimate grounds for complaint, you will drastically reduce the likelihood that the exchange will take a vindictive turn. Frequently repeating phrases like "It wasn't my decision" or "I can't change company policy" will probably only convince the team member that you are more focused on bureaucratic issues than human ones.

If you can, make a commitment to personally look into the issue the subordinate has raised.

➤ *Once you've let the subordinate outline the problem in detail, specify a next step for him or her to take.* If appropriate, ask the subordinate to help you track down the information you need to resolve the problem or move it to the next level of review within the organization. (Bear in mind, however, that the next step *may* be something as simple as arranging a schedule in such a way as to allow two people whose personalities don't mesh well to work out of sight of each other.)

Perspective Check: Responding to the Work Group Problems Your Subordinates Raise

➤ When addressing on-the-job problems raised by a **Lone Ranger,** stop and ask yourself whether you have been attempting to micro-manage this subordinate. If you have, change your approach! Lone Rangers work best when issued a "long leash."

➤ When addressing on-the-job problems raised by a **Sharpshooter,** stop and ask yourself whether you have paid sufficient attention to the many and varied quality-control issues your Sharpshooter has raised. If you have not, change your approach! Sharpshooters who feel their warnings are being ignored often take on the righteous indignation more commonly associated with Old Testament prophets of doom.

➤ When addressing on-the-job problems raised by a **Professor,** stop and ask yourself whether you have been asking this subordinate to undertake tasks that are likely to alienate other members of the department or result in controversial outcomes. If you have, change your approach! As a general rule, Professors are not big on risk taking.

➤ When addressing on-the-job problems raised by a **Cheerleader,** stop and ask yourself whether you have been attempting, consciously or as an indirect result of the work you have assigned, to get this person to minimize his or her contacts with others in the workplace. If you have, change your approach! Cheerleaders tend to be gregarious and to view their deadlines and commitments in terms of their interactions with other people. Asking them to work in a vacuum is a mistake.

HOW TO SMOOTH WORKPLACE FEUDS

Constant, long-term bickering in the workplace drains energy and attention into unproductive areas—and has a severe negative impact even on those team members who aren't directly involved in the feud. That's dangerous, but the act of ignoring the situation is more dangerous still. Acknowledging that such a problem exists among your team is the first step. If you take appropriate action, you can point all that energy into an area that will move projects forward, not drag things down.

Here are four ideas for resolving pointless conflicts so that your team members and colleagues can move on to the real business at hand. They can be applied to any number of situations, but a certain amount of preparatory work is worth undertaking before you try to implement them.

Identifying which of four first-instinct mindsets are in play is always a good idea during your interactions with others, but it is particularly important when you are called upon to resolve conflicts between subordinates (or anyone else in the organization). You may want to review the appropriate sections of Chapter 1 for guidance on identifying, in short order, the Lone Ranger, the Sharpshooter, the Professor, and the Cheerleader. If you have not yet taken the two-part test that appears in Chapter 1, you should definitely do so before trying to employ the conflict-resolution techniques that appeal to particular mindset types. Focusing your efforts on the member of a misidentified mindset group may well make the situation worse!

> ➤ *After identifying the first-instinct mindsets of the participants, try to emphasize components of the problem they are likely to see from the same point of view.* A Sharpshooter, for example, is likely to share a concern for technical detail and accuracy with a Professor. By focusing on the best approaches that will lead to the successful resolution of technical problems— and, perhaps, dishing out a little well-targeted flattery to both parties on how perceptive they each are in this area—you may well be able to identify some common ground.

> ➤ *Where it is appropriate to do so, bring good ideas or productive instincts related to the dispute out into the open.* These will probably take the form of new perspectives on a pressing problem; make an effort to view things from each party's mindset and to develop solutions that will appeal to others of his or her group.

> ➤ *Don't* try to make one person's personal antagonism the focus of a group meeting. *Do* try to address the most legitimate concerns of each participant of the conflict within the context of an appropriate group

forum. ***Warning:*** *This is not the same as attempting to settle the dispute by committee!* The idea is to isolate issues for discussion and help people move beyond the notion that "nobody ever listens around here." This technique will work best when you make an effort to see, and promote, *each* combatant's best instincts in the situation. (If you are dealing with a situation in which there are *no* good instincts—merely a desire to disrupt the workplace and undermine the efforts of others—you are dealing with one or more problem employees. Advice for dealing with these people appears later in the book.)

Rumor and gossip tend to magnify discord and misunderstanding; the relevant issues openly and, so far as possible, without recrimination.

➢ *Regardless of which side you feel is right, reject any personal attacks instantly and inform the person issuing them that such tactics are inappropriate.* Name-calling, obscenity, or otherwise unprofessional language is inflammatory and highly likely to result in a completely polarized situation. Do not allow such talk from your subordinates to stand without a quick reprimand and a firm pronouncement that such remarks are out of bounds.

When your subordinates see you standing up for someone's basic rights as a member of the work group (a third-level Maslow need linked to belonging), they will virtually always lend strong support to your efforts to bring a measure of civility to the conflict.

Draw your "line in the sand" confidently, without apology, and *immediately* after the personal attack occurs (or as close to immediately as is practicable). In so doing, you will help the participants move beyond individual attacks and be in a position to encourage them to develop a set of ground rules for managing the dispute.

Important note: *Beware of taking action in this area with regard to second-hand conversations!* What someone *reports* as another's remarks is not always accurate. Your aim is not to enforce a standard applicable to every possible controversy when it comes to inappropriate language, but to take action and set standards when you are absolutely sure of the facts. (Besides, if you take action in too many "he-said"/"she-said" situations, people will start believing they should appeal to you to resolve ever more minute and inconsequential disputes.)

➤ *Review Chapter 9 for more detailed information on resolving difficult conflicts.* This part of the book addresses the complex and challenging issue of conflict management in greater depth.

Perspective Check: Smoothing Workplace Feuds

➤ When addressing feud-related issues with a **Lone Ranger,** remember that these subordinates may regard even the well-intentioned input of others in the organization as uninformed meddling. Understand this inherent predisposition for what it is; don't try to label it as "good" or "bad" in and of itself. Channel the team member's intensity into positive directions whenever you can, but don't expect lectures or pronouncements to cause Lone Rangers to change their ways when it comes to accepting criticism or incorporating the views of others into their work patterns.

➤ When addressing feud-related issues with a **Sharpshooter,** remember that these subordinates often deliver unsentimental—and unflattering—assessments of the flaws they spot in the work of others. Understand this inherent predisposition for what it is; don't try to label it as "good" or "bad" in and of itself. Channel the team member's passion for accuracy into positive directions whenever you can, but don't expect lectures or pronouncements to cause Sharpshooters to change their ways when it comes to assessing someone else's work (or their own) for errors. Some Sharpshooters learn to couch their critiques in less intimidating language. For others, the verdicts they pronounce may always have something of an edge to them.

➤ When addressing feud-related issues with a **Professor,** remember that these subordinates have been known to drive others to distraction by demanding a seemingly endless series of charts, graphs, and tests before making a decision. (The trait has been known to push the can-do Cheerleaders and Lone Rangers to the very brink of sanity.) Understand this inherent predisposition for what it is; don't try to label it as "good" or "bad" in and of itself. Channel the team member's eagerness to develop workable systems into positive directions whenever you can, but don't expect lectures or pronouncements to cause Professors to stop asking for what they feel to be adequate proof before making a decision.

➢ When addressing feud-related issues with a **Cheerleader,** understand that these subordinates may take their loyalty to "the team" (or to a customer or other business ally) to extremes. More than one Cheerleader has been accused of lacking perspective when it comes to recognizing the limitations of others with whom he or she has built an alliance. Understand this inherent predisposition for what it is; don't try to label it as "good" or "bad" in and of itself. Channel this subordinate's team orientation into positive directions whenever you can, but don't expect lectures or pronouncements to cause Cheerleaders to renounce their willingness to stand up for those who've stood up for them.

Important dispute-resolution note: Demanding that a subordinate within a particular mindset group "give in" on one of the core issues just described is a sure-fire recipe for conflict escalation!

HOW TO TRAIN AN EMPLOYEE IN A NEW PROCEDURE

When it comes to training your subordinates in new procedures, simply tossing a manual at your subordinate and walking away generally won't do the trick. Neither will flipping on the computer, performing a few basic functions, and making some remark about "getting one's feet wet" is the best way to make sense of the system. (This is a favorite "training method" of Lone Rangers and Sharpshooters that tends to leave befuddled—and agitated—trainees in its wake.)

Here are six ideas for helping your team members get up to speed on the systems they have not yet mastered:

➢ *Break the information up into discrete chunks.* Even those of us who know full well that we live in the television-influenced Age of Declining Attention Spans have been known to fall in love with the forty- (or sixty-, or eighty-) minute training session. It's true: You'll probably get the best results if you focus on fifteen-minute "information" sessions, then find some way to vary the pace between these segments. Don't expect all the key ideas of an hour-long lecture to sink in, even if you do pass along a manual at the end of the process.

➢ *Send emotional as well as logical messages.* Simply reviewing all the steps involved in a particular procedure isn't enough. People respond not only to facts, but also to the level of enthusiasm and approval you mix into the message you send along. In addition to covering all the technical points, appeal fourth- (esteem) and fifth-level (self-actualization and positive personal challenge) Maslow needs as appropriate. A fourth-level emotional appeal might sound like this: "You've gotten a good start on this. I think you're really getting the hang of it." A fifth-level emotional appeal might sound like this: "Once you become comfortable with the system, I think you'll find that it will be able to help you develop that organizational graphic design portfolio that you and Sheila were so excited about at the meeting yesterday."

➤ *Explain, in detail, some devastating error you made when you were learning how to use the system.* Relay a self-deflating story—not in a lecturing, "don't-let-this-happen-to-you" tone, but as an acknowledgment that we are all beginners at some point. The specific technical question under discussion will come across vividly to your listener, and you will also humanize the session and encourage the trainee not to overreact to the inevitable problems *everyone* encounters while becoming familiar with a new way of doing things.

➤ *Remove the word "mistake" from your vocabulary while training the person.* We often forget that the words others direct toward us can have a startling impact on the way we perceive ourselves, especially when we are trying to make sense of a new and potentially threatening situation. The word "mistake" tends to freeze people up and bring the thinking process to an abrupt halt. When we tell people they've made a "mistake," even in the nicest possible way, they begin plotting escape routes and preparing defense tactics. So don't tell people that's what they've done.

➤ *If you are a Lone Ranger or a Sharpshooter and are conducting the training yourself, make a special point of following up with the team member to see how things are working out.* Lone Rangers (like the author) and Sharpshooters often take an "anyone-can-handle-this" approach that leaves the people they train feeling more than a little confused. Some of us even confuse "training" with "letting the other person watch you work for a moment."

If you fall into either of these categories, make a point of following up a day or so after the training session just to make sure that the points that seemed so clear to you ended up being just as clear to the person you were supposed to train. Mark the event on your personal calendar.

➤ *Find the nearest Professor.* Short on time? If you've got a Professor on your staff who is well versed in the system in question, there's a good chance you won't have to spend much of your own time—or any of it—training a person who's got little or no background in a particular work area. Professors *love* to help others find the most efficient way of doing things. By hooking them up with someone who's new to the process, odds are you'll make everyone happy. The person in need of the training will learn the essentials (and then some) about the system. The Professor will have demonstrated once again his or her value to you, to the organization, and to humanity at large. And you will have gotten some work done while no one was looking.

Perspective Check: Training an Employee in a New Procedure

➤ When helping a **Lone Ranger** make sense of a new system, emphasize that the ability to master the system will result in greater autonomy and more time to work on critical tasks independently.

➤ When helping a **Sharpshooter** make sense of a new system, highlight the system's ability to help the subordinate spot errors and act on them before they become real problems.

➤ When helping a **Professor** make sense of a new system, emphasize the system's ability to help various "factions" interact harmoniously with one another, with benefit and credit accruing to the Professor as a result.

➤ When helping a **Cheerleader** make sense of a new system, emphasize how doing so will help the Cheerleader get the very best from his or her interactions with others in the organization. (As mentioned earlier, Cheerleaders tend to respond well to tools that make communicating with others in the organization easier and faster. If you can, put this principle to work for you by highlighting these tools first.)

FIVE STEPS THAT WILL LET YOU SAY NO WITHOUT WINNING ENEMIES

A new computer system you don't have the budget to purchase, a top-level meeting on an overexamined topic the head of the company has specifically warned you she's sick and tired of discussing, a more lucrative commission structure for one and only one person—whatever it is, your subordinate really wants it. And no matter how earnestly he or she pleads, the sad reality is that you can't supply it. Sometimes it's a good idea to finesse such requests by asking for some time to "review matters thoroughly," but sometimes your best bet is to get the bad news out on the table in short order.

Here's a five-step plan that will help make telling people no a little easier:

➤ *Let the team member deliver his or her soliloquy before responding.* Even if you've heard the request before, there's a good chance your subordinate has spent a good deal of time fine-tuning the message. A good many subordinates, when strategizing requests they know are likely to be controversial or hard to obtain, will actually go to the trouble of writing down and/or memorizing a speech for your benefit. Don't deprive your subordinate of the opportunity to deliver it. Hear the person out.

Interrupting a subordinate while he or she is delivering a carefully composed request will virtually guarantee ill will and may result in the beginnings of a shouting match. Who needs it? Your decision to listen to the person's request doesn't in the least diminish your role as the final arbiter of the decision. In fact, when you hear the person's aria, you *strengthen* your position as the final judge in the area in question.

If the situation demands it, ask the person to operate within a mutually agreeable time limit. But take the time to listen to the request, especially when you know that your subordinate has spent time developing or refining it.

➤ *If your aim is to resolve the issue once and for all, get the bad news out on the table in short order.* Once the subordinate has finished speaking, briefly *restate* the main points of his or her message, *express your understanding and support* of one or more of the subordinate's goals in making the request, and then *state clearly* that you cannot approve the request. Don't offer a *raft* of supporting reasons for your position *first;* your listener will be monitoring you for a yes or no response. Provide one, and then offer all the reasons that you feel are worth reviewing.

Engaging in lengthy technical or procedural discussions before delivering the verdict (a tactic Sharpshooters and Professors are wont to engage in) may lead your listener to believe that there is a yes at the end of the message. When the team member learns that this is not the case, you may have a good deal more resentment to deal with than you'd bargained for.

Here is what your rejection of the subordinate's request might sound like:

> "*(Restate:)* Harry, I appreciate your taking the time to discuss the issues you've just gone over. It sounds to me that you're concerned about the limitations of the current system, especially as it affects you during cata-logue production time. *(Express understanding and support of one or more of the subordinate's goals:)* You've got an excellent eye for assessing the work-flow in the department, and I really appreciate the fact that you're trying to find ways to help people work more efficiently in Production. *(Clearly state your decision:)* But the budget restraints that we've been forced to work under this year make it impossible for me to even think of approv-ing a new computer system until the next fiscal year. I know this must be disappointing for you to hear, Harry, but I'm afraid we're going to have to make do with what we have for a while."

➤ *Let the subordinate react.* It's only human to feel disappointment at hav-ing had a request rejected. Allow your subordinate the opportunity to briefly express that disappointment.

➤ *Think of something else you know the subordinate is obsessive about and try to point him or her in that direction.* Having turned down the subordinate's request, try to change the subject (or link it) to a matter you know your subordinate feels particularly strongly about. If you can, offer to help the subordinate achieve a goal in this area:

> "Harry, did you ever get the chance to draw up that artwork and photo log you mentioned at the last meeting? You mentioned how tight things are for you in the department now, and I know having to track down missing art probably doesn't do your schedule any good during deadline time. Would it help if I asked Laura to give you a hand setting that up this afternoon?"

➤ *As you move toward concluding the session, emphasize common goals.* Even though you and the subordinate have a different point of view about how best to handle the matter at hand, there is some constructive point or important organizational goal that you both view in basically the same way. Move away from "right vs. wrong" discussions by isolating some piece of common ground and highlighting it:

> "Well, it's obvious we both want to put out the best possible catalogue with the resources available to us. We hope the company will be operating under a spending environment that's a little less restrictive before too long, right?"

Perspective Check: Saying No Without Making Enemies

➤ When denying a **Lone Ranger's** request, close the meeting by giving this team member some goal to work toward that will bring him or her closer to achieving the objective you have been discussing. Lone Rangers are extremely goal-oriented and are likely to take outright dismissal of the request, with no possibility of reconsideration, as a personal affront of sorts. If at all possible, leave the Lone Ranger a little "daylight" to work toward.

➤ When denying a **Sharpshooter's** request, ask for his or her ongoing help in monitoring problems in the area under discussion.

➤ When denying a **Professor's** request, you may be able to make your case more convincing by highlighting a key constituency within the organization that would react badly to the idea the Professor is suggesting.

➤ When denying a **Cheerleader's** request, highlight the greater importance of attaining an imminent team goal—one that the subordinate will play a key role in attaining.

ELEVEN WAYS TO GIVE CONSTRUCTIVE CRITICISM

Remember the *Peanuts* comic strip in which Lucy van Pelt went around the neighborhood collaring all her acquaintances and reciting their faults from an exhaustive list she'd developed? For some reason, her friends didn't react at all well to the well-intentioned experiment.

Even when we have a completely valid point about someone else's performance level, attitude, or communication style, transmitting the message in a way that will allow the other person to understand and act on our observation takes tact, precision, and practice. Simply reciting the fault to the person's face ("You need to increase your keyboarding accuracy; it's the lowest in the department") is likely to backfire!

Here are eleven ways to get the message across to your team members constructively:

➤ *Discuss any changes you expect your subordinate to make during a private meeting.* Do not address sensitive issues with a subordinate or express any form of criticism, in a public forum. It will embarrass the team member whose performance you are trying to alter and let other workers know that they can expect their own errors or mishaps to be addressed publicly. This type of dynamic encourages coverups.

➤ *Avoid stating facts.* Appealing to "matters of fact" when you are trying to change someone's approach to a project can be a dangerous undertaking.

It is often quite pointless to pursue "the facts," even when you are dealing with a set of circumstances about which you are entirely correct. As any good salesperson can attest, human beings are creatures of emotion, hunch, instinct, and impulse—not computers working through elaborate logical chains. (Yes, this is true even of Sharpshooters, though most of them would hesitate to admit it!) The "facts" are likely to be interpreted through your team member's unique set of prejudices, predispositions, and defense mechanisms. You don't want to argue about what is or is not the case; you want to point your subordinate in a new direction and get better results.

Talk in terms of what you believe, what you have heard, what you understand to be true—not what *is*. If you must correct your team member's erroneous information or approach, do so indirectly:

> "I wonder whether the report might not be even stronger if we started thinking about using some color at key points in the text."

Instead of:

> "Black and white reports are boring."

➤ *Find something you can praise before correcting the team member's assumptions.* Another way to avoid the temptation to tell the subordinate he or she is in the wrong is to identify something that is *right* in the subordinate's approach. Then use that as your transition point for the issue you want to address. It might sound something like this:

> "On page four, I thought the return rate was twenty percent, but, you know, the points you make on that page about distribution are right on target."

➤ *Preface any correction with a statement of how much you need the person and appreciate his or her work—and offer appropriate details.* If you truly *don't* need the person and *don't* appreciate his or her work or potential for work, you are, by definition, in a near-firing situation. (See the later section of this chapter for details on how to handle that difficult chore.) Most of the time, however, there's something about the subordinate's work you can find to praise before pointing out a problem.

➤ *Beware of "should."* Telling people what they "should" or "shouldn't" do often comes off sounding imperious and dictatorial. The same goes for "ought." You'll probably get better results if you say something like this:

> "I'm not sure sending that overnight is your best bet. Remember that memo Greeley sent along to everyone about keeping our freight costs down? Why don't we try Priority Mail?"

➤ *Find something positive in the subordinate's effort and praise the guiding idea behind that positive element.* Once you've done that, you'll be in a better position to identify a more productive approach for your team member. What you say could sound something like this:

> "It's really wonderful the way you're pulling out all the stops to try to make this deadline. I think you're going to make it, but I'm wondering if you should schedule some extra time for proofreading the brochure before it goes off to the printer. You've got a lot of copy coming in here at the last minute."

➤ *If the subordinate raises a legitimate grievance during your meeting, assume personal responsibility for following up on that issue.* Many so-called "morale problems" or "productivity problems" are rooted in long-simmering disputes and/or valid complaints. If a meeting with your subordinate leads you to believe that there is a work-related grievance that requires attention, assure your team member that you will personally review the problem and follow up. Doing so will almost certainly result in a rapid improvement in the subordinate's attitude.

➤ *Review the trait you're trying to correct for specificity before you attempt to get the subordinate to change his or her way of doing things.* Is the change you want the person to make too vague to be successfully implemented? One frustrated manager at an art-supply firm had an unending passion for instructing her key people to develop the proper "precision in action." The oft-cited goal was incorporated into numerous heart-to-heart talks with a half-dozen subordinates, but it was repeated so often and connected to so many disparate circumstances, that it eventually lost all meaning.

But what about corporate culture? What about the mission statement? What about those company-wide "marching orders" that use words like "precision," "quality" and "excellence"—and are quoted over and over again to employees throughout the course of the working year?

Mission statements *can* take the form of sweeping, broadly defined initiatives, and they should certainly support all our efforts to improve the work that we do. But mission statements are not the same thing as face-to-face encounters with subordinates who need help in a particular area. The changes we ask subordinates to make in their personal approach to their work should be *specific* and should show that we have gone to the trouble to observe their situation carefully, not merely to recite a popular paragraph from the annual report.

Offering a catch-all phrase we can adapt to any situation that doesn't suit our fancy may allow us to scratch an item off our to-do list, but it won't give our subordinates much to work from. Instead of constantly appealing to the (self-evident) importance of proper "precision," that manager at the art-supply firm could have gotten better results by posing a specific *question* along the following lines:

> "Ernie, I'm concerned about a letter I got from a customer about a problem he had with one of our products. He says he had to make adjustments to the casing on our model S-24 widget in order to get it to fit his frame. Could you take a look at it, tell me whether you think he's identified a problem, and, if he has, draw up a list of the quality-control steps we can consider going over with your department?"

Such a query is just as "direct" as the earnest, unvarying repetition of the "precision" mantra, but it is far likelier to result in positive change.

➤ *When addressing a "character flaw," try ascribing it to someone other than the subordinate before you instruct him or her to change a personal behavior.* Don't tell tales out of school on your colleagues; do remember problematic college chums, former co-workers, former spouses, or anyone else from the distant past whose habits were (or can be made to appear) strikingly similar to the one you want your subordinate to focus on. Casually tell a story that illustrates the dramatic consequences of failing to address the problem in question.

➤ *When you're tempted to explode, ask a question instead.* You'll get further with the subordinate if you express your concern in terms of detached curiosity, rather than righteous indignation. There is inherent power in the phrase "I was just curious"—use it to your advantage, and don't be afraid to incorporate a little *nonsarcastic* humor in the process:

"Joanne, I was just curious—have you given any thought to developing a checklist for the production people to work with, so we don't have to go through the missing-UPC melodrama again with them?"

➤ *Allow failure.* Are you sure you have to try to correct this person now? Sometimes the most interesting solutions and learning experiences arise from so-called "mistakes." Ask yourself: What is the worst-case scenario you can associate with simply letting the team member pursue his or her own way of doing things and then following up appropriately afterwards? An interesting side note: Many members of minority groups report feeling suffocated by managers who are so eager to help them learn to succeed that they are never allowed to fail. Failure is an essential part of the learning process. Don't try to eliminate it from the equation.

If you can, express your concerns from within a context that encourages your subordinate to experiment—and fill you in afterward on what happens.

Perspective Check: Giving Constructive Criticism

➤ When trying to pass along constructive criticism to a **Lone Ranger,** emphasize your gratitude for the person's general ability to get a great deal done when the chips are down. Give examples of this behavior if you can. Make it clear that you've come to count (or if you're dealing with an emerging performer, hope soon to be able to count) on that ability. *Then, as part of your previous statement,* isolate the issue where you hope to see improvement and identify it as a potential, but not a serious, obstacle to your Lone Ranger's growth and success. Close by reinforcing your appreciation of the Lone Ranger's positive traits.

➤ When trying to pass along constructive criticism to a **Sharpshooter,** emphasize your gratitude for the person's capacity to spot potentially catastrophic problems. Give examples of this behavior if you can. Make it clear that you've come to count (or, if you're dealing with an emerging performer, hope soon to be able to count) on that ability. *Then, as part of your previous statement,* isolate the issue where you hope to see improvement and identify it as a potential, but not a serious, obstacle to your Sharpshooter's growth and success. Close by reinforcing your appreciation of the Sharpshooter's positive traits.

➤ When trying to pass along constructive criticism to a **Professor,** emphasize your gratitude for the person's general ability to help things in the area run smoothly, without costly organizational breakdowns. Give examples of this behavior if you can. Make it clear that you've come to count (or if you're dealing with an emerging performer, hope soon to be able to count) on that ability. *Then, as part of your previous statement,* isolate the issue where you hope to see improvement, and identify it as a potential, but not a serious, obstacle to your Professor's growth and success. Close by reinforcing your appreciation of the Professor's positive traits.

➤ When trying to pass along constructive criticism to a **Cheerleader,** emphasize your gratitude for the person's general ability to inspire, and serve as an example for, others in the organization and his or her capacity for acting as a role model in time-sensitive situations when everyone has to pull together. Give examples of this behavior if you can. Make it clear that you've come to count (or if you're dealing with an emerging performer, hope soon to be able to count) on that ability. *Then, as part of your previous statement,* isolate the issue where you hope to see improvement and identify it as a potential, but not a serious, obstacle to your Cheerleader's growth and success. Close by reinforcing your appreciation of the Cheerleader's positive traits.

HOW TO DEAL WITH PROBLEM EMPLOYEES

Every manager has to deal with them, but not every manager can honestly claim to have acted with a cool head when difficult employees "acted out."

> *Note:* The subject here is not people who have serious psychological problems or who have drug abuse issues to resolve or who are coming to terms with a major crisis in life (such as a divorce or the death of a loved one). People in these three categories act erratically and unpredictably, but they do so for a clear reason. The first two cases call for outside counseling and treatment; the last calls for a period of patience and forbearance.

What *is* at issue here is the best way of dealing with those employees for whom freeloading, lying, or baiting or undercutting the boss come to be pastimes of sorts. We are talking about those comparatively well-adjusted subordinates for whom getting away with inappropriate workplace behavior—whether that behavior is directed toward colleagues or superiors—is part of the challenge of the day. These people's energies, can be better directed in other ways, and your job is to find a way to point them somehow toward a constructive outlet for those energies, one that they have a better-than-even chance of actually focusing on.

Here are six suggestions for responding appropriately to those employees who seem to delight in crossing the line. In many—not all, but many—cases, you will be able to use the ideas that follow to take a counterproductive but nevertheless energy-laden set of behaviors and harness them in a direction that will allow this person to function more effectively as a contributor to your organization:

➢ *Remember the "Pygmalion Effect."* Dr. Rick Brinkman and Dr. Rick Kirschner describe this powerful dynamic in their excellent book *Dealing with People You Can't Stand.* Simply stated, the Pygmalion Effect describes the phenomenon whereby a poor typist who is treated as though he were the best keyboardist in the department may show a dramatic improvement in his typing skills. In other words, by simply *assuming* your people excel in a particular area and treating them accordingly, you may be able to help them improve their performance.

The technique has implications in a wide variety of areas when it comes to dealing with promising subordinates, but the Pygmalion Effect presents a host of particularly intriguing questions when it comes to dealing with *difficult* subordinates. What would happen if we stopped focusing on the negative with the department's "head case" and started, just as an experiment, treating him or her with exactly the same deference, enthusiasm, and acceptance we show when talking to our top performer? Could something that simple really turn someone around? Brinkman and Kirschner argue persuasively that it could.

What about situations involving insubordination or inappropriate workplace behavior? Brinkman and Kirschner advocate telling difficult people, "That's not like you"—even when it is *exactly* like the person in question. And they cite some pretty remarkable results.

The Pygmalion Effect is a fascinating example of the power of positive reinforcement, even when it is (from our point of view, at any rate) completely inappropriate, due to the apparent lack of anything positive to reinforce! It couldn't hurt to try the technique—and it could make a world of difference.

➢ *Find some area in which you can acknowledge the problem employee's superior expertise or ability.* Many employees who make life difficult for managers have serious self-esteem problems and believe that others do not respect them or their work. Address this fourth-level Maslow need by pointing out some facet of the job that this person performs better than anyone else—including you. This approach may take a couple of tries to execute perfectly, but many managers have determined that such knee-bending toward the problem employee is a small price to pay for some peace in the workplace. It is quite startling to find out how such an acknowledgment, often of a distinctly marginal aspect of the work, can change someone's outlook. Praising the person publicly for his or her corner of excellence is also highly likely to turn things around for you.

➤ *Don't respond to abusive or attacking questions.* The temptation to respond directly to a question (particularly an obnoxious one) can be overwhelming. We are trained to answer queries from an early age; when people ask questions with premises that challenge our authority or competence, we generally feel a natural inclination to set them straight. But by doing so, we only increase the likelihood of sustained conflict. Keep your cool. Sidestep the question and return to the point under discussion:

> "We're not discussing people's level of education, Mike. We're discussing appropriate and inappropriate language to others in the workplace."

➤ *Refrain from issuing any direct order or instruction to a problem employee.* Barking out orders isn't a great way to treat *anyone* in the organization, but it is fraught with particularly unpleasant possibilities when applied to those subordinates itching for a fight.

At several earlier points in this chapter, we examined the advantages of *indirectly* phrasing directives, suggestions, or criticisms. All that advice goes double when it comes to troublesome team members. Issuing an order to these people means that you are willing to stand behind the letter of the order and enforce it. If you're not willing to do that, keep things on a "have you thought about" and "what if we" basis.

➤ *Try transferring the relationship to paper.* Memos are wonderful things, especially when you have to deal with someone who has a serious problem with face-to-face encounters with authority figures. Many a problem employee has been turned into a productive team member by a manager who knew how to compose an upbeat, humorous, nonthreatening, and *nonsarcastic* memo every working day.

This approach is not the answer to every possible instance of inappropriate workplace behavior, but there are *some* instances where it can achieve truly remarkable results. Many of the people we're discussing have underdeveloped social skills, and their inability to interact well on a face-to-face level may be the sort of problem that more or less solves itself when goals, suggestions, and instructions are limited to the printed page, rather than delivered during one-on-one meetings. Many managers find that this technique can instantly relieve the tension and pressure from the in-person encounters, which often become more socially oriented, allowing the partners to focus on innocuous small talk.

If your problem employee *doesn't* show some kind of improvement, then:

➤ *Get rid of chronic problem employees.* If you've made consistent, long-term efforts to improve the situation and have gotten nowhere with the employee, you should seriously consider cutting the cord. After all, you're running a work group, not a psychotherapy center. If you've given the relationship your best effort and are honestly convinced you're dealing with an employee who seems to enjoy causing trouble, someone who will never work out at your organization, *take action.* Don't bother with halfway measures (like transferring the person to some poor manager who has no idea what's coming). Document what needs to be documented, then initiate the process that will allow you to say goodbye.

See the section on termination near the end of this chapter.

Perspective Check: Problem Employees

➤ When dealing with a **Lone Ranger** who is a problem employee, give the subordinate a specific improvement target to hit within a specified period of time. Then get out of the person's way and see what happens. (Positive-thinking, Pygmalion Effect variation: Is this person capable of taming your next impossible deadline? Would you consider allowing him or her to work more or less alone on the project?)

➤ When dealing with a **Sharpshooter** who is a problem employee, ask the employee to work on committing error assessments to paper rather than delivering them in person (and perhaps inappropriately). (Positive-thinking, Pygmalion Effect variation: Is this person capable of becoming your ace troubleshooter in another area? Would you consider allowing him or her to work more or less alone on the project?)

➤ When dealing with a **Professor** who is a problem employee, ask the employee to develop a series of tests and measurements of his or her own performance in a certain area and to share the results with you regularly. (Positive-thinking, Pygmalion Effect variation: Is this person capable of tackling a troublesome organizational or system issue for you in another area? Would you consider allowing him or her to supervise other people on a temporary basis to complete the project?)

➤ When dealing with a **Cheerleader** who is a problem employee, ask the team member to consider the effects of his or her actions on the morale of others in the department. Appeal to his or her status as a potential leader. (Positive-thinking, Pygmalion Effect variation: Is there a group-oriented product—even a modest one—that you can delegate to this person? Would you consider allowing him or her to take a leadership position on the project?)

SIX IDEAS FOR IMPROVING DELEGATING SKILLS

When people say that someone "hasn't learned how to delegate," it's a good bet that what they're really saying is that the person has problems communicating objectives effectively and providing people with the proper tools. Here are six ideas that will help you get your point across, identify core principles, establish harmonious relationships with the people to whom you hand over projects, and minimize the danger of your project grinding to a complete halt (or, worse, moving in a direction you would never have approved).

➤ *Make your objectives specific and make sure you're communicating them clearly.* Telling a subordinate to "review the report for trouble spots" or "eliminate any errors that still remain" may make you feel as if you've covered everything, but the fact remains that such all-encompassing instructions are devilishly difficult to carry out. Part of being an effective manager is being able to quantify and specify instructions, and it may well be the most important part. Running a close second could be the willingness to take responsibility for a set of instructions you've mangled, return to the situation, let the subordinate know that communication really *is* a two-way street, and say that you missed something the first time around. Many subordinates who fail to master a set of hastily passed-along instructions are left to dangle in the wind for a while, even when they ask for help. The clear implication is that their ability to "understand" is lacking. A manager who is willing to go back to the person to whom he or she delegated things, admit that something slipped through the cracks, and review principles that should have been emphasized the first time around will get better end results—and build trust at the same time.

You and your subordinate will probably both be happier in the long run if you outline what you want in enough detail for him or her to be able to chart meaningful progress toward a particular goal—independently. What you say could sound like this:

> "Could you please take a few minutes to proofread the report for me, then go over it once again to make sure we addressed all the points Mr. Bigg raised? Here are the notes from the meeting we had with him; let me know if any of the points he raised seem tricky."

➤ *Don't simply* instruct *people to do things you know they won't do or will take any opportunity to avoid doing.* If you know your subordinate will take advantage of any chance to avoid or postpone a particular task, or if you strongly suspect that he or she simply loathes carrying out something you're trying to delegate, there are only so many times you can "delegate" the task in question before things will start to backfire.

Giving orders may seem, at first, to be the sort of activity that arises from a position of strength, but the fact is that ordering people around is really a symptom of weakness—especially if you know ahead of time that the order won't be carried out! All too often, "orders" result in "disorder." We don't take into account the conditions our subordinates will be facing or the attitude they will bring to the task. If we set them up for failure or feed a long-standing grudge, we will undercut our own authority.

If your subordinate chafes at the bit every time you try to pass along a particular job, there is a deeper issue for you to discuss. Address it directly before you attempt to cross the item off your list or pass the job on to someone else. Just as a good attorney will never ask a question without knowing what the answer will be, you should never give an order if you suspect there is a better-than-even chance the desired action will never be carried out.

If you have the time, try to get to the bottom of things. Your attempt to address an underlying problem issue could sound like this:

> "Susan, when we talked about filling out the X-43 reports for Ms. Jones last time, I got the feeling you wanted to get a little more guidance on making use of the computer printout to complete the entries. Was I right about that?"

If your guess about the potential problem was right, you'll probably know in short order. If not, you should encourage the subordinate to tell you where the problem lies. (See the bullet that follows for guidance on where to go from there.) If your subordinate consistently avoids important parts of his or her job—or makes your attempt to pass along work a cause for melodramatic exchanges or sarcastic retorts—you are dealing with a problem employee. See the advice in the previous entry.

➤ *Make sure your subordinates have the tools and strategies they need.* Have you given sufficient thought to the question of *how* your people are going to accomplish the goals you've laid out for them? If the task is a complex one, consider setting out all the key steps in a written memo. If there are other people in the organization for your people to contact or persuade, offer some pointers on dealing with these people. If there are new systems to master, take the time necessary to walk your people through the training period, and be sure you've left them feeling comfortable with the procedures before you abandon them to the fates. (See also the advice below on tossing out hypothetical situations before you consider the task delegated.)

➤ *Don't ask a subordinate whether or not he or she "understands" the steps involved in a procedure; instead, toss out a hypothetical situation—in a nonthreatening way—and ask how the subordinate would respond.* It's often extremely difficult for people to admit to a superior that they don't understand something. You'll get better results and waste less of everyone's time if you say something like this:

> "Okay, so that's the basic procedure for handling refund requests from a customer. Let's take a minute to do a little role-playing game. Let's pretend I'm a customer, and I call up and say something like this: 'I placed my order the night before last, and you people said everything was all set for overnight delivery, but my wife didn't get the flowers I ordered for her. I want my money back, and I want it now.' How would you respond to that?"

➤ *Make it clear that a subordinate should ask for help if necessary.* Let's face it, you can't plan for everything. You'll relieve a lot of initial tension and probably increase everyone's confidence level if you let your team member know what kinds of circumstances he or she might run into that will require more input from you.

➤ *Have a backup plan.* What if things don't go exactly as you and your subordinate plan? Have you got a backup plan? Or two? Or three? The act of delegation does not relieve you of the responsibility for making the kinds of contributions that lead to the development of workable contingency plans. Nor does it mean you are at liberty to leave the task of following up entirely in someone else's hands. Even if the person to whom you are delegating the job is a trusted achiever—*especially* if the person to whom you are delegating the job is a trusted achiever—you must be on your guard against complacency. The fact that things have worked out well in the past is no assurance that they will continue to do so in the future. Work out contingency plans with your subordinate before you pass the job along. After you've passed it along, mark your calendar. Ask how things are progressing. Be willing to develop additional contingency plans as circumstances require.

Perspective Check: Delegation

➤ When delegating a task to a **Lone Ranger,** establish key goals, review the resources available, highlight the deadline, and get out of the person's way.

➤ When delegating a task to a **Sharpshooter,** be as specific as you can about the types of problems you want to avoid. Appeal to the Sharpshooter as an expert at spotting these types of problems, and try to find a way to let the person work independently on what you have passed along.

➤ When delegating a task to a **Professor,** ask the employee to help you develop a written battle plan for tackling the problem. If it's possible for you to do so, allow the team member to consult with others as part of developing this plan.

➤ When delegating a task to a **Cheerleader,** find a way to phrase the task as a "we" project the person can coordinate in a relatively short time frame: "Joanne, I'd like to get your help on a direct-mail project; if we can develop a sharp new campaign that will reach women between the ages of eighteen and thirty-four, I think we can make a big splash with the president. Why don't you take the lead role in brainstorming some new ideas with the other team members and get back to me tomorrow on what you come up with?"

HOW TO GIVE A SALARY REVIEW

Important note: Your organization's salary review process may incorporate specific formal steps, or require you to complete particular forms as part of the process. These procedures are there for a reason, and you must follow them to the letter and give them priority over any of the ideas that appear here. (Failing to do so may leave your company open to legal problems—or jeopardize your career!) Consider the suggestions that follow to be points for incorporation in the face-to-face component of the salary review process, but don't skip any of the procedures, written or otherwise, that your company has implemented, and don't cut any corners!

Here are three ideas for making the most of the salary review process—and avoiding potentially unpleasant problems:

➤ *With problem performers, highlight future rewards, those that you can deliver after the team member makes measurable progress toward a specific goal.* The aims here are to accent the positive potential rather than the performance problem. Make it clear that you aren't trying to dodge compensating the team member fairly and that you want to set up standards you can both live with.

The single most effective approach you can follow with problem performers is, fortunately, pretty straightforward: Track their progress toward a *quantifiable* goal (such as increasing the number of daily cold calls, if the team member is a salesperson); check in on a monthly or, preferably, weekly basis to monitor progress toward that goal; and provide a meaningful reward once the team member hits the mark for you. The reward will be most effective if it's financial, of course, but there are other ways to motivate people: flexible scheduling, comp time, or public recognition are three categories you may want to consider. But delaying raises, by making them contingent upon performance advances in a certain area, is probably the most powerful motivator. If your organization allows you to use these "carrots," you'll be in a position to talk forthrightly to your team member. Here's an example of what the verbal portion of the review might sound like; notice how it makes a point of discussing positive points first:

> "Ellen, there are some areas we need to work on together. If we can resolve them, we're going to be in a great position to move your career forward here, because you've got tremendous amounts of energy, a superior knowledge of the computer system, and the kind of ability to interact well with others that makes me think you've got real potential as a manager. But before we can point you in that direction, Ellen, we have to address the issue of overpromising. You told me that you thought the Emerson project could be completed in two weeks; it took you three months, and it backed up a lot of people in the department. I have to be honest with you, Ellen, and remind you that there was a similar problem with the contract negotiations on the Wilson book; they came away believing that we'd purchase 7,000 units after publication, and you had no authorization to even talk about that kind of figure to them. Now, I know we've talked about how there were communication problems on that deal, but I don't think that undercuts what I'm talking about—it only makes me want to reinforce it more. However it happened, you sent some kind of message that led them to believe we were going to be willing to commit to that degree, and it was a real headache for me to sort it all out after the fact. The fact is, Ellen, that this overpromising problem is overshadowing your other talents, which are considerable. So here's what we're looking at. I can only pass along a two-percent salary increase right now, but I'm authorized to pass along an additional six percent, to be paid retroactively, if you can improve your estimation on the time lines for projects in a measurable way. What I want to do is meet with you every week for three months and work on this issue; if at the end of that time period, all your completion estimates for the period are within ten percent of what you tell me they're going to be, I'll be in a position to pass along the full eight-percent increase, which would bring your salary up to [whatever salary figure is appropriate]. That's where we stand, Ellen; I really hope we can work together to overcome this problem and put you on the fast track."

You may also want to work an appropriate appeal to a need in the Maslow hierarchy into your salary review for the problem employee. See the entries that follow for some ideas on this score.

➤ *Appeal to appropriate Maslow needs when trying to highlight goals for the future.* Obviously, a certain familiarity with your team member's outlook is important before you try to associate improvement in a certain area with a certain Maslow need. But the process is worth the effort and preparation necessary.

If an otherwise satisfactory performer needs to work on personal organization and seems to be a good candidate for a fourth-level (self-esteem) appeal, you might say something like this:

> "Adam, I think that, on balance, you're doing a good job for the company in the accounting department. Your work in the collections area is particularly strong; you've helped us to reduce bad debt by about fifteen percent, and that's an extremely important contribution. I think your facility with numbers, when taken together with your strong phone skills, makes you an important team member within the organization. Even for important contributors, though, there's always room for improvement, and in your case I think you should probably take a look at the level of organization in your personal work area. My bet is that you spend more time looking for names and addresses than you have to and that you haven't taken full advantage of the contact management program we installed on your computer to help you with your collections calls. Now, don't get me wrong—I'm quite happy with the numbers you've been posting in this area. I just can't help wondering how much more impressive they might have been if you hadn't spent so much time sorting through scraps of paper, and I think other people in your work group would probably notice and appreciate an improvement in this area (fourth-level Maslow appeal).

> "Sometimes your desk can look a little disorganized, and sometimes I think reports and printouts are delayed because of delays in tracking down information you ought to be able to pull up with one or two keystrokes. So that's an area I think we should work to improve, and I think if we do, you'll find people really looking up to you a lot more in the accounting department.

> "Overall, though, I want you to know that I really appreciate the work you've been doing in your department and I'm in a position to increase your salary to [whatever new level is appropriate]."

➤ *With superior performers, encourage them to shoot for the stars.* Encouraging top-level performers to maximize their contributions—and stay with your company!—is one of the most important functions of the salary review process. Here's one example of what a verbal salary review for a worker who's performing at an excellent level could sound like; as in the previous example, it incorporates a direct appeal to a need on the Maslow hierarchy—in this case, the need for belonging. (Obviously, you will have to target your message to a need that you feel is appropriate for your team member.) Note how this statement gets the good news out very early; many peak achievers will be extraordinarily sensitive to early signs and may misread "balanced" assessments and tune out the rest of your message:

> "David, I'm happy to report that your work level has been excellent over the past year. You've helped to initiate some truly top-notch work in the production department, and I think it's fair to say that you've become an important member of the family here at G&G (third-level Maslow appeal).
>
> "I was particularly impressed with your work developing the packaging for the Tigerware 4.0 release. The logo you developed ended up serving as the basis for the national ad campaign, and as you know, that was a resounding success, as were the in-store marketing pieces you helped to develop. The best thing you can do to a good product is develop good packaging, and I want you to know that I very much appreciate the long hours you put in helping G&G to do that. You've also shown yourself to be an extremely important part of the team when it comes to getting less experienced staff people up to speed. You've really meant a lot to us in this area, and I know Janet and Dominic, in particular, are quite grateful for all your help (third-level Maslow appeal). You've helped them to master some very complex software, and you've done it without losing any noticeable ground on your other projects. Frankly, I'm a little curious about how you pulled it all off; you're going to have to let me in on the secret some day.
>
> "Because you've been with the company for less than two years, the policy book states that the highest salary increase I can request for you is [X level]. I found that a little bit frustrating, and I made a formal request for an increase to a higher level. I can't talk about the figures I have in mind now, but I do want to tell you that I've been told by the president that he and I are thinking along the same lines on this matter. Your two-year anniversary will be rolling around in about a month and a half, and I think we'll have some more good news for you at that time—and perhaps some changes to consider in your job description, too. But that's for later on. For right now, I'm increasing your rate of pay to [X level], and I want to send you an unequivocal message that we are very happy indeed to have you here as part of the G&G family (third-level Maslow appeal), and we hope you'll stay with us for a very long time."

Perspective Check: Giving a Salary Review

➤ When preparing a salary review for a **Lone Ranger,** make an effort to show your satisfaction with specific past occasions when the person has performed in some notable way for you if you can. If you can honestly do so, offer praise on this score *before* you outline future goals or describe areas where there is room for improvement. If you can avoid doing so, *do not* tell Lone Rangers that you want them to work on limiting the urge to handle everything themselves. Instead, try to channel that instinct in the right direction.

➤ When preparing a salary review for a **Sharpshooter,** make an effort to show your satisfaction with specific past occasions when the person has helped you spot serious problems before they had severe negative impacts. If you can honestly do so, offer praise on this score *before* you outline future goals or describe areas where there is room for improvement. If you can avoid doing so, *do not* tell Sharpshooters that you want them to work on limiting the urge to "see the negative in everything." Instead, try to channel that instinct in the right direction.

➤ When preparing a salary review for a **Professor,** make an effort to show your satisfaction with specific past occasions when the person has set up procedures and systems that increased efficiency or eliminated errors ahead of time. If you can honestly do so, offer praise on this score *before* you outline future goals or describe areas where there is room for improvement. If you can avoid doing so, *do not* tell Professors that you want them to work on developing a spontaneous approach or learning how to "think on their feet." Instead, try to channel their caution and concern for establishing and following correct procedures in the right direction.

➤ When preparing a salary review for a **Cheerleader,** make an effort to show your satisfaction with specific past occasions when the person has helped you encourage others to work harmoniously toward important goals. If you can honestly do so, offer praise on this score *before* you outline future goals or describe areas where there is room for improvement. If you can avoid doing so, *do not* tell Cheerleaders that you want them to improve their ability to "work independently" or "waste less time in discussions with others." Instead, try to channel their instincts in these areas in a positive direction.

HOW TO DISMISS AN EMPLOYEE

Conducting a termination interview has to rank at or near the top of any manager's list of unpopular tasks. It's not surprising, then, when we are called upon to deliver the bad news, that we often take steps to soften the blow, both for the about-to-be-dismissed worker and for ourselves. As well-intentioned as these steps may be, they are often ill-advised. You should not, for instance, schedule the dreaded meeting for the first available time slot (in order to "get it all over with") if the first available time slot is Friday afternoon . . . or any other time when the rest of the office's happy pre-weekend departure will contrast unpleasantly with the dismissed worker's exit from the premises. Such grisly scenes may stoke the fires of resentment. Personnel experts wisely counsel that you schedule termination interviews on *any* other workday than the last day before an extended break, such as a holiday or a weekend. This has to do with the happy-workers-streaming-out-the-door problem just cited and with the more ominous fact that Saturdays and Sundays seem to provide the best time for the very recently aggrieved to plan lawsuits against a former employer. Sometimes letting an impending unpleasant task cast a pall over your own weekend is the best available option.

Similarly, trying to "make it easy" on the employee by breaking the news in a restaurant or bar, rather than in an office setting, may seem to be a more compassionate step than it really is. Let's ignore for a moment the potentially explosive effects of alcohol consumption before or during the dismissal. Even if you could be assured of a liquor-free session, bars and restaurants are *not* the best places to go to fire someone. After all, in any setting, the employee who has been given the bad news is likely to appeal to the manager "as a friend" to return to the top brass and plead for another chance. As difficult as this appeal may be to sidestep in an office environment, it is downright excruciating when delivered in a social setting. Don't run the risk of taking part in a drawn-out scene that ends only when you make a half-hearted commitment to "see what you can do." This is the outcome of many firing meetings scheduled outside the office.

Don't duck responsibility for the firing by reporting that the decision has been made by someone else. This is a great way to get the furious former employee to storm into that higher-level executive's office and demand reinstatement. When we say that the matter is out of our hands and helpfully identify the person whose hands *are* controlling matters, the terminated employee often can't resist the temptation to make one last, doomed try to set things right or, failing that, to vent. If there is ranting and raving to be done, it should be done with you; ride out the storm and stick to your guns, as outlined following.

The successful termination interview delivers the organization's decision in a manner that is professional in both setting and style. If you can find an *appropriate* way to smooth the meeting's progress by making an appeal to a Maslow need (by pointing out, for instance, your respect for the person's maturity in the face of a difficult situation—a fourth-level appeal), do so, but tread carefully. You may show understanding, but you may *not* deviate from the job you've been assigned to do. Your delivery and demeanor in this meeting must make it clear that the decision you are passing on is not open to debate or appeal. Avoid well-intentioned but groundless reassurances that are likely only to make an already demoralized person furious. Pronouncements such as "You'll be much better off this way" or "You can find a better job in no time" usually have the effect of enraging, rather than calming, the former employee. Get the bad news on the table as quickly and as directly as possible, acknowledge the pain and frustration the former employee is probably feeling, and outline the next steps the former employee should take. This last portion of the dismissal speech is an important one. A termination that concludes on an unstructured, open-ended note may well leave the dislocated worker in a position to come up with his or her own answer to the natural question "What happens next?"—and that answer may be an unfortunate one for everyone concerned.

Here are some examples of what to say when you sit down to let someone go. The message should be delivered in a closed-door meeting if you are firing someone for cause; if you must pass along a layoff or downsizing notice to a group of people, you should still try to find some way to deliver the news on a one-on-one basis. Sometimes, however, this will not be possible.

➤ *If the termination is taking place as the result of a downsizing or related cost-cutting initiative, it should sound something like this:*

"Nancy, you're probably aware that the organization has made the decision to phase out a number of positions. I have to tell you that your job is one of them. I know you've made some important contributions here, and I know this must not be easy for you—it certainly isn't for me. I regret that this step has to be taken, but the decision has been finalized. This is a letter that outlines the severance package you'll be eligible to receive; I'd like you to take the rest of today off so you can review it. You should also plan on meeting with the people in personnel at ten o'clock tomorrow;

they have some important information about the assistance we'll be offering you and the other people who are affected by this step."

➤ *If the termination is taking place as the result of the employee's poor on-the-job performance or inappropriate behavior in the workplace, it should sound something like this:*

"Scott, it probably won't come as a surprise to you to learn that we've been reviewing your role here closely over the past weeks. I must tell you that we've decided that there just isn't a good match here between you and the company, and today is your last day at Jameson Associates. This is a decision that I know can't be pleasant for you—it certainly isn't for me. But I want you to know that it's one that we've made only after giving the matter a good deal of consideration. We thought long and hard about the possibility of finding some other area for you to contribute in, and the conclusion we've come to is that that would simply be trying to fit a square peg into a round hole. I'd like you to take the rest of the day to clear out your work area and to meet with Fred in personnel before you leave to talk about your final paycheck."

➤ *No matter what the situation—whether you're firing for cause or delivering the bad news about a layoff, whether you're dismissing a recent hire or someone who has been with the company for years—do not make reference to the employee's age, sex, or physical disability (if any) during the meeting.* If you leave the impression that the termination may be the result of discrimination, you will leave your company open to serious legal problems. If you have any questions about whether or not your decision to fire this individual will result in legal action, check with your organization's attorney.

➤ *Be prepared for an outburst of some kind.* Keep your responses measured and professional. Do not discuss specific aspects of the person's job performance. When in doubt, restate an appropriate point from your opening remarks.

➤ *Do not ramble.* Say what has to be said and stop talking.

➤ *Speak empathetically.* Do not use a patronizing or superior tone. Do not use the meeting as an excuse to settle scores. Do not rehash old conflicts. Make the session as easy on the other person—and yourself—as humanly possible.

➤ *Do not make excuses or imply that you would not be taking this step if the decision were up to you.* As outlined a little earlier, this is a great way to get the termination process to drag on forever or to encourage the person to "appeal to the top," something your superior(s) may not appreciate.

➤ *If the former employee expresses a desire to speak to someone higher in authority, say something along the following lines:*

> "Obviously, I can't keep you from trying to contact anyone you wish to, but I have to tell you I think that would not be a good idea. This decision has been finalized through all the proper channels, and it is not going to be reversed. I think the best approach is to focus on the situation we're now facing and to try to make the best of it."

Perspective Check: Dismissing an Employee

> ***Important note:*** *Although not everyone will take advantage of the opportunity, you should probably* assume *that the person you are letting go will need to speak for a few moments about his or her dismissal at some point during your meeting. What the person has to say may not be much fun to listen to, but you should, within limits, allow the former employee to work off some steam. (Better that they should vent to you than to an attorney!) Here are some rough guidelines on what you can expect to hear . . . and how to react:*

➤ When passing along the bad news to a **Lone Ranger,** bear in mind that you are likely to face an extended monologue along the lines of "Look how hard I have worked for you." Avoid the temptation to point out that *hard* work is not necessarily *effective* work; it is too late for that discussion. When the person has had a chance to express his or her emotions for a minute or two, *calmly* restate your own disappointment that the person's work did not represent a good match between the person and the organization and discuss the next steps you want the person to take.

➤ When passing along the bad news to a **Sharpshooter,** bear in mind that you are likely to face an extended monologue along the lines of "It isn't my fault—it's someone else's fault." You should either work up a strategy for wrapping up the meeting after a few moments of this—by having to close things out to attend an important meeting with a superior, for instance—or prepare yourself to settle in for a while. The Sharpshooter's closing aria may feature an abundance of technical detail. Left to their own devices, these people may go on for quite a long period of time; they are probably the hardest group to cut off during a termination interview. When you can get a word in, *briefly* remind the Sharpshooter that the time for assigning blame has passed, and it is now time to take some specific steps; do not engage in a debate over technical details.

➤ When passing along the bad news to a **Professor,** bear in mind that you are likely to face an extended monologue along the lines of "How do you know that the specific area you think is a problem really *is* a problem?" Professors are strongly inclined to check all the data, to probe, to test, and to demand proof before taking a particular step; it's not surprising that they should take the same approach when they are being told they're about to be let go. Politely decline the invitation to justify your organization's decision or to offer a detailed technical analysis. The decision has been made, whether or not the Professor accepts this. Calmly return to the subject at hand and outline the next steps you want the person to take.

➤ When passing along the bad news to a **Cheerleader,** bear in mind that you are likely to face an extended monologue along the lines of "Look how much I have sacrificed for the group." You must walk a fine line; the person you are talking to should be allowed to express the natural disappointment inherent in the situation, but the meeting must not become a laundry list detailing the many times the Cheerleader has gone out on a limb for others. Express your understanding for the person's feelings, but do not allow yourself to be drawn into the specifics of the person's sacrifices. Return to the subject at hand, and specifically outline the next steps you expect the person to take.

Dealing with Peers

Our interactions with peers are among the most difficult ones to handle well instinctively. These exchanges often require us to pay close attention to an intricate series of shifting power balances; when we work together with peers to evaluate new situations and plan reactions to them, we must often know when to let the other person take the lead . . . only to resume the lead ourselves a few moments later.

In the best of all possible worlds, peers cover for each other's "blind spots" seamlessly, with mutual respect and with a minimum of ego involvement. But ours is not the best of all possible worlds.

We can expect crossed wires, mixed messages, and the occasional misguided power play when interacting with those who work at our level in the organization. How we react to these potential trouble spots is the most important thing. Learning to react effectively and in such a way as to minimize conflict and miscommunication is the subject of this chapter.

TEN TIPS FOR EFFECTIVE DAY-TO-DAY INTERACTIONS WITH PEERS

1. *Understand the power of the two questions "What do you think?" and "What are you really trying to accomplish?"* Their power lies not simply in posing the questions, but in listening attentively to the answers that arise afterwards. When you ask peers sincerely for their input by saying "What do you think?" and then listening nonjudgmentally to the response you receive, you not only gain additional information, you gain power. You establish yourself as someone who has the good sense

to seek out a qualified opinion—that of your conversational partner! As for the other question—"What are you really trying to accomplish?"—it is a superb way to get to the heart of a question, especially when your conversational partner seems to be casting about aimlessly. Both questions put you in the driver's seat by pointing your full attention toward the person with whom you're speaking. Both questions (and especially the second one) encourage your conversational partner to open up and provide important facts and objectives. Even if you *don't* need information on a particular topic, these two questions can help smooth your interactions with peers by establishing you as someone who pays attention to important people and events . . . namely, your colleagues and their problems!

2. *Rephrase and restate.* There is nothing quite so flattering as hearing your own words quoted in a complimentary fashion. This is an extremely effective technique for establishing common ground with co-workers: "You know, this reminds me of the time you said we needed to find new ways to allow people time to brainstorm on their own about important projects before we expect them to make meaningful contributions during group meetings. I think we may be facing a similar situation now." Remember, though, that rephrasing and restating a colleague's remarks is *not* the same thing as holding the person hostage to a previous statement in order to win an argument! The first tactic builds bridges; the second is more reminiscent of the way a prosecuting attorney treats a hostile witness.

3. *Recognize the person's preoccupations and encourage him or her to resolve them before you present your own ideas.* Sometimes people *say* they're willing to talk with us about something, but they seem to be on automatic pilot the whole time. Most of us have had the experience of walking out of a meeting with a colleague and saying to ourselves, "I'll bet she didn't hear a word I said." One way to minimize this problem is to develop a sensitivity for when a colleague is preoccupied with another issue and either back off and try again later or, if time permits, encourage the co-worker to discuss whatever's on the top of the list in his or her mind. Trying to go over your own issues when you know your conversational partner isn't really "there" is a waste of time for everyone involved, and it's likely to lead to increased stress levels for both of you. If you decide that the time is right to try to draw your colleague out before you move to your own topic, you might want to do so by asking something like: "You look as if you're really swamped here; why don't we wait on what

I want to talk about. Are you worried about *[X]*?" Let *X* equal some neutral, nonthreatening topic you know your colleague is *not* worried about; he or she will then be in a position to correct you by saying something like, "Oh, no, it's not *X* I'm worried about, it's *Y*; you see, the problem is, I'm supposed to . . ." There will probably follow a brief recounting of the problem your colleague faces; often, by allowing him or her to focus on this for a moment or two, you can win full attention and meaningful input for the question *you* need to discuss.

4. *Don't tell tales out of school.* Sure, you have an obligation to act responsibly when it comes to newly discovered information that bears directly on your professional duties; and there's certainly no excuse for covering up a colleague's unethical or illegal actions. Beyond those situations, though, there is something to be said for allowing your relationships with colleagues to be more notable for their tact than for their headline-drawing ability. It may be tempting to join in the activities of the company "rumor mill," but if you pass along secrets you weren't supposed to, all you'll be doing is building ill will and establishing a reputation for untrustworthiness. That's a high price to pay for the privilege of passing along a juicy story. (And, by the way, once you decide to pay the price, you won't be getting any more juicy stories from that colleague!)

5. *Now and then, be willing to overlook the specifics of what your colleague has to say.* In other words, show the ability to tactfully sidestep conflict by focusing on the positive objectives that motivate your colleague, not on the facts or assertions that have been spoken in defense of those positive objectives. This willingness to yield on specifics and deal with the big goals instead can save you hours of unproductive nitpicking over who actually said or didn't say something about a project. Whenever possible, take the high road and go back to the positive intent that is guiding your colleague. If you can't identify *any* positive intent (a highly unlikely but not unheard of circumstance), see the advice that appears later in this chapter on dealing with difficult colleagues.

6. *Never order people around.* One of your peers is, by definition, an equal. Issuing brusque commands, or camouflaging them by using phrases like: "We'd better get hopping on this" (when it's clear that the person who's going to be doing the hopping) is your colleague is not a good idea. As a general rule, orders *decrease* your actual influence when deal-

ing with anyone in your organization; when barked out to your colleagues, they can be downright dangerous to your career. If you are looking for ways to gain help or support from your peers, see the later entry on "How to Win Support for a New Initiative" and adapt the ideas to your situation.

7. *Nip feuds in the bud.* Workplace feuds between you and a colleague (or colleagues) are draining and potentially damaging to your career. If you spot one developing, do whatever it takes to get out—whether or not you "save face" in doing so. Your energy should be going into the projects and initiatives at hand, not on the best way to engage in one-upmanship with a colleague who's ticked you off. *Make your move on this score early.* Don't wait for a conflict to escalate into a Hatfield-and-McCoy act, and don't ask other colleagues to take sides. When in doubt, apologize and get back to your knitting; this is the single most effective way to outclass the competition.

8. *Don't cut people off.* It's easier to do than you might think—and overt interrupting is only part of the problem. When we look away from a colleague as he or she is beginning to make a point or play with the objects on our desks or use our own laughter as an excuse to take control of a conversation, we're engaging in subtle "interruptions" that may cause just as much resentment as the "hold-on-a-minute" variety.

9. *Stay away from danger words.* In reference to the work of our colleagues, words and phrases like *competence, ability, authority, overstepping, out of line, permission, unacceptable, error, mistake, control,* and a host of others may carry far more negative resonance than we bargain for. Avoid instigating long-term grudges and short-term miscommunication. Stay away from emotionally loaded terminology when discussing your colleagues' performance on the job—or, better yet, remember the old adage that it's hard to regret what you don't say in the first place.

10. *Take a deep breath before giving a peer a "piece of your mind."* With subordinates, we sometimes make a special effort to temper our remarks because we understand the potentially devastating repercussions for team morale if we don't. With superiors, we understand full well that sounding off can cost us our jobs. But when it comes to peers, we may yield to the temptation to tell a person exactly what we think of him or her, especially during times of significant stress. While it may be nice to have a relationship with a peer that features enough trust to withstand the occasional outburst, not all of our contacts with peers fall

into this category. Don't unload on your co-workers. Find another way to address the issue—one that allows you to retain your composure.

Your interactions with peers represent a critical part of your job. Your ability to manage these exchanges will have a great deal to do with how effective you are and how your work will be perceived by others. Because this part of your job is so crucial, and because you are likely to have the time to determine the likely mindset patterns of co-workers you talk to every day, the ideas in the main section of this chapter feature specific, customized strategies for appealing to Lone Rangers, Sharpshooters, Professors, and Cheerleaders in the ways most likely lead to successful outcomes. You'll find these strategies in the sections marked "Perspective Check."

FOUR WAYS TO EARN RESPECT AND ESTABLISH GROUND RULES

The paradox to bear in mind when establishing the parameters of your relationship with peers is this: Outright power plays *don't* get much accomplished; exchanges that subtly (or not-so-subtly) place your peer in a position of influence *do* help you get what you're after. Here are four simple techniques that prove the point. (See also the general notes on effective day-to-day communication with peers, discussed earlier.)

➤ *Learn to admit your own shortcomings and mistakes and ask for help, when appropriate.* Try it. It really doesn't take much in the way of ego-lowering to encounter the stunning power of this technique. Those who have learned the benefit of this approach usually make a point of incorporating it whether or not there is a serious error to rectify. Admitting that you need help and advice makes dealing with the people you work with easier, and outlining what you've learned from an error makes it clear that you're not out to set yourself up as the Supreme Being. You're not really conceding defeat; you're moving forward and securing the assistance of others as you do so. When you say, "I seem to have made a mistake here, and I wonder if you've got any insights on how I should proceed from here," you place your colleague in a position of strength . . . and you win an ally! That's the kind of outcome that puts you in a position of strength.

Apologizing when you realize you were in the wrong after a dispute doesn't hurt, either. It also opens the door for a discussion of future strategy. "I admit it; I've got a blind spot when it comes to trying to get the materials out to the salespeople on time, Marian. I came on a little too strong, and I'm sorry for that. Can you think of some way we can work together to keep things running smoothly in this area?"

➤ *During face-to-face exchanges, try breathing in rhythm with your colleague.* It sounds silly, but the simple act of noticing when your colleague is breathing and *subtly* breathing in and out at roughly the same time can have a truly remarkable positive effect. The technique can help you defuse conflict before it arises, short-circuit attacks that have just been launched, emphasize points of agreement, and build meaningful alliances for the future. Executed properly, the idea is completely undetectable: No one but you will know what you're doing, and that's just fine. This idea is a surprisingly effective interpersonal tool worth considering during your interactions with people at all levels, but because it is first and foremost a technique for establishing common ground, it appears in this part of the book. Don't dismiss it until you've given it a try!

➤ *With older colleagues, don't be afraid to send signals that make it clear you are willing to learn.* You may or may not want to develop a mentor relationship with the person, but it won't hurt to send subtle or overt messages that demonstrate your capacity to listen. See Chapter 2 for a full accounting of techniques you can put to work on this score; in particular, see the advice on using your notepad and a pen as a tool to get another person to really "open up" to you. When you take the trouble to take notes, you show the person that you know what is being said is worth noting in detail. That's a good message to send in any number of situations; it may be a particularly important message to send when dealing with an older, more experienced colleague.

➤ *If you and a colleague are experiencing ongoing conflicts or personality mismatch problems,* disengage *and take the higher road by committing the important details of your exchanges to a neutral written form.* No, this does not mean that you should transfer the conflict into a running "memo battle." It means you should depersonalize the situation and go out of your way to give your colleague the benefit of the doubt—*on paper.* It's often easier to set limits, establish priorities, and maintain spheres of influence with the written word than it is to do so during face-to-face meetings. If you find that things are problematic on an interpersonal level between you and a colleague—and especially if there are age-gap or gender differences that may be standing in the way of harmonious interactions—follow this four-step strategy:

- Write the memo you *want* to write in a *private notebook that you always keep in a safe place, inaccessible to others.* Get everything off your chest; tell your colleague exactly how you feel about the conflicts and problems that are standing between you.

- Put the notebook away in a secure location, one where you and only you have access to it. Wait 24 hours.

- The next day, reread your memo. Make appropriate notes on how your valid points can be communicated in a nonthreatening way and develop new ideas for dealing with the situation at hand.

- *Destroy the first note* by tearing it into tiny pieces and discarding it once it is impossible to read. Write another memo, based on your notes from the previous step; review it for objectivity; leave it in your colleague's mailbox. *Whatever you do, don't skip this final step! Follow it to the letter, exactly as it's laid out!*

Do not compose your first memo on a computer system. Write it out in longhand.

Here is an example of what the twin-memo process might look like. Notice how the second memo moves toward defusing the conflict by approaching problems from a "we" perspective and casually suggesting a noncombative get-together—while still maintaining a certain judicious firmness about inappropriate behavior or remarks.

FIRST MEMO

Dear Bobbi:

Your decision to criticize my ideas for the print campaign in front of my team members today was immature and totally uncalled for. Your repeated use of the word "inept" struck me as particularly unprofessional, and it's caused me a good deal of trouble on the old home front here in Design—not that that matters much to you.

I realize that you've got a few more years of experience in the industry than I do, and I also realize that this account is an important one for the agency. Nevertheless, I feel that I have a right to be treated as an equal and not as someone whose job is to carry out your every whim (or lack of a whim!). I attended the same creative meetings you did on this matter. The fact of the matter is that the central idea for this campaign has never been convincingly outlined for me and my team members. The "Going For It—Big Time" slogan may sound great in the abstract, but it is laughably short on specifics, and specifics are what make for good print campaigns. To date we have received no meaningful input from your end of the agency as to exactly what you think the main visual elements of the campaign should incorporate—or indeed what the central idea we're trying to get across to the target group is.

I may have been here only for a year and a half as Director of Design and Production, but I've picked up a couple of lessons in that time. One is pretty straightforward: There's more to developing good ad copy than shooting down everything someone else suggests. Next time, instead of making me look like an idiot in front of the people who report to me, why not offer up a couple of ideas of your own for me to execute.

Dave

SECOND MEMO

To: Bobbi

Fr: Dave

After brainstorming on this for an evening, I've got some ideas on how we can make some headway on the "Going For It—Big Time" print campaign, but I'm going to need your help in evaluating them.

I know you're as eager as I am to get this pointed in the right direction. How about getting together for lunch on Thursday to go over some new sketches my team and I have come up with? (By the way, the next time there's a problem you want to talk about along these lines, I'd appreciate it if we could go at things in private, one-on-one; our last meeting left a couple of people on my staff kind of shell-shocked, and I think it may have taken the hop off my own fastball for an hour or so, too.)

Obviously, time is not really on our side for this one, so I thought you'd want to get together this week so we could get everything ready for Tom to look at. Let me know if there's another time that's better for you. Talk to you soon!

The first memo gives us the opportunity to express the natural emotions that arise from being involved in a stressful situation. It's wrong to try to bottle these emotions up, but it's equally wrong to use them as weapons against a fellow colleague who's trying just as hard to get things right. Who knows? Maybe *we* go off the deep end once in a (great!) while, as well. It sounds impossible, I know, but it could happen.

Give yourself permission to write the first memo as an essential bridge to the second, but make your permission contingent on a promise to tear the first memo up into tiny pieces once it's served its purpose so that it can never come back to haunt you!

Perspective Check: Earning Respect and Establishing Ground Rules

➢ When trying to establish a good working relationship with a colleague who is a **Lone Ranger,** go out of your way to praise his or her ability to "get things done" and "move mountains" more or less independently. Try to get the person to recount stories to you about the times he or she has acted alone or in a lead capacity to launch or develop important new initiatives.

➢ When trying to establish a good working relationship with a colleague who is a **Sharpshooter,** go out of your way to praise his or her ability to "spot problems before they happen" and "avert real catastrophes" more or less independently. Try to get the person to recount stories to you about the times he or she has acted alone or in a lead capacity to spot potentially disastrous errors.

➢ When trying to establish a good working relationship with a colleague who is a **Professor,** go out of your way to praise his or her ability to "quantify issues" and "establish workable procedures" for the group. Try to get the person to recount stories to you about the times he or she has played a key role in developing important new ways for the organization to tackle recurrent problems.

➢ When trying to establish a good working relationship with a colleague who is a **Cheerleader,** go out of your way to praise his or her ability to "get the best out of others" and "inspire people" on the job. Try to get the person to recount stories to you about the times he or she has played a key role in coordinating and motivating teams or groups of people.

THREE STRATEGIES THAT WILL HELP YOU BENEFIT FROM OTHER PEOPLE'S KNOWLEDGE AND EXPERIENCE

You don't know *everything,* right? Real leadership lies in the ability to coordinate the abilities and experiences of others toward a goal or obstacle that you face. That's an important skill to develop not only with your subordinates (see the notes on listening to employees in the previous chapter), but also during your interactions with colleagues. Here are three ideas for sounding out your co-workers for meaningful advice and guidance:

> ➢ *If you feel comfortable doing so, and the levels of experience between you and your colleague are appropriate, try to establish a mentor relationship.* This is a particularly effective technique when the colleague with whom you are working is an older Sharpshooter or Professor. In all likelihood, this person has built a career around the process of spotting problems; instead of fighting this dynamic or asking your colleague not to indulge his or her natural instincts, put the error-locating mechanism to work for you. Ask your colleague for help and advice—*don't* ask the person to do all the work for you! Your aim is to make a flattering request for this person's insights and begin to develop a long-term relationship that will allow you to consult regularly with your Sharpshooter or Professor colleague. Tailor your request to the pre-dispositions of these two groups; emphasize the potential catastrophes you think may be lurking in a particularly challenging task you face. By doing so, you'll be making a fifth-level Maslow appeal by asking the colleague to bring all his or her skills to bear in evaluating a professional challenge. What you say could sound something like this:

> "Jerry, I'm interested in your thoughts about the Ramon account. I think there are a lot of potential problems in my first draft of the proposal, and I'm really eager to look around every corner on this one. Do you have time to share a couple of minutes on that with me?"

For most Sharpshooters and Professors, the invitation will be too tempting to decline, and it will often lead to a long-term alliance of benefit to both partners. As long as you make it *abundantly* clear that your aim is to hold brief meetings and share in the person's insights—not to dump your work on the other person's desk—you should get good results with the technique. The idea can be adapted to Lone Rangers and Cheerleaders, of course, by focusing on their predispositions, but because the error-alert Sharpshooters and Professors are often the trickiest colleagues to work with on an interpersonal level, this technique can be expected to yield the best results with members of these groups. It offers them the opportunity to channel their natural instinct to locate problems *away* from you and *toward* your work.

Show respect for the instincts and accomplishments of Sharpshooters and Professors who have a few years' worth of problem solving under their belts. You are much better off turning them into allies instead of making enemies of them. Don't overreact to their fault-finding. Put it to work for you.

➤ *Remove the one-upmanship problem by letting the other person feel big, too.* If you're working on a project that may seem to be more important to your colleague than his or her work, you run the risk of being accused of "putting on airs" if you talk about the project at every opportunity. Don't intimidate others with your accomplishments or current assignments; you'll only foster resentment and encourage people to withhold key facts. Find something challenging and exciting about what's on the other person's desk and talk about that; downplay your own work when it seems appropriate to do so.

➤ *When you get static, hostility, or random content instead of the information you need, repeat the remarks in a positive way (this shows that you're listening) and try to hook the colleague's remark up with a nonthreatening question that returns to the subject.* This takes a little practice—after all, you must be sure that you don't come across as someone who parrots another person's remarks unthinkingly. Here's an example of you how might manage one of these potentially challenging exchanges:

> *Your colleague:* I know exactly what you're trying to get done here, Jeff; we tried to get direct access to the consumer problems the customer-service people heard about, too. But it's devilishly tough because the Management Information Services people think they own the company. I was working on a memo for Brian on this idiotic idea they've come up with to cancel the monthly sales report printouts. Have you ever heard of anything so ludicrous?

> *Danger!* *You are about to get drawn into a departmental dispute, one that has nothing to do with your objective: finding out exactly what consumers have to say about your product when there's a problem!*

> *You:* I had no idea. Well, I can certainly see how people in your department rely on those kinds of reports to get their job done, Carol.

You've just restated the person's remark, not by overtly taking sides in the conflict, but by sympathizing with what the other person has to get done.

> *You:* Believe me, I know how hard it is to try to get work done without the information you need.

You've continued by emphasizing the broadly defined *common problem you and your colleague both face.*

You: Listen, I know you're busy here, but what do you think would be the best way for me to track down the details of how the 800-number customer-service people in Arizona actually log the complaints they get from customers?

Attitude is everything here; you want to gently but firmly guide the colleague toward your request for information, not demand that he or she focus on what you have to solve.

Your colleague: Oh, let's see—I think I took some notes on that problem when I was struggling with this last spring . . . yeah, here they are. Let me photocopy this for you; I'll drop it in the box for you later today, all right?

Perspective Check: Benefiting from the Knowledge and Experience of Others

➢ When trying to get information from a **Lone Ranger,** consider setting specific time limits for your conversation. Make it clear that you're not trying to eat up the person's entire day, just a tiny fraction of it. Lone Rangers, as a general rule, loathe long meetings and suspect that *any* meeting has the chance to turn into a long one. They are far more likely to agree to a guaranteed five-minute discussion than to a "chance to review all the important issues involved." Make it clear that you do not intend to add anything to the Lone Ranger's already lengthy "to-do" list.

➢ When trying to get information from a **Sharpshooter,** emphasize that you need their help to spot and eradicate a potentially catastrophic error in something you're working on and appeal to the Sharpshooter's ability to spot problems independently. Make it clear that you are looking for input and experience, not someone to complete the task for you.

➢ When trying to get information from a **Professor,** let him or her know that you don't have enough data yet to feel comfortable making a decision, and say that you'd appreciate his or her input in the process before it moves forward. Make it clear that you are looking for advice and input, not someone to whom you can hand off your project.

➢ When trying to get information from a **Cheerleader,** highlight an imminent deadline that you're working toward and ask for *a specifically defined stretch of time* to discuss how the Cheerleader and/or the team he or she works with has dealt with issues similar to the ones you face.

Your aim is to cast yourself as a "temporary" member of the Cheerleader's team, which he or she will probably think of as something akin to a family. Don't abuse the privilege, however; you must not take more time from the deadline-oriented Cheerleader's day than you say you will, and you must not leave the impression that you are trying to find someone else to do your work for you.

FOUR WAYS TO WIN SUPPORT FOR A NEW INITIATIVE

Gaining the support of colleagues on potentially challenging initiatives can be tricky. Here are four ideas you can use or adapt to help win support for ideas your colleagues are unfamiliar with:

➢ *Make small talk work for you.* Before you outline what you want to get accomplished, ask yourself some questions: Do you really know who you're talking to? Do you know what challenges the person faces on a daily basis? Do you know what nonwork interests he or she pursues? *Before* you outline a project or initiative, make sure that you have established some kind of common ground that has nothing to do with your initiative. This common ground could take the form of a shared passion for a local sports team, a favorite vacation spot you both know about, a hobby (such as Internet surfing) that both of you pursue—the possibilities are endless.

The idea here is to use the seemingly innocuous ritual conversation we all engage in for a practical purpose: ally building. When you use small talk to send the message "I'm a lot like you; I share your interests and concerns on this issue," you're building a bridge. Show *sincere* interest in and attention to the events in your colleague's life and draw parallels wherever you can. By forming these kinds of (genuine, not forced) connections, you'll make your later appeal for help and support more likely to succeed.

➢ *Remember the power of emotional appeals.* Like almost everyone else, your colleagues are—whether they acknowledge it or not—more susceptible to direct personal appeals that relate to their own interests than they are to lengthy logical arguments. We may *ask* for elaborate proofs before important decisions, but we *make* them only when we are certain that we feel comfortable, on a gut level, with the possible outcomes.

Before you set up twenty computer models illustrating the logical soundness of your approach to winning a colleague's support on an important initiative, take a moment to think about what this person wants, in a fundamental sense, out of the job he or she holds in the organization. Is the colleague interested in consolidating what he thinks is a tenuous position within the organization? Try to frame your efforts to persuade them in terms of the new security that may come his way after having been associated with a successful project. (This is, of course, a positively oriented variation on what amounts to a second-level Maslow appeal to safety and security.) Is the colleague eager to be perceived as the very best within her field? Try to make a fourth-level Maslow appeal by highlighting elements of the project that will help her gain prestige in the eyes of others—and remember basketball coach John Wooden's remark about how remarkably easy it is to get things done when you don't care who gets the credit.

➤ *Use humor when appropriate.* Humor is a powerful weapon for building allies, especially when it demonstrates to others that you don't take yourself too seriously and aren't out to make life difficult for others. When discussing a new approach or initiative, don't be afraid to use humor—of a kind that's appropriate to your own personality, your message, and the work environment—to make your points.

➤ *Don't ask directly for support if there seems to be a good chance that doing so will polarize the situation.* Keep an eye on your colleague's body language and focus of attention. If he or she is fidgeting, looking away from you, or otherwise showing signs of discomfort, you should probably back off and elicit input and suggestions for your plan, rather than asking outright for the person's support and assistance. In such a situation, instead of asking "So, can you stand behind this with me when it comes time to discuss it at the meeting?" you're better off asking one or more of these questions:

"In what direction do you think I should be pointing this?"

"Is there some part of this that doesn't work for you?"

"How do you think this could be improved?"

"Do you have anything you want to suggest about what I'm trying to get accomplished in the first place?"

You may or may not want to incorporate the advice you receive as a result of asking these questions, but asking them is a far better alternative than forcing the issue with a question that will leave your colleague no alternatives other than accepting or rejecting what you've come up with.

Perspective Check: Winning Support for a New Initiative

➤ When trying to elicit the support of a **Lone Ranger,** make a point of highlighting any part of the plan that will help him or her, or others in the organization, work more effectively on an independent basis.

➤ When trying to elicit the support of a **Sharpshooter,** highlight the criticial errors you know are waiting to be unearthed in your proposal or initiative; emphasize the dire consequences for the organization if they remain undiscovered. Incorporate the Sharpshooter's "corrections" wherever possible, even if they are of a minor or cosmetic nature.

➤ When trying to elicit the support of a **Professor,** ask for help in developing a new set of procedures for dealing with an unforeseen circumstance. Incorporate the Professor's "corrections" wherever possible, even if they are of a minor or cosmetic nature.

➤ When trying to elicit the support of a **Cheerleader,** try to emphasize some aspect of the plan or proposal that will be of direct benefit to the colleague's contacts with others in the organization. In other words, emphasize some part of what you are undertaking that will make it easier for the Cheerleader to interact with the people he or she encounters regularly. Ideally, your plan should show a clear advantage for the people who report directly to the Cheerleader, or who work with him or her on an everyday basis, an advantage these people will attribute *to* the Cheerleader.

WHAT TO DO WHEN SOMEONE TRIES TO TAKE CREDIT FOR YOUR WORK

Wait a minute! Whose idea was this in the first place? If it was yours, but there's some confusion about the matter on a colleague's part, here are four tips for responding effectively.

➤ *Try to resolve the question by means of a passing reference in an otherwise innocuous memo.* We're not talking about launching an attack on paper here, but about a tactful reminder of the way the situation has evolved that's issued in an offhand way. Where it seems appropriate to do so, incorporate dates, titles, and citations to any paper trail that may exist. Here's an idea of what such a memo might look like:

To: Caryn

Fr: Brent

Re: Forbes Proposal

I thought it might be a good idea to include some sales figures in the appendix here; what do you think?

Maybe we should even incorporate a direct reference to sales numbers on the page that features my idea for the Twist-Em logo; do you think this would fight with the visuals too much? See my original sketch of September 14. (Photocopy attached.)

Let's talk soon about this.

It's important to incorporate a suggestion for a face-to-face discussion at the end of this memo; this will give you the opportunity to reinforce, subtly, your real message: The idea was yours.

This technique will smoke out those who honestly forgot about the lead role you played in developing your concept, as well as those colleagues who will try to take credit for your work only if you don't make any attempt to stand up for yourself. This leaves you with the hard-core problem: those who are willing to lie, to you or anyone else, about whose idea is being discussed. In dealing with such people, you have three options, which follow. Choosing the right approach will depend on your relationship with the colleague, your degree of devotion to the idea in question, and the importance you place on getting your name attached to the initiative.

➤ *In a low-key face-to-face meeting, flatter the person shamelessly, then politely but firmly re-establish the correct attribution.* Follow up your statement of ownership with another liberal dose of appreciation for your colleague's unique talents and insights. This approach may be particularly necessary for women in the workplace; many researchers have found that female workers, who tend to operate from a "we" focus rather than an "I" focus, are often the source of ideas and initiatives later appropriated by male co-workers. By focusing on the positives of the situation— your colleague's praiseworthy attempt to do the best possible job and his or her unique approach to the problem at hand—you may help to defuse a potentially difficult situation.

If you want to take this approach, do so early in the process! Waiting until after your colleague has circulated your idea to others in the organization will only make it more difficult for you to receive credit.

➤ *Elicit your colleague's substantive feedback and input and share credit.* Sometimes the best way to resolve this issue harmoniously is to allow your colleague to pull some of the weight, by offering his or her own ideas on how best to alter or implement what you've suggested, and then presenting the idea as your joint project.

➤ *Withdraw.* It's an option, and it may not be the right one for you, but then again, it just may. You must ask yourself: Which is most important, getting this initiative implemented or receiving sole credit for having come up with it? This is a complicated issue, particularly for women, who must decide when to address "idea-appropriation" issues with male co-workers head-on and when to make a certain sacrifice for the organization. In making your choice, consider the amount of energy you would have to spend to document your "case." In some instances, such as when a major promotion is on the line, that time and energy will be well spent. In others, where there is little at stake except "the principle of the thing," your efforts to prove ownership will only serve to exhaust you . . . and perhaps even frustrate higher-ups, who may find themselves wondering why you can't find anything better to do with your time.

Perspective Check: Dealing with Someone Who Wants to Take Credit for Your Work

➤ If you decide to try to resolve a credit-for-work-or-ideas issue with a **Lone Ranger,** avoid pointing out how much time you put in on the project. Lone Rangers often put in lots of long hours, too, and the exchange may degenerate into a discussion about who is more devoted to the job. That's not the issue. If you can get a discussion of the topic going early enough, you may be able to cast it in terms of your willingness to assume full responsibility for the initiative, given the Lone Ranger's full schedule. Lone Rangers are, as a rule, chronic over-committers; if you can approach the issue in this way, you may be able to carry the day.

➤ If you decide to try to resolve a credit-for-work-or-ideas issue with a **Sharpshooter,** *do not* move into a prosecutorial mode. Your attempts to "prove" that the idea or project is rightfully yours may leave you on the wrong end of an argument with Johnnie Cochrane. Instead, try to get the discussion going very early in the game, and ask if you can count on the Sharpshooter's "continued input on problem areas" as you move the project forward. Sharpshooters often react quite well when appealed to for sage troubleshooting advice. They can also provide you with invaluable advice that will save you from serious errors. Try to engineer an (unspoken!) trade: You get credit for what is rightfully yours, and the Sharpshooter gets a senior advisory role befitting his or her expertise.

> If you decide to try to resolve a credit-for-work-or-ideas issue with a **Professor,** highlight your role as a team player and point out *in a nonthreatening way* how failing to provide you with the credit you deserve has the potential to cause serious disruption in the organization. (Your example may, for instance, serve as a serious disincentive to others to speak up about new approaches they think may be helpful.) If there is any past history or policy, written or unwritten, about the issue of granting appropriate credit for work done, you may want to make reference to it. Professors, as a general rule, like to maintain smooth organizational operation and "go by the book" if there is no persuasive reason to avoid doing so.

> If you decide to try to resolve a credit-for-work-or-ideas issue with a **Cheerleader,** odds are you'll be most successful if you can cast yourself as "one of the team" rather than a rival—and perhaps even talk about how much you hope to learn from your colleague in the future on similar projects. Cheerleaders often respond well to appeals from team members; your aim here is to come across as one of the gang, not as someone whom the person must compete with for influence. Asking for advice on how to handle the potentially awkward situation you face and confessing your uneasiness about the issue of handling who gets credit probably won't hurt. You may want to try this during a private, one-on-one meeting with your Cheerleader colleague; in many situations, the problem will solve itself when the Cheerleader responds positively to your appeal for help. The Cheerleader may "take you under his or her wing," just as he or she would a subordinate.

Important note: In dealing with a colleague from any of the four groups, please remember—there are times when allowing someone else to claim credit for your work can be a masterful strategic move! (Remember, too, that formal credit is a very different thing from informal credit. Many a CEO keeps careful track of the people who put the interests of the organization before their own interests now and then.)

HOW TO RESOLVE INTERDEPARTMENTAL TURF DISPUTES

Who's in charge here? When you and a colleague have differing answers to that question, you need to be sure you proceed with both tact and firmness. Here are three ideas that will help you make sense of those situations when you *both* think you've got the final say:

➤ *As early as possible, try to get the discussion moved to a one-on-one, rather than a public, exchange.* When we have to resolve turf disputes in front of our own teams, things get complicated. We may become more interested in how our team perceives the messages and whether they understand that we "can't be pushed around." We may also, consciously or unconsciously, try to send the message to those who report to us that we are willing to "go to the mat for them" when it comes to defending their interests. These are understandable sentiments, but when two people start pursuing the job of expressing them at the same time, gridlock is often the result. Do you and your colleague a favor; retire to a neutral corner together and talk things through person-to-person, with no audience in attendance.

➤ *Don't get sidetracked by bluster or overstatement.* Does it sound as though your colleague is deliberately challenging you or saying things designed to get you angry? This may be an attempt to get you to stop thinking clearly about the situation or to agree to an arrangement that is not in your interest. No matter how ridiculous your colleague's comments may get, avoid the temptation to escalate the dispute; keep a clear head, even in the face of rhetorical overstatement. (If your colleague is consistently hostile, irrational, or profane as you attempt to resolve who'll handle which responsibilities, bring the matter quietly to the attention of your superior.)

➤ *Try to reduce tension by outlining proposed new arrangements in writing.* Withdrawing from person-to-person conflict and taking the time to compose a memo that outlines a *number* of possible solutions will allow both you and your partner time to decompress and will reduce the likelihood of future conflict. (If you make photocopies, which you should, this approach will also provide you with a paper trail that details your calm, reasoned approach to anyone who may need to intervene in the future.)

Perspective Check: Handling Interdepartmental Turf Disputes.

➤ When trying to sort out a turf dispute with a **Lone Ranger,** make a point of emphasizing those aspects of the project or initiative that will require extensive meetings and consultations with others. Lone Rangers are, as a general rule, extremely wary of the prospect of having their work time siphoned away with meetings and conferences.

➤ When trying to sort out a turf dispute with a **Sharpshooter,** consider enlisting the aid of another Sharpshooter who can act as your consultant. (This assumes, of course, that you are uncomfortable with the idea of incorporating your first colleague in an advisory role of some sort.) Many turf disputes with Sharpshooters arise because of their deep concern over ongoing quality-control issues; by appealing to a trusted team member who shares the Sharpshooter's viewpoint on such issues and incorporating that team member into your working group in some way, you may be in a position to reduce the anxiety level and resume the lead role on your project.

➤ When trying to sort out a turf dispute with a **Professor,** try to highlight another project that requires a new system or procedure—a project that will, if overlooked by the Professor, have the potential to result in potentially catastrophic errors. Ask *nonthreatening* questions that point the Professor toward a question: How much of his or her time would be going to the project under dispute with you and how much of *that* time *should* be going to the project you're highlighting, the one that needs a new system or a refinement on an older one?

➤ When trying to sort out a turf dispute with a **Cheerleader,** cast yourself in the role of one of the Cheerleader's team members, and ask for guidance on the vexing issue of how best to resolve the overlap. During your discussion, highlight an imminent deadline on another project that the Cheerleader faces, then drop *nonthreatening* hints that he or she will be in a better position to help the group meet that deadline by passing the project under dispute off to you.

HOW TO LET A COLLEAGUE KNOW HE OR SHE HAS A PROBLEM EMPLOYEE IN THE DEPARTMENT

Everybody has the potential for a blind spot or two. If an oblivious co-worker is placing full faith in someone who truly doesn't deserve it, you'll do everyone a favor if you can find an effective way to share your concerns. Here are five ideas that may help you get the point across before things get ugly.

It should go without saying that you must not bring up "performance problems" if the real issue is an interpersonal problem you have with your colleague's subordinate.

➤ *Keep your concerns verbal, at least initially.* This is one instance when you *don't* want to move to the written word early on in the process. If you send your colleague the message that you're in a position to develop a "paper trail" about the employee you have a problem with, you may polarize the situation, whether or not you actually intend to keep detailed records of your exchanges with your colleague. Keep your comments informal and private, and deliver them in a one-on-one setting that will make it clear that you take the issue seriously. (A passing remark over lunch may be easy to dismiss; a ten-minute conversation during the workday probably won't be.)

➤ *When discussing the problem employee, preface your remarks with a few observations about the ways in which the person you're concerned about differs from your colleague.* When we develop blind spots about employees, it's often because we draw parallels between their backgrounds, work patterns, and achievements and our own. If you are talking to a colleague who thinks that everyone who graduated from her alma mater can do no wrong, you may need to highlight some of the differences in working style and commitment that exist between your colleague and her subordinate. Don't be afraid to use your colleague's areas of strength as a starting point; stay away from specifics about the problem employee's performance at the beginning of the conversation, but do point out that the person in question "sure isn't like you as far as *(X)* is concerned." Keep things informal and comfortable; make sure your colleague knows that you're acting out of concern for him or her, rather than self-interest.

➤ *Before you deal directly with the performance problems you perceive in the subordinate's work, point out how starkly the person differs from other people on your colleague's team.* Another great potential starting point for blind spots: the echo syndrome. This occurs when we associate the working skills and achievements of a star performer with those of another person who reminds us of that person—but is not in the same league as far as results are concerned. Continue your "contrast attack" by pointing out specific areas in which the employee you're concerned about differs from the colleague's best performers. Stay as vague as you can for as long as you can about the specific shortcomings of the problem employee.

➤ *Let your colleague talk.* At this point, your colleague will probably see where you're headed. Don't try to ram your point home; stop talking and see how your colleague responds. If he or she already knows about the problem, this is the point in the discussion at which you'll be able to tell. If your colleague does *not* know about the problem or shows anger or denial, make one *brief, nonthreatening* appeal to the specifics of the situation, as outlined following.

➤ *Make your point . . . and then make it clear you're not looking for a conflict.* Whatever you say, be sure that it is not delivered in a challenging or authoritarian manner, that it avoids using words like "should" and "ought," and that it allows your colleague the option of considering the matter further on his or her own. State events in terms of your perceptions, not in terms of "the facts of the matter."

Once you've established contrasts between the problem employee's way of doing things and your colleague's, then tactfully pointed out the ways in which the person being discussed is different from the stars in the colleague's work area, you'll be ready to detail *briefly and in a nonaggressive way* the specific problems you perceive about this employee. What you say about that employee could sound something like the following:

> "Jenny, I don't know how much time you've spent with Irene when she isn't working in the reception area, but I can't help wondering if there might be a bit of a productivity problem when she's not around you. Yesterday I came by to use the copy machine; she was making funny pictures of her hands. I decided not to say anything, to come back fifteen minutes later. But Jenny, when I did, it looked to me like she was still at it. Now, maybe this was some unorthodox creative project you assigned to her, but even if that's what it was, there are a lot of things like that that seem to have been catching my eye, and I can't help but wonder how other people in the department may react to this sort of thing."

Important note: Don't demand an immediate decision on the issue. (If you are facing a crisis situation, one that carries serious ethical, competitive, or legal implications for the company, you may decide to inform your colleague that you have no alternative but to bring the matter to the attention of a superior.) Demanding action from your colleague is not likely to promote a reasoned, harmonious discussion of the issue. In most cases, you will probably be better off trying to let your colleague take action independently.

Perspective Check: Letting a Colleague Know About a Problem Employee

➢ When trying to convince a **Lone Ranger** that there's a problem employee in the department, highlight those areas of the employee's work pattern that are going to make demands on your colleague's day. Lone Rangers are likelier to respond to the issue you've raised when they're convinced that the person in question is keeping them from getting to the items in their own in box.

➢ When trying to convince a **Sharpshooter** that there's a problem employee in the department, highlight those times when the employee missed potentially catastrophic problems. Sharpshooters are likelier to respond to the issue you've raised when they're convinced that the person in question cannot flag key errors.

➢ When trying to convince a **Professor** that there's a problem employee in the department, highlight those times when the employee failed to follow established systems and procedures. Professors are likelier to respond to the issue you've raised when they're convinced that the person in question is unlikely to go by the book.

➢ When trying to convince a **Cheerleader** that there's a problem employee in the department, get ready for the long haul. This group may be most difficult to convince of the importance of addressing the issue at hand. Cheerleaders are often willing to overlook even starkly outlined performance problems of employees whom they consider to be "part of the team." If your colleague does not seem capable of responding effectively to the problem you raise, you may need to point out, over a decent stretch of time, instances when the problem employee *adversely affects the Cheerleader's entire team.* The Cheerleader is likely to put the interests of "his people" first and foremost—you may need to approach the question in this fashion over an extended period.

THREE TECHNIQUES FOR ELICITING FEEDBACK ON AN IMPORTANT PROJECT

Sometimes eliciting the ideas of other team members on important initiatives can be a challenging task. How do you get the person to drop what he or she is doing and focus, with full attention, on the project you're hoping to get right? Here are three ideas for gaining meaningful input from your colleagues:

➢ *Pick your battles.* Your colleagues are busy, too. Every one of them knows that, as time goes by, the amount of energy they can put into their own projects gets a little bit smaller. So don't appeal to your colleagues for *every* question; make a point of "asking for help" judiciously. That way, when you do need substantial input on a project, you'll be in a better position to get the person to disengage and focus on your project. If your colleague appears distracted but offers to "listen for a few minutes," don't waste two people's time; come back when you can both devote your full attention to the matter.

Remember that someone who takes time out of his or her day to listen to and offer advice on your initiatives deserves the same courtesy in return.

➢ *Don't get sidetracked.* Don't fixate on the content of what your colleague says about the project, especially early on in the exchange. Sometimes people need to get a couple of lame ideas out of the way before they can start to talk intelligently about something. Tactfully pass by the outlandish or misapplied concept; focus on what's workable in your colleague's comments and verbally reinforce those elements. ("Uh-huh." "Yes, you're right." "I see what you mean.")

➢ *Take notes.* As pointed out previously, this technique has the triple advantage of flattering the person with whom you're speaking, encouraging that person to open up on the topic in question, and providing you with a detailed record of the exchange.

Perspective Check: Eliciting Feedback on an Important Project

➢ When trying to elicit feedback from a **Lone Ranger,** you may want to ask *one important question at a time,* one that will take you only a few seconds to phrase. Once you've received your answer, if your colleague does not invite a full-scale discussion of the issue, disengage, let the Lone Ranger get back to work, and follow up concisely at a later time. As a general rule, members of this group despise long meetings and review sessions. Don't get involved in multi-level analysis before you get to the point; ask the key question, take note of the answer, and take the hints the Lone Ranger drops about when it's time to wind things up.

➢ When trying to elicit feedback from a **Sharpshooter,** highlight some internal flaw or oversight you've found in the project or initiative, then ask the Sharpshooter to help you amplify or expand on those points.

Presenting the problem as a good-natured, understated, and brief exercise in logical competitiveness is probably your best bet. You've found one problem, and you want to make sure the Sharpshooter doesn't see any more. Let the Sharpshooter win the contest.

➤ When trying to elicit feedback from a **Professor,** highlight some way in which what you're planning is not going to make sense for other people who have to make sense of it, then ask the Professor to amplify or expand on those points. Don't be surprised if the Professor asks for time to review the project or asks you to develop additional data before engaging in an in-depth discussion.

➤ When trying to elicit feedback from a **Cheerleader,** highlight some part of your project that will make it easier for the Cheerleader to work more effectively with his or her team, or with other members of the organization, in the face of an imposing deadline. Then ask for input based on "what would and wouldn't work for you (and/or: your people)."

HOW TO OFFER SUGGESTIONS CONSTRUCTIVELY

Constructive suggestions fall into two categories: one for when you have reason to believe a catastrophe is imminent, and one for all the other situations. Here are some suggestions on how to deal with each category:

➤ *If things are not at a potential crisis level . . .* try to phrase your suggestion in the form of a question, preferably an unintimidating one that proceeds from a position of (apparent) blissful ignorance. Direct statements can be intimidating, whether or not they're intended that way; they're often intended as direct orders. Holding forth with a series of facts is *not* the best way to offer criticism. Consider the difference between the two approaches that follow:

> "We've got a planning problem here, Mike. Your people are constantly monopolizing our color printer with last-minute projects; you ought to get your own, because there's certainly money in your budget for it. I don't know why you keep putting it off."

> "Mike, your people must be going nuts trying to elbow your way into our place to get out all your time-sensitive proposals. Have you considered a color printer for your department? [Let your colleague respond.] How do you think Emma would react if you made a requisition request? [Let your

colleague respond.] Do you think there's still money in the budget? [Let your colleague respond.]"

The first approach stakes out territory; the second gently guides your colleague toward an understanding of the situation you both face . . . and points the way toward one possible solution. Note how the issue of changing the department's way of planning projects has been moved to the background. It's far better to focus on systems and events that affect you directly than to deliver unrequested sermons to your colleagues. Your unspoken message will probably get across more effectively this way than if you acted on the urge to tell your colleague to "shape up."

Using tactful questioning, as outlined, also lets your colleague know that you aren't under any illusion that the option you're outlining is the *only* possible solution. Keep an open mind to new ways of looking at the situation as your colleague responds to your questions. Remember, too, that the tone you adopt in these exchanges is just as important as the content of the message itself. Even a careful syntactical phrasing of a nonthreatening question can backfire if you deliver it in an uncompromisng, staccato style.

➤ *If you truly believe catastrophe is imminent,* say so openly . . . but leave your colleague the opportunity to rectify the situation without having to capitulate to you. One effective way to do this is to cite, during a one-on-one meeting, parallels between the situation your colleague faces and a bad experience you've had in the past. Tell your own sad story before coming to your main point: It's going to be in the colleague's— and the organization's—best interests to change the present approach to things. What you say could sound something like this:

> "Jill, I wanted to take a moment to talk to you about the Johnson proposal. I know things are crazy in your department now while you're assembling this, but I just wanted to share something that happened to me a couple of years ago, something that I sure hope you don't have to go through. I was setting up a proposal very similar to this, and I put off photocopying a draft for Legal for review before setting things up in the final draft. I had meant to get a copy out to them for weeks, but I neglected it until the day before our meeting with the client. Well, everyone in Legal was out with the flu that day, so I ended up making a presentation the lawyers never signed off on. It was one of the biggest mistakes of my career, and it ended up costing us about two hundred thousand dollars because we guaranteed something to the client that we shouldn't have, and we had to knock our price down as a result. It was a pretty grim cou-

ple of days. I mention this incident because I think your project is, if anything, more complicated than the one I was working on. If you can't get this to the people at Legal a good week or so before you have to meet with the client, I'd strongly suggest that you postpone the meeting. I hope you don't mind my mentioning this, but I thought you might want to enter this on your checklist before you get stung as badly as I did."

Making the effort to develop a parallel such as this one, even if you have to stretch a bit to make your connections, is worthwhile. Telling this kind of story uses self-disclosure to reassure your colleague that you're not pursuing the subject for the purpose of one-upmanship. (The one-on-one setting for such a talk is, obviously, essential.)

Perspective Check: Offering Constructive Suggestions

➤ When trying to offer constructive criticism to a colleague who is a **Lone Ranger,** cite your own shortcomings when it comes to "taking charge and making things happen independently" before you suggest any possible area for improvement.

➤ When trying to offer constructive criticism to a colleague who is a **Sharpshooter,** cite your own shortcomings when it comes to "spotting the most important problems" before you suggest any possible area for improvement.

➤ When trying to offer constructive criticism to a colleague who is a **Professor,** cite your own shortcomings when it comes to "setting things up so they make sense for other people" before you suggest any possible area for improvement.

➤ When trying to offer constructive criticism to a colleague who is a **Cheerleader,** cite your own shortcomings when it comes to "coordinating things on a one-on-one basis with other people" before you suggest any possible area for improvement.

Even if you have to exaggerate your own shortcomings in order to deliver your message in a nonthreatening way, that's preferable to simply delivering the bald message "You need to improve" to a colleague.

Important note: *If a colleague's working pattern does not directly affect you and does not represent a serious threat to the organization, your best option is probably not to offer constructive criticism unless you're asked, in no uncertain terms, for your opinion.*

HOW TO OVERCOME PROCRASTINATION ON THE PART OF A COLLEAGUE

Suppose you have to hand in a report this Tuesday and your colleague has had the materials you need for the past three weeks. Here are some suggestions on how best to move past procrastination on the part of the people you work with, without ruffling any feathers:

➤ *Acknowledge that your colleague is overworked, then try to set up a specific time obligation.* Even if your co-worker does have a time-management problem, it's a good bet that he or she sees the situation as one in which far too much work has been passed along in the first place. Don't challenge that assumption. Put it to work for you. Place it at the beginning of your exchange, then outline a specific time commitment. *Set an outer limit* to the time you will need to resolve or address your issue, then do your level best to honor that estimate.

> "Shelley, I know how crazy you've been going with the conversion to the new system; it's a real monster, and to tell you the truth I don't quite know how you've been keeping up with it. I understand how hard it's been for you to get to some of the other things on the list over the last couple of weeks, and I have to tell you that I really respect anyone who can make sense of the job of connecting the two systems (fourth-level Maslow appeal). Because I know your time is pretty tight, I wanted to suggest that we get together for half an hour to go over those notes on the consumer mailing. Ms. Potter said I should develop the figures by Friday, and that's coming right up. Could we shoot for tomorrow at eight-thirty? That way, we can wrap up by nine, and you can get back to conquering the computer beast for everyone."

➤ *Ask for time commitments in writing or, failing that, write them down yourself and pass along a copy.* If you're dealing with someone who can't seem to say no to anything and has all the attendant overcommitment problems, you can make their commitment to *you* stand out by asking them to put it down on paper. In a pinch, you may have to summarize the discussion in writing yourself, but you should try to persuade your colleague to "jot it all down and pass along a copy" if at all possible. The physical process of writing down the deadline in such a way that another person will be able to read it has a galvanizing effect. It strengthens memory of the deadline, emphasizes personal accountability, and may even help the person get a start on some of the organizational and strategy issues involved in attaining the goal.

➤ *Make sure you're not dealing with a hesitation issue.* Many people assume that their colleagues have "procrastination problems," when in fact all they have is a different way of assessing questions of risk. Some people spend more time in "fact-finding" mode and conferences with others before taking a potentially hazardous course of action. To many colleagues, and particularly to those for whom such "hesitation" is a sign of both inaction and weakness, it may take a while to recognize this process as something other than procrastination. You may want to make an effort to build a little extra time into your time estimates when dealing with such colleagues.

Perspective Check: Overcoming a Colleague's Procrastination

➤ When dealing with a **Lone Ranger** who has time-management problems, bear in mind that this person tends to focus on one project at a time. Negotiating for ways to get your project on the table now may work; negotiating for ways to get your project, and only your project, on the table at a specific later time may work. But asking the person to "get to it as soon as possible" or "keep it in the back of your mind" won't.

➤ When dealing with a **Sharpshooter** who has time-management problems, emphasize the worst possible outcome that could result if errors or flaws in the project in question go undetected.

➤ When dealing with a **Professor** who has time-management problems, "getting it all down on paper" may be your most effective approach. Members of this group are generally more attuned to formal (that is, written) commitments, policies, and procedures than members of the other three groups.

➤ When dealing with a **Cheerleader** who has time-management problems, ask for a (reasonable!) direct promise about when your project is likely to be finished. In other words, ask for the Cheerleader's word; keep the pressure up, tactfully but firmly, if you meet with disclaimers or escape hatches. Try to get the verbal "on-my-honor" commitment during a time when you and the Cheerleader are making direct eye contact. Members of this group get most of their work done through one-on-one interactions with others; unless you are dealing with someone you know or strongly suspect to be dishonest, you can generally count on a promise from a Cheerleader. Don't go overboard! The aim is not to stare at the person until he or she makes the commitment you want, but to establish a personal connection as fellow professionals who can depend on each other.

SEVEN WAYS TO TURN AN ENEMY INTO AN ALLY

Sometimes, of course, you won't be able to win over a colleague who is bound and determined to bring a hostile approach to all his or her interactions with you. Even when you're dealing with particularly ill-tempered and aggressive colleagues, however, you can minimize the adverse effects of these exchanges. Here are seven techniques for making the most of a relationship with a colleague who seems to have it in for you:

> *Identify the positive intent in what the person is communicating and respond to that.* In other words, if your colleague has a way of sniping about perceived errors in your department, find a way to focus on your shared concern for quality control—rather than entering into a prolonged debate over what does and does not constitute an error. In *almost* every barbed remark, there is a positive objective lurking behind the rhetoric. If you can do a little digging and determine what that positive objective is and how it can help you move forward constructively in the discussion, you will go a long way toward defusing the antagonistic episodes that may come your way.

> *Don't be afraid to admit you're wrong.* Even if the *way* your colleague is getting the message across doesn't exactly have you jumping for joy, you should always be willing to concede a point if the person you are talking to has raised an issue of valid concern. No, this doesn't mean you have to capitulate every time an overaggressive colleague launches an attack; but you should consider the message first, and the messenger second, and you should strive to be objective about the feedback you're getting, even if it isn't being delivered in a particularly objective fashion. (And here's a little secret to bear in mind: Admitting you're wrong often carries the advantage of getting your colleague to stop haranguing you. It's among the classiest ways to produce stunned silence.)

> *Focus on the other person's victories.* Even your colleague's nonwork-related accomplishments can serve as an opportunity to build bridges. Remember that showing genuine interest in the activities and attainments of others is a way of showing respect and appreciation—and, thus, a subtle third-level Maslow appeal. Many a hostile exchange has been brought to a quiet conclusion by one partner's decision to focus not on the literal terms of the dispute but on the other person's strong suit. If your colleague is being driven by ego and control issues, you may be in a perfect position to defuse the conflict by acknowledging

his or her mastery of a certain aspect of the job. By the same token, if
your colleague wants to boast about something, is there really any disadvantage to allowing him or her to do so?

➤ *Ignore hostile or threatening questions.* "Who on earth do you think you
are?" "Didn't they teach you anything at that fancy school of yours?"
"Have you ever heard of a little thing called contingency planning?"
These questions, and their innumerable unpleasant variations,
aren't requests for information at all; they're attempts to get you to
lose your poise and equilibrium. Don't respond passionately to
them. Don't respond to them. Simply pretend they never escaped
your colleague's lips and return to the subject at hand: what you perceive (not what *is*), what you plan to do, and how you hope to do it.
By denying your colleague the opportunity to rattle you, you will
probably decrease his or her reliance on these types of threatening
questions.

➤ *Repeat the message you're hearing back to your colleague to be sure you've gotten it clearly.* Whether or not you agree with what your colleague is passing along, it represents his or her perception of the situation and
deserves to be treated with respect. It could sound something like this:

> "If I understand what you're saying, George, you feel that we haven't been
> putting enough time into developmental work before passing the projects
> on to production, and you think we're spending too much time and
> money fixing things very late in the cycle—things that you feel could have
> been caught earlier. Is that a fair assessment of what you're saying?"

This tactic can work wonders; it is an essential tool for anyone whose
aim is to reduce polarization in a one-on-one exchange. Your colleague is far less likely to overreact or react aggressively if you make it
abundantly clear that you *do* hear the message that's being passed
along and that you aren't simply waiting for your turn to shout.

➤ *Let the colleague know that you need him or her.* Whether or not you actually do is, of course, a separate question. The idea here is to take
advantage of the pleasant glow of heightened self-esteem that accom-
panies such an admission, to move beyond the potentially polarizing
exchanges, and to minimize or eliminate future rivalry or resentment.
Cite two or three areas where your colleague's input and guidance are
essential to your work. If you have to reach a little to identify these
areas, your colleague probably won't protest too much about it.

➤ *Follow up attentively and responsibly.* After you and your colleague have concluded your discussion, keep in touch about the subject you've been examining. Highlight, either on paper or verbally, any new perspectives you gained from the exchange, and make it clear that you value appropriate input from your colleague on this or any other topic. If you feel comfortable doing so, incorporate an element of humor in your follow-up, one that will make it clear that you are eager to pursue constructive, rather than antagonistic, exchanges over the long haul.

Perspective Check: Turning Enemies into Allies

➤ When trying to turn a **Lone Ranger** into an ally, point out times when you have helped to smooth the path toward his or her most pressing project. Acknowledge the person's ability to "move mountains" for the organization; do not try to cast yourself as someone who works harder or puts in longer hours.

➤ When trying to turn a **Sharpshooter** into an ally, don't swim against the stream—give him or her something to correct! By acting on the problems your colleague identifies, you will broadcast your respect for his or her (often considerable) flaw-finding prowess. Telling the person not to correct you will often leave him or her without a primary means of communication and may lead to considerable frustration. Instead, channel your colleague's often overpowering instinct to find errors and mistakes into some innocuous (or not-so-innocuous) area.

➤ When trying to turn a **Professor** into an ally, demonstrate your ability and willingness to "go by the book." (Professors tend to view people who "rock the boat" with a certain skepticism or even outright hostility.) If at all possible, find some aspect of a system or procedure your colleague has introduced or developed that has affected you directly; point out how this system has made your work easier and more efficient.

➤ When trying to turn a **Cheerleader** into an ally, point out, if at all possible, times when you made life easier for your colleague—or, perhaps even more important, members of his or her team. If you can, focus on group initiatives on which you and your colleague share the same interests. The idea is to present yourself as a member of the team, just like the Cheerleader. (If you feel comfortable granting the Cheerleader a lead role on that team, so much the better.)

HOW TO DEAL WITH CO-WORKERS WHO HAVE PERSISTENT ATTITUDE PROBLEMS

They're out there: the colleagues who, for one reason or another, just can't resist the temptation to act like jerks, usually at the most inopportune moments. These people aren't actually out to *get* you; they simply possess very poor people skills and don't mind doing things that get on your nerves. Here are four ideas for making life a little more bearable when such colleagues are around:

➤ *If you are repeatedly interrupted, resume your point from exactly where you left off.* Occasional interruption is one thing; relentless badgering is another. If you find that a colleague makes a habit of cutting you off and you're looking for a direct but not overly confrontational way to send the message that you don't appreciate it, this is probably your best bet. Take a short pause before resuming your point, then briefly make eye contact with your colleague to let him or her know that you are not willing to pretend that the interruption didn't happen. Usually, this technique is enough to help you get the idea across.

➤ *Don't be afraid of silence.* The temptation to fill conversational pauses can often be quite strong, but there are times when you are best advised to resist it. If a colleague is engaging in juvenile humor, inappropriate remarks about others in the office, or any other form of communication you feel is beyond the pale, consider the power of a nice, stony hush in response. It's often the most eloquent reply you can make.

➤ *Draw the person out after an attacking, ill-considered, or just plain inappropriate remark.* When colleagues launch verbal missiles, especially in public or quasi-public settings, they often do so in the confidence that the conversation will continue after their remark. In some instances, you may decide to try to question the person directly, rather than let the remark pass in silence, as outlined above. For instance, in the case of a thoughtless racial slur that's aimed toward your ethnic group, you might decide to fix your gaze calmly on your colleague and say, "Fred, I find it hard to believe you really think that's amusing. Do you?"

➤ *Finally, make peace by praising the person's better side.* If there's been a bump in the road between you and your colleague, dismiss the matter once it's been addressed directly or indirectly by saying something along the lines of, "That's really not like you, Carl. You don't usually play games like this." Even if it is *exactly* like Carl to play such games, you won't get much of an argument from him. This is the Pygmalion Effect (discussed earlier) in action. Dr. Rick Brinkman and Dr. Rick Kirschner describe this remarkably effective technique in their book *Dealing with People You Can't Stand*. The idea is simply to praise that aspect of the person's approach that is either sorely lacking or totally absent. The act of praising the person for the (supposed) virtue you are trying to cultivate often brings about improvement in the area in question. Try it—it works!

Perspective Check: Dealing with Co-workers Who Have Persistent Attitude Problems

➤ The **Lone Ranger** colleague who has a persistent attitude problem is likely to demonstrate a very healthy ego mechanism. Don't get into a one-on-one confrontation with this colleague if you can possibly avoid it; when this person is on deadline, very little in the way of rational appeal will make a difference. In the name of "wrapping up the project," the Lone Ranger may come off as demanding, sarcastic, or downright unprofessional as he or she pursues a key goal. Wait until the storm passes and the latest crisis has receded for a moment; then try to point out how changes in the way the Lone Ranger interacts with you can make things smoother for everyone.

➤ The **Sharpshooter** colleague who has a persistent attitude problem is likely to fall into two categories: the one who picks everything apart in an effort to prove a superior mastery of the topic at hand (often at your expense), and the one who seems to spend most of the day figuring out why whatever initiative you're trying to pursue cannot be accomplished. It bears repeating that many Sharpshooters can be distracted by appeals to their technical prowess. You may be able, over time, to turn the constant criticizer into an ally by making regular attempts to praise his or her superior troubleshooting skill in a particular area. The person in the second category, the Sharpshooter who constantly bottlenecks your efforts, may simply need *something else to bottleneck*. Provide him or her with the opportunity to do this by asking for a review of the problems in a new, uncharted area. Then briefly, casually, at the end of the exchange, inform your colleague of the actions *you* are planning to take to overcome the obstacles that you face in the area you are truly interested in. It sounds like a bit of a guerrilla action, and perhaps it is, but the sad fact is that there are some Sharpshooters for whom the best strategy is finding a way to get them out of your way.

➤ The **Professor** colleague who has a persistent attitude problem is likely to present you with a legalistic, "throw-the-book-at-'em" mindset. For some Professors, it seems, every situation must be guided by a regulation, and every regulation must be attached to some situation. Your best approach here is not to challenge the systems-and-procedures approach of the Professor, but to show your colleague that you are willing to proceed through whatever formal channels exist to attain your goal(s). What some people consider spontaneity and creativity, the Professor is, in his or her worst moments, likely to view as chaos. For these colleagues, you may have to "translate" your initiative into a rulebook-friendly undertaking by citing parallels and precedents extensively and by specifying the formal provisions that exist for what you're trying to do. *Do not* attempt to introduce new and unfamiliar facts into the situation; this will only put your Professor colleague on the defensive.

➤ The **Cheerleader** colleague who has a persistent attitude problem is likely to be a gossip-monger. For Cheerleaders, face-to-face interactions with others are the most important means of communication. A number of them succumb to the temptation to spread unflattering stories, true or false, about others. The habit can be extremely difficult to overcome, and you probably should not expect your colleague to make a change in this area. Your best bet is to appeal, during a private meeting, to your status as fellow team members and to briefly but unhesitatingly lay out your personal standards when it comes to talking about people behind their backs: You don't do it to others, and you hope no one will do it to you. After you've tactfully made your point, find some way to loosen up the meeting, perhaps by telling a humorous, self-deprecating story about yourself that shows you know how to take a joke.

Important note: In dealing with persistent attitude problems with colleagues, you are better off trying to mirror the person's attitude or outlook than you are trying to change that outlook. You should not, for instance, expect the Sharpshooter to "stop being so picky." A better course of action is to demonstrate that you, too, have an understanding of the importance of attention to minute details.

Dealing with Superiors

Understanding all the dynamics underlying your relationship with your boss is a long-term undertaking, something that probably can't be mastered overnight. No single idea in this chapter will make for harmonious interactions where there is mistrust, misunderstanding, or running conflict; but by applying appropriate techniques that appear here, you'll be in a position to improve or solidify your position with a superior.

Review the ideas on listening that appear in Chapter 2; keep an open mind; allow your superior to change course without having to feel as though doing so represents a personal defeat; and customize your approach. If there is any group for which it makes sense to alter your appeal based on a conversational partner's status as a Lone Ranger, Sharpshooter, Professor, or Cheerleader, it is this group.

TEN TIPS FOR EFFECTIVE DAY-TO-DAY INTERACTIONS WITH SUPERIORS

1. *Keep your appeals brief.* Odds are that your superior has a pretty impressive list of time commitments. Respect them. Get right to the point. When appealing to your superior for action on a particular issue, do your best to reduce the issues at hand to a single-page memo. (Although they may from time to time ask for more detailed analyses, top-level managers quickly learn to appreciate subordinates who can compose good one-page memos.)

2. *Stick with the facts you can backup, and don't try to use "weasel language."* What is weasel language? Basically, it's any qualifier, condition, or excep-

tion that drains a statement of the meaning it seems to convey at first glance. The disclaimer that whizzes by in tiny type during a television advertisement, for instance, is a prime example of weasel language. If all that legalese didn't undercut the message the advertiser was trying to get across, why would they make it so small and run it past you at one-hundred-twenty-miles per hour? The higher the position your superior occupies in the organization, the more likely it is that he or she is a past master at ferreting out such "escape hatch" words as *nearly, virtually, almost, approximately, roughly,* and *generally.* If you want to score ponts with the boss, make statements you won't have to apologize for, then stand behind them.

3. *Interpret the data.* It's likely that your superior must sift through mountains of information every day. Instead of simply dumping the numbers on his or her desk, provide a brief written or verbal assessment of what you think the facts you are passing along *mean.* If a new product has been the subject of two hundred customer complaint calls over the past three months, how does that stack up to the first three months of *other* new product launches in the company's history?

4. *Know when to offer help without being asked for it.* Realizing when to *offer* assistance, rather than forcing a superior into the position of *asking* for it, is an ability that has launched many a fast-track career. Many top-level managers—particularly males, and more particularly males at the very top of their organizations—have come to equate uncertainty with weakness, and have, accordingly, learned to surround themselves with people who will fill in the blanks for them virtually unbidden. Asking for help or admitting a knowledge gap, after all, might be seen as an opening for a rival to exploit! When working with higher-level managers, understand that a need for power and control may be coloring your exchanges: many a plea for help comes disguised in the form of a complaint or a new set of standards for others to meet.

5. *Don't tell tales out of school.* If passing along workplace gossip you hear from colleagues is tactless and unprofessional, revealing confidences that affect your superior is close to suicidal. It is certainly true that a good many managers still operate in the "give-me-someone-whose-neck-I-can-wring-when-something-goes-wrong" mode, and it's also true that the temptation to share one's deepest feelings about such a superior's weak moments can occasionally be quite strong. But if you're working for the person, you're working for the person. Don't betray

confidences; if the working relationship you and your superior have developed over time is unhealthy, find another situation. But don't undercut the most important professional alliance on your list while you're still on the roster. Take the heat, and find some way to work off the stress that doesn't involve telling stories on your boss.

6. *Don't take everything literally.* Immediately following a less-than-successful airport press event, President Richard Nixon once stormed past a group of aides and ordered that there be "no more airport landings." After the President left the room, his lieutenants pondered their situation; how on earth were they to fulfill such a directive? Was the rest of Nixon's term really to be carried out without air travel? Should someone be dispatched to inform the President of the impossibility of his demand? Could Nixon's aides *ignore* a direct order from the President of the United States? After a good deal of hand-wringing, one senior aide came up with the solution to the problem: He composed a memo that addressed the President's core concern: There were to be no more *unsuccessful* airport landings, and in order to fulfill that objective, there was to be a renewed focus on the organization of press events. Sometimes, reading and acting on the *intent* of a superior's pronouncement is more important than following it to the letter.

7. *When in doubt, assume personal responsibility.* Many top-level managers hear quite a bit more buck-passing than they'd care to from the people who report to them. One of the simplest and most effective ways to make yourself stand out from the others your superior comes in contact with can be boiled down to five blissfully accountable words: "I'll take care of it." Once you promise to do so, keep your superior posted on your efforts and of the results he or she can expect within a specific time frame.

8. *In tough times, take the blame and move on.* This note doesn't necessarily apply to *every* boss, but it is true that for some top decision makers (especially those who are Professors and Sharpshooters), finding someone who is willing to assume the blame is not so much a matter of occasional censure as a habitual way of conducting day-to-day operations. For these superiors, holding people accountable is a way of life. Usually, there's nothing personal. If you can keep your poise, adapt to your boss's way of working, and demonstrate that you're willing to take the heat without becoming less effective, you'll probably be in a good position to distinguish yourself from others in the organization. If you

are uncomfortable with this communication dynamic, try to find another superior to work for.

9. *Identify a shared nonwork-related interest.* If small talk is important in your interactions with colleagues, it can be doubly so in your discussions with your boss. That's why it's important to search out some kind of social (rather than professional) context for the "intro" and "outro" portions of your day with your superior. The topic might be sports, a favorite television program, or even an academic passion, such as American history. (Believe it: Once two Civil War buffs discover each other, they'll never lack for conversational material!) Your relationship with your boss will go smoother when he or she has some framework for evaluating you as a fellow human being, not just as a subordinate. You may decide to quietly offer a topic a day until you find one that makes your superior start beaming. Even second- and third-generation workaholics have been known to light up at the mention of a particular type of popular music they favor (say, Beatles records). Try whatever topic seems appropriate, and keep at it on a "slow-but-sure" basis. Eventually, you'll hit on something that gets your boss talking. Once you do, follow his or her lead.

10. *Take notes.* The importance of the proper use of this technique has been discussed earlier, but there may be no more appropriate place and time for it than during discussions with your superior. When you pull out a notepad and jot down your superior's observations and instructions, you send a series of important messages:

> "I'm listening."

> "What you're saying is important enough to record in a permanent medium."

> "You can feel free to lead the conversation."

> "You don't have to remember all the points you pass along; I'll consult them at a later time."

> "There's no doubt about who's in control of this exchange."

> "What happens next is going to be a direct result of what you're telling me right now."

Your interactions with superiors will probably have more impact on your career success than your contacts with any other individuals within your organization. Because your communication style with these people is so crucial and because you are likely to have the time to determine the likely mindset patterns of superiors with whom you deal every day, the ideas in the main section of this chapter feature specific, customized strategies for appealing to Lone Rangers, Sharpshooters, Professors, and Cheerleaders in the ways most likely to lead to successful outcomes. You'll find these strategies in the sections marked "Perspective Check."

HOW TO ASK FOR A RAISE

Timing is everything when it comes to asking for more money from your boss. Here are six ideas for managing this potentially tricky exchange to your advantage:

> *Make sure your appearance is working for you.* This is not the occasion to wear jeans and a tee shirt to work, even if it is dress-down day. Be certain that the personal image you're projecting is one of poised, confident professionalism.

> *Take a few moments to scope out your superior's mindset before you sit down to talk things over.* What has your boss had to deal with in the last twenty-four hours? What will he or she have to focus on in the *next* twenty-four hours? You probably can't get definitive answers to these questions, but you can develop some best-guess scenarios. If you've got a good idea that your boss is addressing a sudden crisis, preparing for a major event or presentation, or, heaven help you, trying to make sense of a budget overrun, then you need to think twice before raising the issue of increasing your salary. Wait until the seas are smooth before you begin your journey. (If you have to, approach your superior on another matter and use his or her reaction to determine whether or not the time is right.)

> *Keep the tone light.* You may feel nervous, but you need to find some way to approach this exchange in a confident, upbeat manner. One good way to do this is to offer a status report on a successful project you are coordinating—and use that report as your bridge to the formal request for a salary increase. Even if you feel you are significantly underpaid, you must avoid polarizing things. Do not make the mistake of beginning your discussion of salary issues with sarcasm, inappropriate humor, or accusing language. Stick with happy stories.

> Using the proper tone is extremely important. You don't know how this request is going to be dealt with; if you come on too strong, a

denial may leave a long-lasting feeling of bitterness between you and your boss. The idea is to make a reasoned, professional appeal—not to permanently alter the relationship for the worse.

➤ *Be prepared to quantify your accomplishments and to offer an anecdote that supports your request.* How much money have you saved the company by doing something new, something that no one had anticipated you would be responsible for? Be as specific as possible and appeal to a third-party reference to back up your claims if the situation permits. Then (preferably before your superior weighs in with an opinion on the matter) move directly into a story that shows exactly how you got things done and how your inspired approach saved the company time, money, or both. Try to follow up the hard facts with the anecdote, because effective stories are far more likely to do the persuading for you than the hard facts are. You *need* the hard facts, of course, but they should serve as a precursor to the main portion of your request, which is the success story.

Remember that you are asking for *additional* money, and so you must illustrate how you have performed in a way that is *above and beyond the formal expectations of your job*. Even if you consider your present salary to be below average or unacceptable, you must take your superior's view of the situation here: You have been paid X dollars to perform Y function and now you want Z dollars. Unless you've been making a habit of doing more than Y on a regular basis, or unless you plan to do noticeably more than Y and can cite compelling evidence that this is likely to take place, most superiors will ask you to postpone your request or decline it outright. Some people will argue that you should appeal to factors such as the industry salary average for someone in your field during your discussions with your superior about salary. You may certainly do so if you wish, but a good many bosses—especially those in smaller, entrepreneurially oriented firms—won't much care what the average rate of pay is and may even suggest that you try to find work with a firm that is more likely to pay you the amount you're after.

Here's an example of what your request for a raise might sound like:

"Mr. Fredericks, do you have a couple of minutes to go over something? Thanks. I wanted to talk for just a moment about some of the things I've been working on here in Customer Service. As you know, I was hired last year to train people in making sense of our computer system, and I feel very confident that I've been doing an excellent job of that. The entire team got up to speed on the 3660 software very quickly, and I felt they had an excellent grasp of the kinds of product and service questions they were likely to encounter when on the line with people who use what we make. When it was time to design and implement the new system, I feel I made a significant contribution there, one that really wasn't incorporated in my formal job description. I met with the software developers, spent a great deal of time helping them to debug the program, and *helped them bring in the final version two weeks ahead of schedule, which I estimate saved the company something on the order of fourteen thousand dollars.* I think it's fair to point out that I did this while *maintaining all my other responsibilities with the new trainees and helping to reduce absenteeism and tardiness by twelve and fourteen percent, respectively, compared with last year.* Now that we have the new system in place, I'm spending a lot of late nights working to develop the manual that will help new people get up to speed with this system, just as our present team members have. *You know, Mr. Fredericks, when I was working with the software designer last week, he told me that he had never worked with a training person who had as strong a grasp on the technical aspects of a new system as I did.* Because of all the extra work I have done and am doing on implementing the new system, I feel justified in asking for an increase in salary."

➤ *Stop talking.* Relax. Superiors know it takes courage to bring up something like this. Most of them won't leave you hanging for too long. You demonstrated an appealing self-confidence by raising the question; show the same trait by waiting patiently for your boss's response. It may be extremely uncomfortable for a brief moment, but you should ride out the silence. Don't specify a figure you're after. Don't tell the same success story over and over. Don't change the subject or apologize for having brought it up. Wait for your boss to respond to the issue you've raised. Your objective is to get your superior to say something along the lines of, "Well, what kind of a raise did you have in mind?"

Let's be realistic; your superior may say this or may start off on a speech of his or her own about how tight budgets are or how fortunate you are to be working at a company with growth potential. But by making a compelling case, in the way just outlined, and then leaving unanswered the obvious question of how much more money you're looking for, you will probably increase the odds somewhat that your superior will focus on this question. If and when this happens, you should respond with a *range,* rather than a specific figure, that represents the low-end figure you will accept at one end and an "optimistic" figure at the other end.

You should not mention a low-end figure that you consider unacceptable. You should not mention an "optimistic" figure that is wildly unrealistic given your company, the industry, and the financial state of the company.

➤ *If your superior declines the request or asks that you put it off until the formal salary review process comes around . . . well, you tried, right?* At least you've positioned yourself properly for the annual review. Keep careful notes of the conversation (jot things down in a notebook immediately after the meeting), and, when the promised day comes around, remind your superior of what he or she said back on such-and-such a date. (If your own livelihood doesn't merit careful record-keeping, nothing does!)

Perspective Check: Asking for a Raise

Important note: *When asking your superior for a salary increase, play directly to the predispositions of his or her mindset group! Even if you don't share the boss's category, you may want to consider* pretending *that you do (for rhetorical purposes, that is—don't exaggerate any part of your record). As you prepare the material you will share with your boss at this meeting, keep this fact in mind: People like to help the careers of those subordinates whose work patterns resemble their own!*

➤ When asking a **Lone Ranger** for a raise, highlight those parts of your work record when you've taken the initiative on a project and "moved mountains" more or less independently.

➤ When asking a **Sharpshooter** for a raise, highlight the times when you spotted serious problems in time to prevent them from becoming catastrophic setbacks. If you can, demonstrate by means of hard, verifiable numbers exactly how you have increased efficiency or reduced error rates.

➤ When asking a **Professor** for a raise, talk about the (formal or informal) systems and procedures you have suggested that have made your interactions with others in the organization more productive and less prone to error. If you can, demonstrate, by means of hard, verifiable numbers exactly how you have increased efficiency or reduced error rates.

➤ When asking a **Cheerleader** for a raise, highlight those aspects of your work record that show you to be a superior team player, someone who has made important contributions to group goals during "crunch time." Flattering quotes or endorsements from others, either inside or outside the organization, may be particularly effective with this group.

(Regardless of the manager you're talking to—Lone Ranger, Sharpshooter, Professor, or Cheerleader—be sure that the person you're quoting has no problem with your repeating the remarks if you decide to do so as part of the salary negotiation process.)

Note: *The ideas outlined in this section can easily be adapted to a request for a promotion, as well.*

HOW TO MAINTAIN A HARMONIOUS WORKING RELATIONSHIP WITH YOUR BOSS, EVEN IN DIFFICULT TIMES

Crises come, crises go; you want your superior to know that even if things get difficult, your aim is to keep all operations running smoothly, with a minimum of miscommunications. Here are five ideas for maintaining a harmonious working alliance with your boss even when the going gets a little rough:

➤ *Take notes.* The point has been made earlier in this chapter (and elsewhere in this book), but it bears repeating. Thoughtful, attentive note-taking will send all the right signals to your superior, will give you a permanent record of key points and instructions, and will earn you a position of distinction over time. If you adapt nothing else from this chapter in altering the way you deal with your superior, you should incorporate this habit into your daily routine.

➤ *Don't get paranoid about silences.* Many managers use silence as a rhetorical device or as a means for displaying control of the conversation. Don't let this spook you. Indulging the temptation to "fill the void" by repeating yourself or making innocuous comments usually won't win you any points. Unless you have something appropriate to add to the conversation, ride out the silence with your superior. (Often, he or she will simply be composing the next thought.)

➤ *Don't oversell an idea or engage in doubletalk.* The higher up in the organization your superior, the less tolerant he or she is likely to be of exaggeration and excessive use of meaningless catch phrases. (Experienced managers remember all too well what it's like to get burned by "overoptimistic" projections or misled by fast talk.) Make promises you intend to keep; use words that have clear meanings for everyone in the room.

➤ *Address the intent, not the content, of overblown rhetoric or challenging questions.* "So—are we going to have to wait for the Second Coming before these sales figures hit the levels you forecast?" What a question! But what your boss is *really* asking, even though it may not sound like it at the moment, is this: "What steps are you currently taking to help us hit the numbers we were talking about?" Answer the second question and appeal to the Maslow need that may be guiding it (such as a need for optimum performance and achievement, a variation on the fifth-level self-actualization need). Even if you have to do a little silent translating beforehand, respond to the question's intent—don't take it literally. And whatever you do, don't reply sarcastically in turn!

➤ *Use time lines.* Managers get tired of hearing people talk about initiatives that will happen "in the foreseeable future," "eventually," or "in the long run." (Once, when Franklin Delano Roosevelt was assured by an economist that the massive unemployment of the Great Depression would correct itself in the long run, the President remarked caustically that "people don't eat in the long run.") Set yourself apart from the backpedalers. Use specific time lines, ones you feel confident you can stand behind: "Even though we've had some setbacks, the project will be completed and on your desk by September first; I don't anticipate there will be any problems on that score, but in the unlikely event that there are, you'll hear from me at least two weeks beforehand."

Perspective Check: Encouraging Harmonious Relations During Tough Times

➤ When working through tough times with a superior who is a **Lone Ranger,** make *realistic* commitments to deadlines and then follow through as promised. Lone Rangers tend to perceive the working world in terms of deadlines tackled independently; they often expect others to perform just as heroically as they can during "crunch times." You may lose serious points if you overpromise or underdeliver.

➤ When working through tough times with a superior who is a **Sharpshooter,** demonstrate a fanatical attention to quality control and error eradication. These are the elements of the job your boss is likely to react most dramatically to if they are overlooked in the heat of the moment. For the Sharpshooter, a dozen missed deadlines are, in the final analysis, preferable to a lapse in quality that could come back to haunt the organization. (One Sharpshooter of the author's acquaintance was given to making statements like, "What I'm particularly concerned about is avoiding problems of a catastrophic nature"!)

➤ When working through tough times with a superior who is a **Professor,** provide quantifiable data and appeal to past tests and trial runs; follow established procedures wherever possible, and *do not* attempt to "follow a gut instinct" in resolving a critical problem. Professors get nervous around people who follow hunches and make up their own rules as they go along. (Lone Rangers, by contrast, tend to welcome them—as long as they deliver results.)

➤ When working through tough times with a superior who is a **Cheerleader,** *don't make waves.* During difficult periods, the Cheerleader's nightmare is that the carefully nurtured "all-for-one-one-for-all" mentality he or she has established among team members will fall apart. The image you want to project is that of a conscientious team member who knows how important it is to pull together as a team during difficult stretches. Put off any question or issue that is not consistent with this image; address such problems after the dust has settled.

Important note: During crisis periods, you may have to make a (silent) effort to compensate for your superior's blind spots. If your superior is a Lone Ranger or a Cheerleader, you may need to focus with greater attention than normal on quality-control issues. If your superior is a Sharpshooter or a Professor, you may need to put greater emphasis on deadline and time-management questions than you usually would. When things get rough, superiors, like the rest of us, tend to focus almost exclusively on primary objectives and predispositions and to "tune out" issues that don't relate directly to those objectives and predispositions.

WHAT TO DO WHEN YOUR BOSS IS BYPASSED

Your superior has lost an internal debate on an important new initiative, and he or she doesn't appear to be taking it too well. Here are three ideas for making it through this potentially challenging period:

➤ *Allow for a period of disappointment.* Now is not the time to ask for input on a trivial matter—or, for that matter, an important one! It's human nature to sulk a bit after a defeat. If you press your superior for a decision on something now, you may get an answer you don't like or feel less than comfortable implementing. Unless you are facing a truly time-sensitive situation, let your boss have a day or two to decompress before you throw another problem on the desk.

➤ *Watch that small talk.* It's human nature to want to discuss recent events in your work environment, but during this period when your superior is likely to be sensitive to any comments about the battle just lost, steer clear of any issue even vaguely related to that battle. Some supervisors are likely to perceive even the most innocuous comments as personal attacks.

➤ *Keep your thoughts about the recent battle to yourself.* Others in the organization may be inclined to pass along "all the dirt" on the recent decision that didn't go your superior's way. Resist the temptation to engage in story-swapping. It could backfire spectacularly on you.

Perspective Check: Dealing with a Boss Who's Been Bypassed

➤ When interacting with a **Lone Ranger** superior who has just lost an internal battle, mention past initiatives, unrelated to the recent dispute, that your boss executed without a hitch.

➤ When interacting with a **Sharpshooter** superior who has just lost an internal battle, mention past instances, unrelated to the present dispute, when your boss personally spotted a critical error that could have had devastating consequences for the organization.

➤ When interacting with a **Professor** superior who has just lost an internal battle, mention past systems and procedures, unrelated to the recent dispute, that your boss tested and implemented successfully.

➤ When interacting with a **Cheerleader** superior who has just lost an internal battle, mention past instances, unrelated to the recent dispute, when your boss has inspired others to meet a seemingly impossible deadline.

HOW TO PRESENT YOUR IDEAS TO SUPERIORS

You've got a great idea! Now all you have to do is win support from your boss or from other key people in the organization. Here are five ideas for getting your idea the attention and exposure it deserves. Consider incorporating them into the initiative you present to your boss or to other upper-level management people.

➤ *Develop extensive backup and fallback options.* Any manager worth his or her salt is going to ask the question "What if it doesn't work?" This question can break down into any number of specific queries. What if your sales or revenue estimates are off by, say, 50 percent? What if it takes twice as long to train people in the new procedure you're outlining? What if the amount of time it takes to design the new product you're talking about is three months, rather than one month? These are the questions good managers will be asking you or others in the organization (and Sharpshooter and Professor managers can be expected to ask these types of questions in a bewildering variety of forms). Address such issues directly and in as much or more depth as your manager would. After all, *someone* is going to have to think about what to do if things don't go as planned; if it's you, you'll prove yourself to be a forward-thinking team player, and you'll increase the likelihood that the idea will be adapted more or less as you outline it. (If it is, your claim for full credit will be taken more seriously.) Be prepared to outline a detailed set of contingency plans and fallback options, rather than simply focusing on a "best-case" scenario.

➤ *Stay away from the word "profit."* Sales trainer Anthony Parinello, author of the excellent book *Selling to VITO,* points out that top decision makers tend not to react well to people who toss this term around a lot. The fact of the matter is that profit is an elusive concept, one that even the top person in the organization may not grasp fully. (Parinello also points out that the person who *does* have the most fully developed idea of the organization's profitability, the head of accounting, is often among the least powerful of the company's senior managers.) Talk about contribution to overhead; talk about revenue; talk about net sales. But don't talk about profit. Managers in general, and high-level managers in particular, will probably be turned off. (A good many of them honestly do not know how profitable their organizations are until the people in accounting tell them.)

➤ *Get it down in black and white, incorporate a strong visual element, and consider using color.* More and more, these days, we find ourselves living in a visually oriented society—with little time on its hands. No, there's nothing wrong with informal chat sessions about your projects, but on initiatives you truly feel strongly about, it's worthwhile to bear in mind that ideas tend to become more tangible when they're committed to paper. People have to *do* things with paper proposals—whereas they can promise to "think about" verbal suggestions and then never follow up. As you assemble your initial proposal, consider the advantages of a compelling one- or two-page summary that incorporates color and graphics, rather than a lengthy, full-scale assessment of the subject that will take your boss half an hour or more to get through.

There are two advantages to being brief: Your intended audience is more likely to read your document, and you won't waste too much time preparing an in-depth treatment that turns out to be pointed in the wrong direction. If you do decide to develop a concise, compelling color document, be sure that it broadly outlines the various backups and contingency plans you've developed (just mentioned). You should be able to summarize these verbally when your boss asks, or supply a detailed, point-by-point review after you've achieved the necessary "buy-in" from upper management.

➤ *Highlight tangible benefits.* If you think you can increase revenues, say how much. If you think you can reduce downtime, estimate by how many days. If you think you can lower temporary-personnel costs, explain how, and outline how many temp workers you think could be eliminated.

➤ *Don't get hung up on yes or no answers.* Some of the best ideas hang around for a while before being implemented. Pressuring your superior for an immediate decision may do both of you a disservice. It's better to wait until you've had the chance to work out all the kinks and your boss has had the chance to digest the idea completely. Don't be afraid to retrieve an idea you truly believe to have merit out of the mothballs every week or two, because this pattern of persistent fine-tuning may be just the way to build up the foundation of planning that makes successful execution possible.

Perspective Check: Presenting Your Ideas

➤ When presenting an idea to a **Lone Ranger,** focus on a single big concept that you know or strongly believe will appeal to this person. Don't get bogged down in detail; keep the strokes broad and respond to the questions that arise. Multi-layered appeals are often lost on these managers, who may develop a certain blissful tunnel vision over time.

➢ When presenting an idea to a **Sharpshooter,** consider incorporating quotes from respected third parties, prospective customers, or members of sample research groups. Managers in this group have learned from experience the importance of establishing a "comfort level" before proceeding with a project; endorsements from trusted sources or people who closely mirror the target audience will help you earn trust from the Sharpshooter.

➢ When presenting an idea to a **Professor,** be prepared for a long-term discussion, and don't be surprised if the Professor asks for lots and lots of data on a follow-up basis. Many Professors are simply uneasy about making decisions in the first place, and new initiatives have a way of frightening them at times. Instead of simply saying no to everything (although that is an option more than one Professor seems quite comfortable with), their typical response is to ask for more charts, more analyses, and more testing. As frustrating as this cycle can be, accept it as a fact of workaday life when your superior is a Professor. Document everything; gather it into an expandable binder at each round, so the Professor can tell that he or she is now looking at page 34 of 117 of your most recently amended, research-intensive proposal. Don't try to execute an "end run" around your superior by presenting the idea to someone else unless you discuss this with your superior first.

➢ When presenting an idea to a **Cheerleader,** make an effort to show your satisfaction with specific past occasions when the person has helped you get the best from other team members (or from third parties such as employees in other departments, vendors, or customers). Do this *before* you offer criticism on any point. Highlight the help you need in "rallying the troops" in the face of an important deadline.

HOW TO GET AN EXTENSION ON A DEADLINE

Yikes! The project is due next week, and you're sure you're not going to be able to wrap it up by then. Here are three ideas for managing the potentially tricky meeting when you ask for an extension:

➢ *Project confidence.* When supervisors have to evaluate situations like this, they're usually asking themselves whether they're looking at a temporary setback that's likely to be overcome within the time frame you indicate or whether the project is simply out of control. Do your up-front research work, find a new deadline you can work with and stick to (one that includes a little downtime), and then show your boss that you believe in what you're saying. Send the right body-language signals: sit up straight, look the boss right in the eye (but don't stare), and don't fidget. When answering questions about the project, *don't hesitate or backtrack.* Give your best assessment of the current situation without leaving stretches of "dead air."

➤ *Overcome potential gender communication problems.* Avoiding hesitation is particularly important for women who report to male superiors. As Deborah Tannen points out in her book *Talking from 9 to 5,* many men gauge a person's competence by monitoring his or her apparent certainty—and, often, by undercutting subordinates who appear weak because they ask "too many questions." Female workers generally take a more thorough fact-finding approach to complex tasks than men do, which can pay off nicely in the long run but may work against them when they need to extend a deadline. If you are a woman with a male boss, especially one who tends toward brusque, no-nonsense exchanges in assessments of important matters, it is in your best interests to adopt your superior's direct, unhesitating communication style when requesting more time. A good many male supervisors will see responses along the lines of "We need to look at that" or "I'm not sure yet" as signs that you do not know how to manage your own time. Your best bet when dealing with such superiors is probably to make frank, straightforward estimates, demonstrate that you've done your research work, and quickly close up any potentially awkward silences that follow a question from your boss.

➤ *Put it in writing.* Your superior will take a written commitment to a new deadline more seriously than a verbal one. Find a date you can stand behind and outline it in a crisp one-page memo to your boss.

Perspective Check: Getting an Extension on a Deadline

➤ When asking a **Lone Ranger** for an extension, highlight your intentions and objectives before you outline the obstacles that have forced you to ask for more time. The self-sufficient Lone Rangers have little patience for excuses and may measure your efforts against their own substantial abilities to "get things done." You probably won't win that contest, so stick to the matters you can win agreement on: What you've learned, what you hope to get accomplished, how you're planning to get it accomplished, and how much time you'll need. Project the same independence, autonomy, and confidence your supervisor would if he or she were in the same situation.

➤ When asking a **Sharpshooter** for an extension, point out how the additional time you're asking for will help you to avoid or minimize a potentially serious error. Quantify the expense or time that that error would have resulted in if you'd rushed the project through.

➤ When asking a **Professor** for an extension, follow the same advice just outlined for the Sharpshooter, but augment it, if possible, by citing a parallel situation similar to your own that worked out well. (Professors feel better about authorizing extensions and overruns if they have something to compare them with that did not result in a catastrophe.)

➤ When asking a **Cheerleader** for an extension, consider recruiting one or more co-workers and making a group appeal. Cheerleaders have difficulty turning down reasonable requests from "the team." If you cannot incorporate another person as part of your appeal for an extension, emphasize a person-to-person commitment on your part to meet the new deadline you are proposing.

Important note: Estimate your time requirements responsibly, and don't go to the well too often! Make a commitment you can deliver on. Your first request for a deadline extension may not be much fun, but it's generally a good deal more enjoyable than your second request.

HOW TO DECLINE AN ASSIGNMENT

This is a tricky one, and you may not always be able to pull it off. Nevertheless, there are definitely times when you are best advised to try. Here are four suggestions on how best to tell your boss that you're not the best person for the task he or she has in mind:

➤ *Try to get a sense of the level of importance your superior attaches to the task.* Are the organization's quarterly financial results hinging on the successful completion of what you're being assigned to do? Or is this project a "back-burner" matter that your supervisor has finally gotten around to after weeks or months of procrastination? Once you've gotten a sense of how high a priority the project is for your superior, you can follow the advice set out below.

➤ *If the project represents a high-priority or urgent item for your supervisor, tread cautiously and ask nonthreatening, nonpolarizing questions* (i.e., "Are you interested in discussing some alternate approaches on this?"). If you can find or develop an opening, sketch out *at least three* detailed alternate scenarios for successful completion of the task and summarize any productivity or time advantages these alternate approaches may carry. This may do the trick. (If it doesn't, you're probably stuck with the job. Further attempts to extract yourself from the assignment may not be in your best career interests.)

➤ *If the project represents a low-priority item for your supervisor, ask for a few moments to discuss the matter, then approach things directly.* Give your boss an idea of the nature of your misgivings about the project. (These misgivings should, of course, point toward something other than a simple distaste for the work involved!) Explain the valid reasons you have for wondering whether you're the right person for the project, outline one or two rough outlines of possible alternate approaches, and ask directly for your supervisor's guidance on the issue.

➤ *In either case, you may want to make a subtle or direct appeal to the fact that you could be performing more effectively for the company by focusing on something else.* If you can, develop a dollars-and-cents estimate of the benefit to the company of your working on other tasks; allude to this glancingly if the project you're trying to get out of is a high-priority one for your boss and make a direct appeal on this "bottom-line" basis in other situations.

Perspective Check: Declining an Assignment

➤ When trying to decline a project that has been passed along to you by a **Lone Ranger,** consider trying to put the focus on another, more important project that you are personally responsible for one that has an earlier deadline.

➤ When trying to decline a project that has been passed along to you by a **Sharpshooter,** consider trying to put the focus on another, more important project that you are personally responsible for that features potentially serious flaws with long-lasting implications.

➤ When trying to decline a project that has been passed along to you by a **Professor,** consider trying to put the focus on another, more important project you are working on with others, a project that features potentially serious flaws with long-lasting implications.

➤ When trying to decline a project that has been passed along to you by a **Cheerleader,** consider trying to put the focus on another, more important project you are working on with others, a project that has an earlier deadline.

WHAT TO DO WHEN YOU AND YOUR BOSS DISAGREE

You and your superior are human beings, and human beings have a habit of viewing things in conflicting ways from time to time. Here are four suggestions on keeping the lines of communication open during the times when you and your boss can't seem to see eye to eye on a project:

➤ *Stick with what you can quantify.* This is an especially important point to bear in mind if your superior is a Professor or a Sharpshooter, but it is a tactic worth considering during *any* disagreement with *any* superior. The idea is to stay away from generalizations and opinions and to emphasize instead those events, statements, and patterns that can be proven. This is not to say that you shouldn't expect your *boss* to use the occasional sweeping generalization; you should! But when it comes to presenting your view on a subject under dispute, you're better off reinforcing your faith in and respect for your superior's gut instincts (a fourth-level Maslow appeal), then shining the spotlight tactfully on a part of the puzzle that doesn't quite fit in with your superior's approach. In other words, avoid saying things like "I don't think the sales figures you're forecasting are realistic." Instead, you might choose to make an observation like this:

> "Mel, we're forecasting this product to sell fifty thousand units in the first year; that's a nice aggressive target to shoot for, but I can't help wondering whether or not it might be a little on the high side. You know, over the past year, we've only had three releases that moved that many units, and that's out of over a hundred twenty releases. Are we sure we want to assume that this product is going to be among the two or three top performers of the coming year?"

➤ *At the same time, remember that logic has its limits.* The idea is not to mount an elaborate intellectual assault on your superior's position—that's definitely a bad idea—but to use facts that aren't in dispute to *gently* guide your boss toward another way of looking at the situation. Once you have made your tactful appeal to what you perceive to be the most telling facts of the situation, consider shifting out of "logic mode" and giving your superior time to assess the circumstances from the new vantage point you've identified. (You might decide to offer an appealing, nonaggressive anecdote that supports your way of approaching the situation.)

➤ *Use positive phrasing.* Even if you disagree with the position your superior has staked out, do not use antagonistic language in assessing it—or, indeed, at any point of your exchange with the superior. Stay away from words like *danger, unworkable, unstable, flawed, error,* or *mistake* when discussing an option your superior supports. (It's easier to let such words creep into the conversation than you might think.)

➤ *Know when to back off.* There's a time to press your point and there's a time to remember who's the boss. If you've been unsuccessful in your efforts to highlight, tactfully, the problems you associate with the approach that your superior favors, think seriously about turning down the volume and following your superior's lead. The messages you've been trying to get across have been heard, or at least acknowledged. The ability to pick your battles is an essential component of career stability and success. Don't establish a pattern of constantly "holding out on principle," as this may lead to an unpleasant series of escalating disputes between you and your superior.

Perspective Check: Handling Disagreement

➤ When you find yourself in disagreement with a superior who is a **Lone Ranger,** tactfully highlight any portion of the plan that you favor that represents a more direct, bureacracy-free approach to the question under discussion than what your boss has in mind. Lone Rangers can sometimes be swayed if they are convinced that an initiative represents the most direct, streamlined approach. If you can show how your proposed solution does not have to incorporate input from a number of team members at various levels of the organization or will deliver results more rapidly, you may win the Lone Ranger's interest.

➤ When you find yourself in disagreement with a superior who is a **Sharpshooter,** tactfully highlight any portion of the plan that you favor that represents a more accurate or error-free approach to the question under discussion than what your boss has in mind. Sharpshooters can sometimes be swayed if they are convinced that an initiative represents the likeliest way to move toward a zero-defect outcome. If you can show

how your proposed solution delivers fewer deviations or flaws than what the boss is proposing, you may win the Sharpshooter's interest.

➤ When you find yourself in disagreement with a superior who is a **Professor,** tactfully highlight any portion of the plan that you favor that represents a more tested, proven way to attain the goal than what your boss has in mind. Professors can sometimes be swayed if they are convinced that an initiative represents the most thoroughly "road-tested" approach. If you can show how your proposed solution has been implemented elsewhere in a similar situation, you may win the Professor's interest. (But don't be surprised if your boss asks for even *more* testing before implementing what you've suggested.)

➤ When you find yourself in disagreement with a superior who is a **Cheerleader,** tactfully highlight any portion of the plan that you favor that represents an approach that is likelier to lead to greater workplace harmony than what your boss has in mind. Cheerleaders can sometimes be swayed if they are convinced that a particular initiative represents the approach least likely to lead to disruption among team members in the organization. If you can show how your proposed solution will offer less potential for miscommunication, misunderstanding, and antagonism among the people he or she deals with every day, you may win the Cheerleader's interest.

HOW TO COMPLAIN TO YOUR BOSS

There's a problem, and you genuinely feel that you should speak up directly about it. *How* you do so will have a great deal of impact on the way your superior responds to your appeal. Here are three suggestions for getting your boss to stop, look, and listen to what you have to say:

➤ *Drop blatant hints.* Bear in mind that "blatant" is not synonymous with "rude." Everyday hints are the ones people may or may not pick up on; blatant hints are the ones that fairly scream "There's a problem here" but still allow the recipient the option of pretending that he or she picked up on the issue without prompting. We're not talking about showing your boss up (blatant hints should only be dropped in private) or using the situation as an excuse for taking out your frustration about other issues. What we're talking about is an impossible-to-dismiss reference to the problem you see on the horizon. It could sound something like this:

"You know, that conference is only three days away, and Mark was asking me this morning about the plane reservations. I know you'd wanted me to hold off on arranging things until after the meeting with the people at Bensonworks, but there may be an advantage to getting together with everyone now to nail down who's going and who's not. Is today a good day to look at that?"

Note that this is a very different message from the complaint we probably formulated mentally:

"You're always putting things off until the last minute. Why on earth couldn't we have resolved the travel arrangments last week, the first time I brought it up?"

Following the first example will get you moving in the direction you need to go; following the second could well get you fired. When we "complain" to a superior, what we're really doing is translating the general message ("You always leave things until the last minute") into a nonchallenging, but unignorable, appeal to address a specific course of action related to that message ("It's time to nail down the travel plans"). If you send the message correctly, without antagonism, you may even be able to point your boss, over time, toward changing the larger behavior pattern that causes problems in the first place. But don't demand change from your boss, unless you're willing to track down another one!

➤ *Remember the ten-second rule.* People who deal with top-level business and government officials regularly often follow a simple rule: When you want action, keep your request or observation under ten seconds in length. The principle is worth incorporating when trying to get your boss to take action on a troublesome issue; it puts the focus directly on the issue at hand and makes it clear that your aim is action, not a large chunk of the boss's day. Sometimes, crafting a powerful, nonthreatening message that fits into the ten-second slot takes a little work, but it's usually worth the effort.

➤ *If you're facing a pattern of overt harassment, discrimination, or abuse from your boss, tackle the problem head on.* In most cases, if you look the boss in the eye, explain that you perceive a problem in the area in question, and politely but firmly point out that you're going to be a lot more effective on the job if the two of you find another way to interact with one another, the behavior you're unhappy with will disappear. Just in case, though, make some notes of the exchange, including the date and time. In the unlikely event your supervisor resumes the objectionable behavior, meet with your boss again, mention that you've been taking notes on the problem, and reference the date and time of your previous conversation. This sends the message: "You're leaving a paper trail." If your boss *still* doesn't pick up on the problem, you may be working for the wrong boss. Consider a transfer or lodging a formal complaint with a company representative or looking for work elsewhere.

Perspective Check: Complaining to Your Boss

➤ When trying to get a superior who is a **Lone Ranger** to focus on your complaint, consider *tactfully* highlighting those elements of your appeal that focus on your need to "devote full attention to the job at hand." Lone Rangers will, as a general rule, be able to identify with this desire; it's one that they themselves have experienced from time to time.

➤ When trying to get a superior who is a **Sharpshooter** to focus on your complaint, consider *tactfully* highlighting your discovery of significant inefficiency, duplication of labor, or error in a particular phase of the job, and ask for change based on a new way of doing things. Where possible, document your discovery; point out ways that you think the change you are suggesting will result in reduced error or overlap.

➤ When trying to get a superior who is a **Professor** to focus on your complaint, *tactfully* phrase your suggestion in such a way as to emphasize a need to adapt part of a successful, existing procedure—something now up and running somewhere else—to *your* system. Professors feel more comfortable incorporating systems that have been proven than they do implementing something they regard as untested. As with the Sharpshooter, document whatever inefficiency or overlap you can if doing so will help you make your point.

➤ When trying to get a superior who is a **Cheerleader** to focus on your complaint, consider *tactfully* phrasing your suggestion in a way that emphasizes how a new way of doing things will improve group cohesion and lead to a better work atmosphere for everyone. Point out—in a nonaggressive, optimistic way—how the current way of approaching things may be having a demoralizing or disruptive effect. Cheerleaders are, as a general rule, eager to find ways to keep their team members happy.

BREAKING BAD NEWS, PICKING UP THE PIECES: HOW TO DEAL WITH A BOSS WHO THINKS YOU HAVE A QUALITY OR PERFORMANCE PROBLEM

If your boss thinks there's a problem, guess what? You've got a problem. Here are five ideas for handling situations in which your boss questions your performance or the quality of your work.

> ➤ *Be up front.* Admit what you know . . . and what you don't know. If you try to convince your superior that you have knowledge in an area where you don't, you will only deepen the cycle of mistrust. It's better to identify a need for help in an area where you have a skill gap than to spend all your time and energy trying to camouflage that skill gap.

> ➤ *Approach your situation from a problem-solving mindset.* Don't grovel. Don't spend the whole meeting apologizing. Don't fixate on the past. Demonstrate to your superior that you are just as interested in finding a solution to the problem that's been identified as he or she is, and make it clear that you're eager to hear suggestions about how you can improve your approach.

> ➤ *Never identify a problem without offering at least three potential solutions.* Be ready to do whatever work is required to identify three potential solutions for problems that are identified for you. Put yourself in your supervisor's position. How eager would you be to have someone come up short on a project? You'd probably feel as though the problem were being dumped in your lap. Instead of worrying about how you plan to defend yourself or developing elaborate explanations for why someone else was at fault, develop some workable strategies for making the situation look better. Sketch out the options and make it clear to your supervisor that you are taking full responsibility for improving matters. The number three carries a certain rhetorical magic; when you outline the three options you've developed, you send the message that you've taken a fairly detailed approach to the problem. For some reason, when we hear that we have three possibilities to choose from, we assume there's a decent chance that one of them may work out all right.

> ➤ *If you have to address a subject you know is going to be difficult for your supervisor to deal with, issue a simple "warning statement."* This is a good technique for minimizing the possibility of a blowup—but it shouldn't be overused!

The idea is simple. Instead of responding directly to a question whose answer incorporates information you know won't be welcome news, incorporate a brief preliminary statement that will alert your boss to the fact that there's some rough news ahead. Once you've flashed your warning signal, accept appropriate responsibility for the current situation and offer your three options, as just described. Here's what it might sound like:

> "Mel, I've reviewed all the postings for the last three months, and I want you to know that I found something that probably isn't going to make you very happy, because I know it certainly didn't make me happy. There's an addition error that first slipped in in August, and I missed it. Last quarter's reports were off by thirteen thousand dollars—we were in the red, not in the black, last quarter. I've come up with three possible ways to address this problem—do you want to hear about them?"

After breaking the bad news, you may need to let your superior vent for a little bit about what's happened. Don't try to rush your way through to the possible solutions you've outlined. After the dust settles, you'll still be a step or two ahead of your superior because you will have given some thought to the question of what to do next and he or she will not have. At that point, it's a good bet that your boss will want to hear about the options you have to suggest.

➢ *Keep your chin up.* Even if you made a mistake, you're not a bad person. Don't act like one, and don't roll over and play dead, either. Keep your poise, even if it means doing a little deep breathing on the spot to regain your equilibrium. If you show signs of wilting under the pressure of your boss's internal reprimand, he or she may conclude that you simply don't have what it takes to overcome external obstacles, of which there are plenty in the business world. And bear in mind that more than one manager makes a point of monitoring how subordinates respond during difficult exchanges—like discussions about work-related oversights—when measuring grace under fire. How you *react* to the situation is far more important than the specifics of the problem you face. Make it clear to your boss that you'll overcome whatever problem he or she has identified for you, even if there was a bump in the road a mile or so back—with his or her help, of course. (If you play your cards right, you can turn a reprimand into a fifth-level Maslow appeal. Helping to develop the careers of junior associates, even those who make mistakes from time to time, can be an important part of the self-actualization process.)

Perspective Check: Dealing with a Boss Who Has Problems with Your Work

➤ When addressing a quality or performance problem during a discussion with a superior who is a **Lone Ranger,** find an appropriate opportunity to highlight stories from your past that show how you overcame significant obstacles to attain important goals, more or less on your own. These stories will almost certainly resonate strongly with the Lone Ranger, who has no doubt collected anecdotes along the same lines over time. By sharing these accounts, you will help to reassure your boss that you are in fact the kind of person who can make it through a difficult stretch.

➤ When addressing a quality or performance problem during a discussion with a superior who is a **Sharpshooter,** find an appropriate opportunity to highlight stories from your past that show how you spotted potentially catastrophic mistakes in time to forestall dire consequences. Such stories will very likely earn you points with the Sharpshooter, who has almost certainly amassed anecdotes along the same lines over time. By emphasizing these events from your past, you will help to reassure your boss that you are in fact the kind of person who can be counted on to review important matters.

➤ When addressing a quality or performance problem during a discussion with a superior who is a **Professor,** find an appropriate opportunity to highlight stories from your past that show how you developed a new system or procedure for a previously unforeseen contingency, and emphasize the terrible things that might have happened if you hadn't set up the new way of doing things. Such stories will probably earn you a measure of respect from the Professor, who has almost certainly had similar experiences. By emphasizing these events from your past, you will help to reassure your boss that you are in fact the kind of person who can be counted on to maintain smooth operations in the workplace.

➤ When addressing a quality or performance problem during a discussion with a superior who is a **Cheerleader,** find an appropriate opportunity to highlight stories from your past that show how you helped to resolve a problem by emphasizing the importance of a team goal. Such stories will very likely earn you points with the Cheerleader, who spends much of the day trying to figure out how to get people to look in the same direction. By emphasizing these events from your past, you will help to reassure your boss that you are in fact the kind of person who can be counted on to help the team achieve important objectives.

HOW TO DEVELOP YOUR SELF-REVIEW

Whether or not you are required to compose one, you should compose a written salary review when annual raises are being considered. Pass this along to your superior. Having something on paper makes your contributions over the past year more tangible, and it will allow you to organize your thoughts coherently. The great benefit of getting *any* initiative down in black and white is that doing so gives the recipient something tangible—a piece of paper—that he or she must do something with. There probably isn't a part of your job more deserving of the benefits of this dynamic than your own compensation.

Here are five tips for developing an effective written self-review. You can use them as laid out or adapt them to the formal procedures of your organization if it requires a written self-assessment at salary review time.

> ➤ *Quantify, quantify, quantify.* Don't just point out that you performed *X* task; do a little digging and find out approximately how much money your employer saved as a result of your doing that rather than the average person. Don't just talk about your work in the marketing department; talk about the total revenue the department generated through its campaigns and break down (responsibly!) estimated numbers associated with specific initiatives for which you were responsible. *Don't* make up numbers out of whole cloth; *do* devote the time and effort necessary to provide a hard-numbers, bottom-line analysis of your contributions.

> ➤ *If there was a train wreck, don't pretend that it didn't happen.* Your managers won't react well to a self-review that omits all reference to a crisis or performance-related problem that arose during your watch. Acknowledge what happened, outline what you learned from it, and move on to the next topic.

> ➤ *Don't commit to paper a specific raise amount you think you should receive.* That's the manager's job. If you specify an amount that's too high, you may make your manager "tune out" the rest of your message. If you specify one that's too low, you will almost certainly remove the possibility of getting a better raise.

➤ *Close by offering your assessment of the areas in which you hope to grow and improve.* If you don't do this, you will leave yourself open to charges that you can't be objective about your job.

➤ *Offer* telling *details, but don't go into* too much *detail.* Odds are your boss is a busy person; if you can, keep your self-review to one or two pages. (One page is best.) A manager who has to wade through a massive, incredibly detailed self-review may ask where you found the time to write it from scratch—and what you should have been doing instead!

Here's an example of what your *concise* self-review might look like:

> "Self-review: Sharon Butterworth. This year was an exciting one for me; I was able to take a lead role in developing *sixteen new campaigns,* more than any previous person in this position has done in a single year. The Martin and Valu-Plex campaigns alone represent *four hundred thousand dollars in new business to the firm.* I was particularly proud of the concept and execution of the Batterymate campaign; because the project had to be completed while our pre-production position was open, I coordinated all that work at no extra cost to the company. Hiring a special consultant to handle this work over a six-week period would have cost something on the order of *ten to twelve thousand dollars.* As I begin the next year, I want to improve in the following areas: improving my computerized graphic design skills; working more effectively with the people in design; and improving the work flow through my area by responding more quickly to phone and e-mail messages. All in all, I feel I have been a significant contributor to the company's success this year, and I hope to continue on as a team member at Conroy Advertising for as long as the rewards and challenges are appropriate ones. I anticipate that this will be the case for many years to come."

Perspective Check: Developing Your Self-Review

➤ When developing a self-review for a supervisor who is a **Lone Ranger,** highlight your independent accomplishments and your ability to meet key deadlines with little assistance from others.

➤ When developing a self-review for a supervisor who is a **Sharpshooter,** highlight your ability to identify, more or less on your own, errors that would have cost the organization large amounts of money if they had gone undetected.

➤ When developing a self-review for a superior who is a **Professor,** highlight your ability to develop intelligent approaches to situations other people must work through on a regular basis. You should also consider isolating those instances you went out of your way to verify and fact-check before proceeding with an initiative, and isolate any potentially catastrophic errors you may have detected as a result.

➤ When developing a self-review for a superior who is a **Cheerleader,** highlight your ability to interact well with others and sacrifice personal objectives and interests for those of the team. You should also make a point of emphasizing your specific contributions to important group initiatives.

HOW TO WEATHER A STORM

Your boss is on the warpath! With some superiors, there seem to be times when there's no way to do the right thing. Whatever you say is perceived as a roadblock, and whatever you do isn't what you were supposed to do. Here are five ideas for getting through the day unscathed—and maybe even improving your odds for tomorrow:

➤ *Let 'em vent.* Interrupting a superior who's delivering an impassioned soliloquy is not the best idea. Do not attempt to defend your position. Wait your boss out; before long, the tirade will pass. Rank has its privileges, and one is the right to sound off every once in a while. Respect that privilege; doing anything else will probably be perceived as a challenge.

➤ *Don't back down.* It will only encourage your superior. This is not to say that you should attempt to match antagonistic remark for antagonistic remark. Far from it! Arguing with a superior on a point-for-point level is not your aim; in fact, "defending yourself" as such is not even on the list at times like this. The idea is to show that you're capable of remaining cool and calm, even when the boss can't. Maintain appropriate *intermittent* eye contact (don't stare), wait for the tantrum to pass, and send the right signals with your body language: head up, back straight, hands at the side (or occupied with a pad and pen, taking notes). By showing that you're more than up to the task of waiting the tirade out, you demonstrate to your boss that you're capable of making sense of tough situations. (You also set a subtle example about the right way to respond to stressful situations.)

➤ *Hook in.* As tempting as it may be to disengage or shut down when you're being subjected to a verbal barrage, you must find a way to broadcast an "I'm listening and I understand" message to your superior, even if what he or she is saying is incomprehensible! You can do this by maintaining appropriate eye contact, delivering occasional verbal reinforcements (such as "okay," "yes," and "uh-huh"), and by nodding now and then as your superior reaches a point that appears to him or her to be important. Many superiors will simply turn up the volume, like tourists accosting strangers in a foreign airport, when they think the message isn't getting through. This is a dangerous and counterproductive cycle, one you must avoid at all costs. Don't withdraw. Do whatever it takes to send the "I'm listening" message (and remember the advice that appeared earlier about the power of taking notes during in-person meetings).

➤ *Once your superior reaches a stopping point, play back the main message.* Restating the other person's key idea to show that you received it is an essential technique for good communication; in this situation, it may just get you out of the line of fire. In the case of incoherent or para- noid superiors, you may have to do a little deft "translating" to *identify* the key idea. What you say could sound something like this:

> "Jane, if I understand what you're saying, you're very concerned about the proofreading process and you want me to institute a checklist system that will help us make sure that the kind of mistake that happened on the pull-out coupon never happens again. That's what I'm hearing from you; is that a fair assessment of what you want me to hear?"

➤ *After you restate the message, let your superior know that you've gained some- thing from the exchange.* This may take some work, but it's essential. If your superior has gone over the edge and *doesn't* realize it, he or she will be expecting some tangible result from the "discussion" and will want evidence that the same problem will be unlikely to arise again. If your superior has gone over the edge and *does* realize it, there's a good bet he or she feels awkward now and is looking for a graceful way to get out of the situation. You must provide that graceful exit.

Whichever situation you're dealing with, you must, after restating your boss's message as outlined above, *specify something you've learned* from your exchange with the boss, *admit any errors* you feel are appropriate to assume responsibility for, and *outline how you'll approach such situations differently* the next time you face them. Once you've done this, your superior will, in all likelihood, retire to a neutral corner—for a while.

Perspective Check: Weathering a Storm

➤ When facing a tirade from a **Lone Ranger,** understand that one of the underlying reasons for the eruption may be simple fatigue on your boss's part. Lone Rangers are often notorious workaholics, and they may be sharing their stress load with you. Follow the advice just outlined and bring the exchange to a conclusion as soon as possible. Don't take personally any unfortunate remarks that may come your way. Once your superior gets past the current deadline, gets a little sleep, and regains the ability to speak in coherent sentences, you'll probably be in a position to get the best from each other once again. The average Lone Ranger doesn't have the time or inclination for tirades with other people and is unlikely to indulge in them unless things are going poorly on some other front.

➤ When facing a tirade from a **Sharpshooter,** *take notes.* You are likely to get some very specific pointers on the best ways to do things. Go out of your way to remark on the Sharpshooter's mastery of technical detail. Do whatever is necessary to let your boss know that each and every point raised will be followed up. The Sharpshooter's nightmare is that something will slip through the cracks, and he or she probably wouldn't be taking the time to throw a tantrum unless this seemed to be a realistic prospect. The message you want to get across is a simple one: "I've got it all down in black and white and nothing is going to be overlooked." Then follow up and make this promise a reality!

➤ When facing a tirade from a **Professor,** the advice about *taking notes* is just as appropriate as it is with the Sharpshooter. In addition, you will probably, near the end of your exchange, need to incorporate a promise to *run tests and follow up with their results* if the Professor is concerned about a new system or procedure *or* make an iron-clad vow to *follow the rules to the letter* if the Professor is concerned about a violation of the established way of doing things. If your Professor superior is concerned about the latter issue, you must, after the tirade, initiate a quiet campaign to broadcast your adherence to the rules and regulations. Professors get very nervous when they must supervise people they consider to be heedless rule-breakers.

➤ When facing a tirade from a **Cheerleader,** emphasize your desire to work as a team player and cast your willingness to make changes in your work patterns in that light. Cheerleaders tend to respond best to people who (1) follow their lead, and (2) encourage cohesiveness within the group. So send messages that you are willing to take on the task being discussed in a way that achieves both those goals.

HOW TO DEAL WITH A TYRANT

Unfortunately, some bosses have chronic people-skill problems that have the potential to make your life miserable. Because these bosses are the least likely to react well to any comment even vaguely resembling criticism, your chance of enouraging meaningful personal change is pretty slim. Even though you can't *change* such bosses, however, you can learn how to *manage* them better. Here are five ideas for retaining your sanity and productivity if you have to report to a tyrant:

➤ *Learn the person's habitual body language.* If you watch your boss carefully, you'll probably learn that he or she has certain predictable physical patterns that precede an outburst—or similarly predictable gestures that mark the onset of a deceptively quiet period of Not Exactly Looking Out for Everyone's Best Interests. Does your superior cross her arms when she perceives a challenge? Does she start tapping her foot before she starts planning exactly how she's going to dress someone down? It may seem far-fetched at first, but these instinctive preliminary gestures are known as "tells," and they are common enough for professional poker players to monitor them closely (and silently) in fellow players. "Tells" can serve as uncannily accurate predictors of high stress, and they could be your best clue as to when Mount Vesuvius is about to blow. It may take a week or two of casual observation to spot such a physical habit, but once you do, you'll know when you should deftly change the subject and find something else to focus on that's out of blast range.

➤ *Master the art of transferring discussions to paper.* At various points throughout this book, you've been pointed toward the many advantages of transferring discussions to brief written form. In addition to being more convenient, leaving you with a personal record, and removing strategic "memory lapses" as an option from the person on the receiving end of the memo, putting things in black and white allows you to overcome personal chemistry problems and distance yourself emotionally from one-on-one interaction patterns that could be counterproductive. If you're working for a boss who seems to want to make life difficult, the ability to compose direct, one-page written memos will become something of a survival skill. If you are uncomfortable about your writing abilities and have shied away from this option when you encountered it elsewhere in this book, rest assured that this is the time to put this technique to work for you. You say you have trouble composing more than a sentence or two at a time? That's no problem. Your concise, unchallenging memo probably doesn't *need* to be much longer than that. Here's an example of what it might sound like.

To: Pat

Fr: Brian

I reviewed the order breakdowns as you requested and left the totals with Tom. He said he should be able to incorporate them into the quarterly report without too much difficulty.

That's pretty straightforward—and if you work for a difficult boss, popping such a note into your boss's mailbox *the instant you complete the task* is far preferable to waiting for her to circle past your desk on a blame-assignment mission. You know the kinds of questions you'll face:

> "Did you wrap up those order breakdowns?" (If "yes":) "Well, what on earth did they say? I can't believe you didn't come in early this morning to go over this with me. We've got to get this moving, you know." (If "no":) "Good God, how long have you been sitting on this? Don't you know we've got a quarterly report to wrap up?"

With some bosses, you can't win—or even play for a nice, mutually satisfying draw—during face-to-face encounters. If you want to square away some time in which to complete all those assignments your boss has thoughtfully dumped in your lap, you'll need to learn the fine art of moving matters forward on paper. If you don't, you may spend all day wading through a mass of your superior's unprioritized "gottas" and defending yourself for the way you dealt with whichever one happens to have popped into her head in the past half hour.

➤ *Monitor breathing.* If you're dealing with someone who specializes in and makes a habit of rattling others, you are well advised to monitor your own breathing very closely. Especially in stressful or challenging situations, make a point of breathing low, slow, and deep. This will help you retain composure in the face of an attack from your boss. (Bear in mind, too, that breathing *in rhythm with your superior*—in a way that does not call attention to itself—may help to encourage harmonious interactions between the two of you.)

➢ *Avoid counterattacking at all costs.* Even though you may be sorely tempted, it won't do you a bit of good to mount an assault of your own when your boss sends a heat-seeking missile your way. Stand your ground; acknowledge valid points openly; focus on common intentions. But don't indulge in the luxury of pointing out your boss's oversights for the sake of scoring points. That won't win you any allies, and it certainly won't help you depolarize the exchange in which you're involved at the moment.

➢ *Remember that some bosses just need to get things off their chest.* Nobody's saying you have to volunteer for human punching-bag status, but you should ask yourself whether there's really any reason to suspect that personal animus is the foundation of your superior's intimidating communication style. Usually, it isn't. As difficult as the task may seem at first, it is possible to develop an ongoing relationship with a tyrant without going insane. The key lies in acting on the *intention* of the person's words, rather than their content. Let your boss expound on whatever is the obsession of the moment until a sizable pause ensues, then ask yourself: What is the main objective here? Your response should address that objective directly in a solution-finding, rather than problem-finding, manner.

Perspective Check: Dealing with a Tyrant

➢ When interacting with a tyrannical superior who is a **Lone Ranger,** do your level best to help "clear the decks" and allow this person to work independently, without distraction, on whatever the next deadline-oriented project may be. Lone Rangers tend to descend into fouler and fouler moods when they are not allowed to tackle the project that's ticking away on their desk. Your boss will be happier if you find a way to win him or her a few hours of uninterrupted time, and that means you'll be happier, too.

➢ When interacting with a tyrannical supervisor who is a **Sharpshooter,** constantly remind yourself that finding errors and assigning blame represent, in all likelihood, this person's primary approach to evaluating the world of work. This approach will not change. Instead of pushing yourself to the wall in a futile attempt to deliver something that cannot possibly be picked apart, consider offering broad outlines and themes for your superior to review before proceeding beyond the initial stages. The aim here is to give your boss something to shoot down. If you outline five possible ways to proceed with a project and come away with two still more or less intact after a meeting with your Sharpshooter superior, you'll be doing fairly well.

➤ When interacting with a tyrannical supervisor who is a **Professor,** make an attempt to benefit from your boss's technical knowledge (even if, in the event, it is no more impressive than yours). Overbearing Professors can often be tamed by the simple act of turning them into mentors. Appeal to your boss's instinct to develop error-free solutions for other people by making it clear that you are hoping to learn as much as you can from him or her about the systems with which you both work. For most Professors, the prospect of passing along their accumulated knowledge to a supplicating underling is enough to soften the occasional hard edges of the relationship.

➤ When interacting with a tyrannical supervisor who is a **Cheerleader,** you will probably be facing a situation in which the boss has either determined that you represent a challenge to his or her primacy or concluded that you are a destabilizing force within the work group. Cheerleaders who take a dictatorial tone with their subordinates are rare, but they do exist; as a general rule, they are engaged in one-on-one feuds with team members whom they do not trust. Overcoming this antagonism may take time, and it may take some doing. You will need to send appropriately submissive signals to the Cheerleader to demonstrate that you do not relish the idea of conflict, and you should also find ways to pass along stories that illustrate your willingness to subordinate your personal goals in favor of those of the group.

HOW TO END YOUR RELATIONSHIP WITH A BOSS WHO IS NOT RIGHT FOR YOU

You've decided that it's time to cut the cord; you and your supervisor don't have a harmonious, healthy relationship, and it seems unlikely in the extreme that you'll ever be able to develop one. What do you do? In the final analysis, there are three options—which follow—but there are probably no easy choices.

You may determine that one of the options is right for you, in which case you should carefully review the "Perspective Check" section that follows. This section will outline the best ways to manage your departure from the supervisor in a way that keeps lines of communications open, emphasizes growth and challenge for both parties, and avoids unpleasant exchanges.

Whatever you decide to do, *don't* see your decision to head out the door as an excuse to express openly any frustration you may feel at your working relationship with your former supervisor. In the long term, you will accomplish nothing by giving anyone "a piece of your mind," and you may seriously damage your career prospects.

If you are determined to close out your relationship with your supervisor, these are your three main options:

➤ *Negotiate an internal transfer.* Only you can judge the best way to accomplish this within your organization, but a few words of warning are in order. Politics can be a treacherous thing, and even a supervisor with whom you do not communicate well may view a request on your part to leave the department as a black mark of sorts against his or her management style. There is a chance, of course, that your current boss may be just as eager to alter the situation as you are. If you have a strong sense that this is the case, you may be in a good position to discuss the matter openly with your supervisor. In many cases, however, you will have to engage in the very delicate maneuver of sounding out another manager on the topic of transferring to his or her work area—and hoping that your request to keep the conversation confidential will be respected. This is a very tricky operation, but if your situation seems to you to warrant it, you may conclude that it is worth the risk involved. *Initially, you should keep your requests informal, private, and verbal.* Don't make a formal written request unless you feel comfortable with the idea of your current supervisor hearing about your action.

➤ *Apply for another position within the company that does not require you to report to your current supervisor.* A great way out, and one that you need not apologize for, but by no means a certain bet. Then again, you may wish to use your current work situation as an inspiration to prepare some dramatic new presentation as part of your interview for an internal position elsewhere in the company.

➤ *Resign from the company.* Do so gracefully, without appearing to attack your superior or anyone else in the organization. (You'll want a reference.) But bear in mind that those who apply for work while still employed elsewhere probably stand a better chance of being perceived positively by prospective employers. In some situations, however, resignation will definitely be the best option. For some ideas on unorthodox—but effective—ways to find work at a new organization, see my book *303 Off-the-Wall Ways to Get a Job,* published by Career Press.

Perspective Check: Ending the Relationship

All these suggestions will help you disengage from your relationship with your superior in a positive, harmonious way. Don't burn bridges! Follow the advice laid out.

➤ When terminating your relationship with a **Lone Ranger,** show undiluted appreciation for the specific past occasions when the person has "moved mountains" for you or others in the department. Do not offer criticism on any point. Emphasize how the superior was always someone you could count on to help you overcome seemingly impossible odds. Find some way to ask for a written letter of recommendation *before you move on to your new situation,* and make it clear that you respect the superior's input and advice on where your career should go from here.

➤ When terminating your relationship with a **Sharpshooter,** show undiluted appreciation for the specific past occasions when the person has helped you identify potentially devastating errors. Do not offer criticism on any point. Emphasize how the superior was always someone you could count on to help you put the focus where it belonged: on quality and attention to detail. Find some way to ask for a written letter of recommendation *before you move on to your new situation,* and make it clear that you respect the superior's input and advice on how to avoid mistakes in career planning.

➤ When terminating your relationship with a **Professor,** show undiluted appreciation for the specific past occasions when the person has helped you find ways of working with others efficiently. Do not offer criticism on any point. Emphasize how the superior was always someone you could count on to help you put the focus where it belonged: on group productivity and intelligent strategies for overcoming common obstacles. Find some way to ask for a written letter of recommendation *before you move on to your new situation,* and make it clear that you respect the superior's input and advice on how best to set up your career plan. (***Important note:*** *Professors are often excellent networkers!* Make every effort to keep this person on your side; he or she may be a source of important referrals in the future.)

➢ When terminating your relationship with a **Cheerleader,** show undiluted appreciation for the specific past occasions when the person has helped you work harmoniously with others to attain important goals. Do not offer criticism on any point. Emphasize how the superior was always someone you could count on to help you put the focus where it belonged: on pulling together as a team and hitting targets as a group. Find some way to ask for a written letter of recommendation *before you move on to your new situation,* and make it clear that you respect the superior's input and advice on how to attain important career goals. (***Important note:*** *Cheerleaders are often excellent networkers!* Make every effort to keep this person on your side; he or she may be a source of important referrals in the future.)

Dealing with Clients and Customers

As anyone who's had to negotiate an airport terminal, rent a car, or straighten out problems with a hotel reservation can attest, we live in a society in which true concern for the customer is at times all too rare. In this chapter, we'll take a look at the best ways to project the kind of genuine attention and concern that builds long-term business partnerships.

TEN TIPS FOR EFFECTIVE DAY-TO-DAY INTERACTIONS WITH CLIENTS AND CUSTOMERS

1. *During face-to-face encounters, take notes.* Yes, this is the same advice that is most important for encouraging effective day-to-day interactions with your superior. That's no coincidence. The best way to build long-term alliances with your clients and customers is to treat them like the boss. (In the final analysis, that's what they are!) Accordingly, you will want to take detailed notes during your face-to-face meetings with clients, customers, and people you *hope* will turn into customers, *without asking permission to do so.* This invaluable advice comes courtesy of corporate sales trainer Stephan Schiffman, a tireless advocate of the note-taking technique as an effective sales and customer service tool.

   When you take notes, you send all the right messages. You tell the customer or client that you are listening, that what he or she is saying will be the key factor in what happens next, and that you care enough about the exchange to keep a permanent record. Don't skip this step. Keep detailed notes during all your face-to-face meetings with clients and customers, *whether or not* you think you will need to refer back to the specifics of the meeting at a later date.

2. *Keep your client or customer updated: Return calls promptly and follow up within the time line promised.* The most common fear we all have in dealing with representatives of other organizations is that *nothing is going to happen* as a result of our contact. (This is, alas, perhaps the most common outcome when we deal with seemingly impenetrable bureacratic structures.) If we take on the responsibility to see the client's or customer's issue through the organization, it is incumbent upon us to take on responsibility for communicating progress reports, as well. The simple act of returning phone calls and responding as promised—politely and in an upbeat, optimistic fashion—is often far more important than the message we are passing along.

3. *Stay abreast of the changes in the client's or customer's industry.* Ask about current trends and challenges; take an occasional (or more than occasional) trip through the pages of your customer's industry trade magazine. You should really be reading this magazine already, as it almost certainly has a direct impact on your own industry. If yours is a book-printing business, for instance, you should know what trends are emerging in the publishing business: what forecasts are being touted, and how those forecasts can be expected to affect your customers' ordering and payment patterns.

4. *Try to work from a* we *position.* You and *I* are terms that can be set into opposition; it's tougher to do that with the pronoun *we.* Wherever possible, phrase your questions and suggestions in *we* language. Here are some examples:

    "Can we talk a little bit about inventory storage in the coming year?"

    (*Not:* "What do you think your inventory storage needs in the coming year are going to look like?")

    "What types of projects do you think we should be focusing on in this discussion?"

    (*Not:* "What types of projects are you looking for?")

    "What should we try to emphasize about the Babson campaign?"

    (*Not:* "What do you want me to emphasize about the Babson campaign?")

5. *When in doubt, ask what the client or customer wants to get accomplished.* There is great power in asking, preferably early on in the relationship, something along the following lines: "What's the main goal here?" or "What are the benchmarks for success on this project?" By asking some variation on this "what-are-you-trying-to-get-accomplished" question

and allowing the client or customer to respond in as much detail as he or she feels is appropriate, you'll lay the foundation for a long-term business alliance.

6. *Visit the office.* Your chances of keeping business relationships alive in the long term increase dramatically when you visit your customer's workplace regularly. You'll put the odds even more dramatically in your favor if you can get the customer to agree to enjoy a meal with you now and then. (Of course, you should pick up the tab!)

   Don't misunderstand. Personal interactions are no substitute for bottom-line performance, and you must deliver that, as well. But your customer's loyalty to you will increase if you can establish a one-on-one human connection, associate a face with the voice on the telephone, and get a sense of who your customer really is and what he or she faces every day at work.

7. *Provide updates that detail your contributions.* Sales trainer Anthony Parinello suggests that, during an in-person meeting, you supply both old and new customers with a notebook, preferably one bearing your customer logo, and then supply printed hard-number updates on the ways you are adding value to the organization. By taking this proactive approach and quantifying your contributions—instead of simply assuming that a sale that's "closed" needs no further input—you're far likelier to survive the budget cutbacks and organizational shuffles that are a part of business today. In order to develop a meaningful long-term partnership with your client or customer, you must commit to delivering—and broadcasting—value on a regular basis.

8. *Show personal concern.* As with superiors, it is important to develop shared, nonwork-related topics of discussion with your clients and customers. Ask about hobbies, avocations, or vacation pursuits; try to pin down some area in which you and the customer are enthusiastic about the same topic. Then ask questions that encourage your conversational partner to expound on that topic. Don't monopolize the conversation!

9. *Ask to see the president.* Relax. They're just like everyone else. This is another great idea passed along from sales trainer Tony Parinello, and one that's less intimidating than it might seem at first. By politely, but persistently, asking to meet for even a brief time with the top person at the organization, you will give the chief of the company a name, a personality, and a face to match up with your company name on the

list of vendors. These days, that counts. For more information on the best ways to deal with the heads of companies, see Parinello's book *Selling to VITO (The Very Important Top Officer)*.

10. *Smile.* People like to spend time with others who are enjoying themselves, and it's easier to conclude that you made the right purchase decision when your main contact seems to be having a good time. Ease off the hard sell; take a break from crisis mode; make it clear that you enjoy doing what you do for a living. It's the best one-on-one advertising you'll ever engage in.

SEVEN WAYS FOR MANAGERS TO ESTABLISH CREDIBILITY WITH LONG-STANDING CLIENTS AND CUSTOMERS

You've inherited an account. The person who came before you probably enjoyed a comparatively strong, or at least not disastrous, relationship with this account (given their status as a customer). How do you make sure the relationship continues to work out well for everyone? Here are seven ideas that will help you make sense of the situation you've inherited—and keep your clients and customers happy:

➤ *Take care of the little things—show up and shake hands.* Have you ever noticed that a good deal of the business we all seem to conduct these days is on the telephone, rather than in person? It may seem like a modest step, but keeping in touch through brief person-to-person meetings (i.e., visiting the client's facility, inviting the client or customer to company events, inviting people out to lunch, and undertaking other forms of personal contact) can have a dramatic effect on your organization's ability to retain business. Such "externals" can lend a structure or form to an otherwise amorphous relationship. Put more simply: It's harder to cut someone off who's made an effort to develop a relationship in person. One manager I know took the time to go down his list of suppliers and realized that, even after a round of budget cuts, the vendors who were still on the list and receiving the most business were *all* people who had taken the trouble to actually show up and develop a face-to-face relationship. And yet how many of the people our organization does business with do we know personally, on a face-to-face basis? This may *seem* like Salesmanship 101, but sometimes it's the blindingly obvious points that are the easiest to miss. (And, yes, in case you were wondering, managers, in addition to salespeople, have a role to play as well in the area of relationship-building with clients). When *we* have a problem with a vendor to whom we can't attach a face, isn't it second nature (at least in a good many cases) to assume that the easiest way is simply to switch to someone else? Do the little things. Visit the plant. Shake hands. Take the person who signed the purchase order out to lunch. Be a face, not just a voice. You'll probably find that the time required is time very well spend indeed.

➤ *Is there a problem? Remember that listening is the single best way to keep clients and customers satisfied.* Review the advice in Chapter 2, and see the advice earlier about the importance of taking notes. If you don't take the opportunity to listen to your customers, you are putting your relationship in grave danger. The temptation to talk at length about "what you can do" for the person may seem overwhelming, but you must overcome it. Let the client or customer lecture *you* first about the challenges and obstacles he or she faces.

➤ *Ask questions that encourage long monologues.* You can do this by asking "tell-me-all-about-it" questions before you focus on more pointed, specific queries. Tell-me-all-about-it questions sound like this:

> "What are the main things you're trying to do on the retail bookstore front?"
>
> "So what's the main goal for this year?"
>
> "What kinds of customers are you trying to attract?"

➤ *Ask for priorities.* In addition to asking broad, open-ended questions about business philosophy and direction, be sure to ask about the client's or customer's objectives where you, specifically, are concerned. The question might sound something like this:

> "Mr. Allen, let me ask you something, what are the three or four most important things you'd like me to focus on as I start to take a look at your organization? What are the key areas where you want to see results from us?"

Write down the answers you receive in a notebook, right then and there!

➤ *Keep ego out of the picture.* That means relinquishing any claim to victory in "right/wrong" or "correct/incorrect" outcomes. If you are a Sharpshooter or a Professor, you may need to temper your instinct to find flaws or flag erroneous information. Although it may seem to you an incidence of error correction is for the customer's benefit, there is a strong likelihood that your comments may simply polarize things. Let your client or customer take the lead in the exchange; do not challenge the other person's conception. Instead, offer to do a written follow-up report based on your conversation and tactfully incorporate your suggestions for improvements on paper.

The irony of the world of sales—one that a good many managers fail to grasp—is that it is sometimes your organization's duty to be incorrect. That is to say, when you allow the customer to correct you, to point out an inconsistency or an instance of poor fit between your organization and his and then you act accordingly to resolve the problem that's been raised, you don't *lose* points in the customer's eyes. You gain points. The cliché in this area is that "the customer is always right." That's a misleading saying; the customer *isn't* always right about the best way to approach a problem, but there's precious little to be gained by pointing that fact out. What the customer is unfailingly correct in identifying is *how his organization perceives its own goals.* There is a world of difference between isolating your client's or customer's priorities and discussing the technical aspects of a solution your organization is ready to propose. In the former case (that which has to do with what the customer wants to get accomplished) your background, opinions, and technical knowledge won't count for much. In the latter case (that which has to do with how a particular problem should be resolved), your background, opinions, and technical knowledge will probably count for a great deal. In *both* cases, however, you must relinquish the notion of "convincing" your customer of anything! People who set out to "convince" their customers of the unassailability of their position may win arguments, but they will often lose sales as a result.

Forget about who's right and who's wrong. Forget about past achievements. Forget about how many times you've seen something just like what the customer or client is describing. Check your ego at the door and set about the business of building and sustaining a relationship under which you supply the solutions to problems as your customer defines them.

➤ *Give them 24-hour access to your organization.* This may mean pointing your customer toward someone who will be "on call" during off hours, or it may mean passing along your own home phone number as a backup. The latter option may seem a bit extreme, but the vast majority of the people you give your number to will not abuse the privilege—and *will* appreciate, and remember, the gesture.

➤ *Treat your new contacts as though they were your superiors.* Guess what? They are! Review the applicable ideas in Chapter 5 and make an effort to determine which mindset category your clients and customers fall into: Lone Ranger, Sharpshooter, Professor, or Cheerleader. Then follow the "Perspective Check" advice that appears in the appropriate section. If there is any group of people worthy of the same time, energy, and attention you would expend in learning how to deal effectively with a superior, it is your customers.

HOW TO CULTIVATE NEW BUSINESS

A full discussion of effective sales techniques could fill another book the size of this one, but it is worthwhile to focus here on some of the best ways to use your exchanges with current clients and customers to develop new business. Here are five ideas that will help you do just that:

➤ *Offer quantifiable success stories.* Anecdotes are powerful things; when you pass one along to your current clients and customers that illustrates how you added value to someone's business, you not only strengthen your position on the current project, but also increase the likelihood of future business coming your way. Be specific; appeal to hard-number, bottom-line results, just as you would when preparing a series of anecdotes for a superior who is conducting an annual salary review. (See the section devoted to this topic in Chapter 5 for some pointers on structuring your anecdotes.)

➤ *Ask for referrals.* That's right; ask directly for the names and phone numbers of other people your contact may know of who might benefit from what your organization has to offer. Of course, you will want to structure your question in such a way as to allow your contact to pass along the name of someone other than a direct competitor. But a good number of the people you keep happy may well be able to point you toward prospects in other industries or in related, but not identical, fields of business within the same industry.

➤ *Ask for permission to use a quote or endorsement.* Your ears should perk up when you hear a client say something like this:

"I think you people did an excellent job."

"You really saved our bacon that time."

"I didn't think you'd be able to pull it off."

Whenever complimentary phrases like these come your way, respond by asking, "Mr./Ms. So-and-so, may I quote you on that?" Make it clear that the person's complimentary assessment of your performance will be part of an effort to contact other prospective customers. In the unlikely event that your contact seems uncomfortable with the idea of being quoted, you may want to stipulate that you're happy to limit the quote's audience to people in organizations not competitive with your contact. In most cases, however, your client or customer will be extremely flattered by the request. (It is, in essence, a sign of respect that equates with a fourth-level Maslow appeal.)

➤ *Update your client or customer with industry-related news items he or she may have missed.* Keep up with events in your industry that may be of interest to your client or customer; send along appropriate photocopies and press clippings that he or she is unlikely to have spotted in the trade journal that focuses on his or her industry. By doing so, you will be more likely to develop a mutually advantageous networking relationship, and you may help to solidify your company's position as a vendor or service provider.

➤ *Think in the long term.* Sales trainer Stephan Schiffman argues persuasively in his seminars that the suppliers likeliest to survive reorganizations, budget cutbacks, and strategy shifts are those who make an effort to become part of the *long-term* planning process with their clients and customers. This takes work, but it is probably not as difficult as you think. By asking appropriate future-oriented questions, Schiffman maintains, and focusing on delivering tailor-made solutions dictated by the client's specific requests, rather than your catalog or operation's manual, you can, over time, develop a true business partnership rather than a short-term alliance. Ask your clients and customers what they hope to accomplish within the next three to five years and how you can help them get there. You'll be building the kind of business alliance that Schiffman advocates is essential in our era of profound, unremitting economic and technological change.

HOW TO KEEP YOUR ORGANIZATION'S NAME UPPERMOST IN THE MINDS OF CURRENT AND PROSPECTIVE CUSTOMERS

Whether the issue is people you're *currently* working with or people you *want* to work with, name recognition counts for a great deal. Here are four good ideas for increasing your company's visibility in the information-overload age:

➤ *Send creative one-page letters.* How much of the mail you receive gets right to the point, incorporates some unique graphic element, employs a bit of wry humor, and takes less than thirty seconds to read in full? If you said "hardly any," you're in some pretty good company. But it is exactly these kinds of letters, rather than exhaustive brochures or multi-page appeals, that are likeliest to open doors for you at organizations you have not yet contacted—and keep them open for you at organizations where you do have established business relationships.

In my book *303 Off-the-Wall Ways to Get a Job,* I pass along the story of a job seeker who taped a dime to the lower right-hand corner of her cover letter . . . and began the letter with a headline that said "I Can Turn on a Dime to Master Your Computer System." Beneath the headline, she detailed three or four supporting points. She got the job. Before you dismiss adapting such innovative efforts to your marketing work as "stunts" unworthy of your time or your organization's image, ask yourself three questions:

1. Which do people seem to be paying more attention to these days: words or pictures? (If you answered "words," consider the rise of MTV, the mushrooming popularity of the graphically-oriented part of the Internet known as the World Wide Web, and the relative importance of paid television advertisements and paid print advertisements in political campaigns.)

2. When was the last time you received a multi-page business letter from someone you did not know—and read it from beginning to end? (If you did so recently, you have more time on your hands than most decision makers do.)

3. Does the average person's attention span seem to you to be expanding in length, contracting, or staying about the same? (If you feel it is expanding or staying the same, you should consider that national advertisers are investing millions of dollars in television campaigns that are geared toward an audience that is used to focusing on concepts for durations measured not in seconds but in *fractions* of seconds.)

I am not, of course, arguing that you must duplicate the approach of the person who taped the dime to her cover letter. I *am* arguing, however, that there are distinct advantages to a marketing campaign that uses a one-page letter that incorporates some kind of visual appeal, doesn't waste the reader's time, and isn't afraid to feature an appropriate joke to win attention. Developing a letter that is right for your organization may take a little testing, but this will be time very well spent. (**Technical note:** The leading word processing programs allow you to incorporate—or create from scratch—color graphics within your document. If you are not using these tools to their full capacity, you're missing out on an opportunity to develop new business alliances or solidify existing ones.)

➤ *Make the fax machine work for you.* Monopolizing the target organization's available fax time will surely win you more enemies than friends; but judiciously using fax messages to introduce yourself and your company, follow up on written appeals, or request input on proposals can help you track down new business. As with your mailed messages, be concise and don't be afraid to incorporate some form of mild, visually oriented humor.

The fax message has a distinct advantage over other written forms of communication: It is often viewed as urgent by the receiving organization and placed directly on the addressee's desk. Don't abuse the medium by sending along an unending chain of messages. Let the assumption that an incoming fax must be acted on immediately work in your favor by appealing to this medium only occasionally.

➤ *Harness the power of e-mail.* These days, the world seems to be dividing up into two camps: Those who passionately embrace things like e-mail and Internet surfing and those who have no interest in these topics and have heard enough about electronic communication media to tide them over for the next several decades. If you fall into the latter category, consider making a *temporary* change in your outlook for marketing purposes only. The reason? Those who check their e-mail every day are often addicted to the medium, and a good many consider answering e-mail to be more fun than getting back to what other, more cynical types might consider to be "real work."

Find out more about the Internet. Developing a chatty, informal sentence-or-two-at-a-time e-mail relationship with a top prospect won't eat up much of your time, but there's a very good chance it will help you build a relationship that could turn into a sale.

➤ *Set up a site on the World Wide Web.* As of this writing, something like 25 percent of private companies are maintaining Web sites, which are graphically oriented electronic "pages" in cyberspace that not only offer information, but also point readers toward other sites of interest. (You've probably noticed the tiny writing at the bottom of advertisements these days that reads something like this: "http://www.new.page.on.the.web.com"—those are all addresses on the World Wide Web.) The amount of the up-front investment required depends on the complexity of the page you intend to set up, but if you run into a consultant who tells you that you're going to have to spend tens of thousands of dollars to get your Web site up and running, you should strongly consider finding another consultant. (You may decide to buy one of the inexpensive software packages available that do the job for you; one of these is INTERNET CREATOR, about which you can find out more by calling the manufacturer at 1-800-223-1982, extension 700.)

HOW TO MAKE YOUR ORGANIZATION MORE RESPONSIVE TO CLIENT AND CUSTOMER NEEDS

Everyone talks about developing an organization that's accountable to the customer, but actually doing this is an elusive goal. Here are six ideas for helping your organization improve its customer focus. (See also the section on enhancing customer orientation among your subordinates that begins on page 76.)

➤ *Set up a Mystery Customer program.* We touched on this idea briefly earlier, but it is worth reviewing in this part of the book, as well. The Mystery Customer campaign is a great (and simple) way to keep people on their toes and combat lax customer service work in person or on the phone. Make an announcement that every couple of weeks, but on an irregular schedule, someone will make contact with your firm and ask about some aspect of your product or service. What's so unusual about that? This person will be a short-term company representative, a spy whom no one in your organization will have ever heard of or encountered before, who will report the details of the exchange directly to top management. The program works best if you reward exemplary service extended to the Mystery Customer, but he or she can also alert you to weak links in the customer service network. If you want to identify those times when your organization is likeliest to deliver slipshod or abusive service, the Mystery Customer program is one way to go. (But see the note that follows before attempting to discuss any problem areas with colleagues or subordinates.)

➤ *Beware when "passing along the feedback."* Simply informing colleagues or subordinates about negative customer perceptions or passing along verbatim accounts of customer reactions in situations where there was clearly room for improvement may backfire. It is human nature to defend one's work and that of one's department or work group. "Stating the facts" is not enough. The "facts" should be prefaced with an acknowledgment of good intent on the part of the person you're talking to if you hope to avoid focusing the person's attention on how to defend an attack, rather than making an improvement in that area. Your acknowledgment of good intent (which you should incorporate even when dealing with hard cases who *don't* intend much in the way of customer accountability) could sound something like this:

> "Sally, I realize you want to give the people who depend on us for service the best possible information, and I want to help you do that. I thought you'd want to take a look at this letter I got from a customer about a call she made last week; once you've had the chance to take a look at it, let's talk about the best way to proceed."

Prefacing the customer's feedback in this way is far preferable to simply tossing the letter on the team member's desk and saying, "Do you have anything you want to tell me about this?" Such an approach cannot be perceived as anything other than an attack, and people generally don't think well or constructively when they believe themselves to be under attack.

➤ *Follow the Ramundo Rule on telephone interactions.* Renowned customer service expert Michael Ramundo takes a straightforward approach to eliminating the phenomenon of customers' "getting the runaround" when they land on the company switchboard. Under Ramundo's plan, it is a violation of company policy to transfer a customer or prospective customer to any member of your organization without having first briefed that team member in detail on the reason for the person's call—and gotten *clear acceptance* from that team member of responsibility to take on and resolve the problem. In other words, the customer may spend a little more time on hold during the initial phase of the call, but he or she will never, under any circumstances, have to explain the same problem to four people in a row. The person responsible for resolving the caller's problem may or may not be able to do so while the caller is on the phone, but he or she *must* advise the caller of an estimated resolution time for the problem and *must* take the initiative to make contact if that schedule looks likely to slip. Ramundo's refreshing approach makes it impossible to "pass the buck," and it makes the organization responsible for understanding the customer, rather than the other way around. If you're serious about instilling customer accountability in your company, you'll find some way to implement the Ramundo Rule at all levels of your organization. (And if the organizational hurdles to doing so seem imposing, simply ask yourself this question: Which company would you rather do business with—one that follows the Ramundo Rule or one that doesn't? The answer should help you motivate yourself, your colleagues, and your superiors.)

➤ *Run informal intelligence-gathering missions on the front lines.* Are you in publishing? Then spend half an hour every other week monitoring the purchasing patterns of customers at a local high-traffic bookstore. Talk to the clerks. Talk to the manager. Talk to the customers. Do you work as a consultant to manufacturers of consumer goods? If so, you should spend some time at a local supermarket—and take notes to see how your predictions and analyses shake out in the real world.

➤ *Don't punish the messenger.* How are people who put the focus on customer-related problems in your organization likely to be treated? If they admit a mistake or spot a manufacturing problem late in the process, are they likely to feel better or worse after having alerted someone to the problem? If the culture of your organization is one in which employees perceive that the bearers of bad news are always dealt with harshly, chances are you're not going to hear much bad news—until it's too late. Then your customers will be sure to pass the word along. You may need to enlist the help of high-level allies in order to bring about a meaningful change in your organization's culture, but the effort will be worthwhile.

➤ *Adopt an incentive program.* Reassigning team members who can't adopt a customer focus is only part of the equation; your organization must reward those who go out of their way to improve customer-perceived quality. Tying salary increases to quantifiable, frequently measured indicators of customer satisfaction is one excellent way to go.

HOW TO HANDLE AN IRATE CUSTOMER

Whether the contact is made on the phone or in person, someone in your organization is likely to have to respond to a customer who's in high dudgeon. Here are five ideas that will help you make things less tense for everyone:

> *Ignore personal challenges.* In most cases, these are rhetorical flourishes designed to capture your attention. Don't get sidetracked by them. As long as your customer isn't likely to do harm to himself or anyone else, you should . . .

> *Allow the customer to vent without interruption for at least a moment or two.* If your customer was at the tail end of a two-week, one-city-per-day business trip, and you were standing behind the counter at eleven at night explaining that her bags had been misrouted on the next-to-last connection of the trip, it would be a little unrealistic to expect your customer to take this news in stoic silence.

Let's face it; there may well be legitimate grievances for your customer to come to terms with. Even if there is no extraordinary circumstance resulting from a slipup on your organization's part, there may be other pressures at work that affect your customer's outlook. Attempting, at the outset, to interrupt the customer will only serve as further proof that you and your organization cannot listen. If you can, *take notes* on everything and let your customer roll until the storm passes. If, after a few minutes, you are convinced that this storm is highly unlikely to pass no matter how long you wait, wait until you can get a word in edgewise and move on to the next step, which follows. (By the way, if you are *constantly* interrupted by an abusive customer after you have made a good-faith effort to allow the venting process to run its course, stop talking the second the other person cuts you off. This serves as an effective signal that no real progress is going to be made unless the customer allows you to speak.)

> *Assume appropriate responsibility.* In the vast majority of cases, a ranting, raving customer is aiming to hear four simple words: "We made a mistake." Unless specifically instructed otherwise by someone in your organization, you should probably say those words if the situation warrants. Apologize for that portion of the situation where your organization dropped the ball. If you can, make it clear that you, personally, will do your level best to see that the problem is resolved to the customer's satisfaction. (The "personally" part is important—another contributing factor to the customer's fury is, in all likelihood, a feeling that there is no one individual who is truly accountable within your organization.) Here's what it might sound like:

"Mr. Davis, it turns out that your connecting flight from Atlanta didn't arrive in time for the baggage to be transferred, and I am very sorry about that. The delay wasn't your fault, it was that of the airline, and because of that I'm going to work to make sure that we get them rerouted through to Boston just as quickly as we can."

➤ *Outline a plan.* Tell the customer what you plan to do, how you plan to do it, what steps you will take to provide progress reports, and what you will be doing to make sure that an aggressive but realistic time line for completion is adhered to. Many people shy away from this step because it involves taking responsibility. In most cases, it also requires you to pass along your name and your contact information, which puts you in the hot seat as far as delivering on the specifics of the plan. But the issue is keeping the person as a customer, isn't it? And it's hard to imagine how that can happen unless *someone* takes full responsibility for shepherding this customer's dilemma through the organization. If you're talking to the customer and supposedly trying to resolve the issue, it will do no good to talk about intentions and hopes unless you are also willing to draw up a battle plan that you, personally, are willing to see through the system. What you say could sound something like this:

"Here's what I'm going to do to make sure that your bags show up at your door just as quickly as possible. I'm going to file a tracking order immediately, which means that we'll be able to track down exactly where the bag is in the system within approximately ninety minutes. Once we determine where the bags are, we're going to put them on a van and make every effort to deliver them to your home within no more than six hours of their arrival here at the airport. My estimate is that we'll have someone at your doorstep before eight tomorrow morning. If that's not convenient, we can schedule the delivery for later in the day. If you would like to have the bags dropped off at your front door without having to wake up and answer the doorbell, all you have to do is sign this release. In any event, if you'll just give me your home address on this sheet of paper, we'll be able to get the process moving for you."

You should also *volunteer* your name and contact information and the name and contact information of anyone who is likely to be covering for you when you are not on duty. (Be sure to bring this person up to date on all pertinent details related to this customer's problem.)

➤ *Make a conscious effort not to sound like everyone else on the block.* That means avoiding common mistakes such as: laying the responsibility on another (absent) member of the organization; trivializing the event (e.g., "Hey, it happens"); focusing on another customer while supposedly attending to this one (by, for instance, talking to one person while you're on the phone to another); emphasizing problems rather than solutions (especially important if you are a Professor or a Sharpshooter); and citing rules and regulations (which your customer neither knows about nor cares to know about).

None of these approaches will make your interaction with the irate customer any smoother, and any one of them can be counted on to win business for your competition.

HOW TO RESPOND TO A COMPLAINT LETTER

Written complaints may be a little easier on the ego than face-to-face encounters with furious customers, but they can carry serious legal implications for your organization. Someone who has taken the trouble to write is, consciously or unconsciously, establishing a paper trail that may be important in future civil or regulatory action. In addition, a person who takes the time to write a complaint letter is statistically more likely to appeal to judicial or government bodies to take action against your firm. If that's not sufficient motivation to handle the complaint properly, nothing is!

Here are five suggestions to follow if you want to keep a simple complaint letter from turning into a major legal wrangle:

➤ *Respond promptly.* Yes, this is easier said than done, but it is worth tackling nonetheless. If there are administrative hurdles that prevent you from even seeing the letter for the first month of its life, it may be time to consider some internal changes in your organization. Think about it. If the author of the complaint letter doesn't hear from you for six to eight weeks, you are almost certainly increasing the chances of this customer's defecting to the competition—or bringing legal action against your firm. But don't assume that you must necessarily respond with a letter, because your best course is probably to . . .

➤ *Respond by phone if at all possible.* This approach is quick, personal, and strategically sound—in that it helps keep the exchange from turning into a battle of increasingly vitriolic letters. Telephoning the person who wrote the letter with a proposed solution lets your customer know that the decision to write the letter *worked*—action took place as a result. That's a message you want to get out as quickly as possible. (If the letter does not include a telephone number, look it up.)

It is to the *litigious customer's* advantage to develop a paper trail.

It is to *your organization's* advantage to resolve the matter by phone.

➤ *No phone tag.* The classic bureaucratic dodge of having "left a message" doesn't cut it when you're talking about retaining customers (or, for that matter, keeping them from suing you). If you must leave a message on an answering machine, leave one that makes it clear that you are committed to moving the process forward on a one-on-one basis.

> "Hi, Mr. Allen, this is Ted Winter at ABC company. I'm calling in response to your letter of September nineteenth. I'd like to get in touch with you to let you know about the status of your refund request. I can be reached between the hours of eight in the morning and twelve noon, Monday through Friday, at 617/555-4627. I look forward to talking to you soon."

➤ *Put the customer in touch with someone who will assume personal responsibility for resolving the problem to the customer's satisfaction.* That means following all the steps just outlined for dealing with an irate customer on a face-to-face basis. (In the unlikely event that you cannot reach your customer by phone, your organization's written response to the customer should serve as an introduction to the team member who will serve as the personal contact for resolving this issue, and should include that team member's direct extension. *Important note:* Written admissions of wrongdoing on the part of your organization should be cleared with superiors.)

➤ *Keep it light.* The customer may have used sarcasm, veiled threats, or inappropriate language in the original letter. Pretend you never saw those parts of the message. Make sure that all your communications with the customer assume an optimistic, upbeat, and professional tone. *Never* respond in kind, even (especially!) if the customer is dead wrong.

HOW TO WIN BACK A CUSTOMER WHO GOT LESS THAN YOUR BEST

A while back, there was a little problem. Actually, there was a *big* problem. You lost a customer. Can you ever get the business back? Here are four suggestions that may help you do so:

➤ *Make a bold, unconventional appeal.* Your first goal is to win back attention—and interest—on the part of your customer, and you may need to employ a technique that breaks a few barriers in order to do that. A dash of humor may help you underline your main message: Whatever problems there were in the past won't be occurring again. If your client moved on because of an antagonistic exchange with a misinformed front-desk person, for instance, you might decide to send along a teddy bear dressed as a Boy Scout, along with a card bearing this message:

> "This bear is courteous, thrifty, brave, clean, and reverent—and he also knows when not to recite the rule book chapter and verse to important customers. We will follow his example from now on—scout's honor. I'll be calling you tomorrow morning to discuss some of the ways we can help you increase your company's revenues; hope we can discuss some of the bear essentials of the new approaches we can take to help you."

Is such an approach guaranteed to win the customer back? Of course not. Is it a better way to go than simply writing the account off for all eternity? Absolutely.

➤ *Put it in writing.* Assuming that you won't incur any legal problems from your company as a result of doing so (check with your company's lawyer to be sure), you should strongly consider putting your assessment of what went wrong down on paper—as well as the specific steps you've taken to make sure that the problems your customer encountered won't happen again. Follow your own best instincts on this score when it comes to admitting past lapses. The best approach is usually to outline the problems with an open mind, without dwelling in unnecessary detail on the past problems, and identify what you've learned from them. Do this for the best reason: Because it very often makes sense to share such lessons with the most important business partners. Although you may want to *concisely* state your desire to resume a business relationship with the former customer, make it clear that the main reason for composing the letter is your hope to make a clear assessment of the events that led to the end of the relationship. If you follow these steps and send copies to all the individuals involved with the decision (and perhaps a few higher-ups as well), you will probably be in a good position to regain the customer's trust. You may find that this forthright approach is a much better (and less costly) means of regaining lost business than slashing prices or taking a loss on your next assignment.

➤ *When you resume discussions with the customer, make a guarantee.* Don't hedge or insert slippery disclaimers. Members of this group don't want to hear about "maybe" or "approximately" or "roughly" or "probably."

They want to hear about promises, and they want to see them delivered. Make a striking, quantifiable guarantee—one with a specific time line—and then stand behind it.

The ability to stand behind one's word is a rare business quantity these days. The sheer shock of having run into someone who will promise—and then deliver!—results may be enough to jolt the account back over to your organization's side. But be sure you come through on the promises this time around! If your "second chance" results in a second fiasco, you can probably forget about doing business with this customer for the foreseeable future.

➤ *Offer endorsements.* This is especially important if there were significant lapses in quality in the past. You will need to obtain permission to use quotes from third parties who attest to your new way of doing things— or, better yet, put your client or customer directly in touch with the person who's backing up your claim to have improved operations. The idea is to increase the comfort level of the person who's formed an opinion about the way you operate, and there's no better way to do that than to supply compelling, objective "reviews" that show your organization in a positive light.

Dealing with the Media and the General Public

Any organization that overlooks the role of television, radio, and print in influencing future events and perceptions runs the risk of encountering some unpleasant surprises. And your organization's contacts with noncustomers—contacts that may be brought about by positive or negative media coverage but that you may be able to influence more positively by a stronger role as a good corporate citizen in your community—are no less important.

Members of the media can help you outdistance the competition, and they can also turn upstarts into players you and everyone else in your industry must suddenly take seriously. Anyone who's ever seen an episode of *60 Minutes* knows the sobering consequences of running into a powerful journalist who's concluded that you or your organization would make a great "bad guy" in an upcoming exposé.

In this chapter, we'll look at some of the major pitfalls to avoid and opportunities to exploit when dealing with representatives of the press. We'll also discuss a number of techniques for helping your organization take its place as a responsible member of the community. Such steps, when undertaken quietly but intently, may help you to penetrate the social fabric of the city, town, or locale where your organization operates long before troublesome news stories emerge on any front. That may just be the best press management strategy of all.

Let's deal with the main topic first: Interacting effectively with print and broadcast representatives.

TEN TIPS FOR EFFECTIVE DAY-TO-DAY INTERACTIONS WITH MEMBERS OF THE MEDIA

1. *Understand that they've probably got a lot on their plate.* Only those without much experience in dealing with the media will expect editors and reporters to drop everything they're doing and focus solely on a single issue. Unless you're a superstar or a major national political figure, expect to be apportioned a *brief slice* of your contact's day and get right to the point when you finally do connect. Adopting any other approach will brand you as a rookie and severely limit the exposure you receive.

2. *Don't make extravagant claims.* Journalists are, by nature, a skeptical bunch; if you make claims you can't back up or leave people with the impression that you're trying to turn a hard news story into a paid commercial message, you will either be cut short or subjected to a nice, energetic attack. Yes, you have a message to get across, but the reporter has a job to do, too. If you come across like a used-car sales-man and make no accommodations for either the angle the reporter is pursuing or the requirements of the format in question, don't be surprised if the attention you get is not the kind or duration you'd envisioned.

3. *Remember that a local angle may help win attention for any news item.* It is much, much easier to win media attention for an item that takes place within 100 miles of a given station or newspaper than it is to win cover-age for a story that does not feature a local angle. You may be able to use this principle to your advantage by pitching your story's local aspect to a nationally respected paper. Let's assume, for the sake of argument, that your organization is located in the metropolitan New York City area. If you highlight some local angle appropriately, you may be able to win coverage in the Metro section of a New York paper, which will lend prestige to the rest of your campaign. Why? Because . . .

4. *Coverage begets more coverage.* The more attention other media outlets are paying to your story, the likelier you are to convince any given paper that you represent a significant, timely news item. But you must act quickly and highlight, in your press kit, the most prominent sta-tions and publications that have covered your story.

5. *Don't count too heavily on initial early positive signs from major media outlets.* The bigger they are, the more likely they are to change their minds.

No matter how promising your initial contact, a story can always be cut and an interview can always be bumped. This principle is especially important to bear in mind when dealing with respected national news organs. Legend has it that singer Janis Joplin was slated to appear on the cover of *Time* magazine, but former President Dwight D. Eisenhower passed away during the week that had been reserved for her. "Five years I've been working to get that cover," Joplin supposedly lamented, "and the guy has to die on my $#@$! week."

6. *Realize that drama means heroes and villains.* This means that not all the press attention you and your organization receive will necessarily be positive! Journalists are an intrinsically cynical lot—not because they're less sensitive than the rest of us, but because they've learned from bitter long-term experience that many of the people they deal with are interested in concealing key facts and presenting only one side of a story. Exposing the shenanigans of such people has a double benefit: It reinforces to the reporter that he or she is doing the job effectively and ethically, and it provides interesting, dramatic material with which to fill up newspaper pages and broadcast segments. It is, therefore, imperative that you make clear to any reporters you deal with that you are not a villain! You can do this by approaching issues in a fair, even-handed manner, by occasionally acknowledging errors and oversights, and by emphasizing your regard for the concerns and interests of the average citizen. (The "little guy"—read: the reporter's audience—is in fact a looming presence of immense influence to both local and national media. The amount of attention the "average citizen" pays to a journalist's newspaper, magazine, or newscast has a direct impact on that journalist's career and the bottom-line performance of the company for which he or she works.)

7. *Bear in mind that a good "hook" doesn't take more than a sentence or two to express to another person.* If it takes you longer than one long sentence or two short ones to get your "big idea" across, you still have some work to do. A story that has a hook is one that points in an immediate and compelling way to something that is of prime interest *to the audience of the publication or broadcast you're targeting* because of the direct benefit, or unusual nature, or both, of what you have to say. If your efforts to win media attention are meeting with little or no success, it is probably because what you are passing along has no brief, compelling hook for the news media to turn into a story. If you are attempting to win coverage for your organization, it is *your* responsibility, not the

reporter's, to identify the hook inherent in your appeal. "HELP FOR LOCAL VICTIMS OF INSURANCE OVERCHARGES" is an example of a good hook. "ABC COMPANY OFFERS REVISED APPROACH TO INSURANCE ADJUSTMENT OVERSIGHTS ON ELIGIBLE POLICIES DURING CURRENT FISCAL YEAR" is an example of a poor hook. For more ideas on developing a good hook for your press materials, see the next section in this chapter.

8. *Write for short attention spans, because people in the media have to.* Most reporters and journalists work under tight deadlines and put in very long hours. That means they don't have time to read through a fifty-page report for a single newsworthy fact. Feel free to include appropriate *supplemental* materials for an interested reporter, but get across the sum and substance of what you have to say in one page or less.

9. *Don't be afraid to do the person's job.* The best press release is one that's reprinted verbatim, and the best interview is one that follows the questions you provide for the interviewer's use. It is possible to develop appeals to the press that result in such outcomes (or outcomes very close to these), but you must be willing to show the same objectivity, persistence, and professionalism in preparing your materials that a good reporter would in tracking down a story. Suggestions on preparing customized media materials appear throughout this chapter.

10. *Be willing to work with the jerks.* Many of the people you'll run into have gotten where they are *because* of, not in spite of, the fact that they possess abrasive, overbearing personalities. (This is especially true of certain members of the broadcast media.) In some cases, reporters or anchor people will come on very strong or use tactics that are of questionable taste. This does not necessarily mean that you are under attack, only that you are dealing with a person who works in a medium in which the greatest sin is being boring. In most cases, you will get your point across by playing along with the show's format. Failing to do so by disengaging or shutting down may earn you a reputation as a "lousy guest." (***Important note:*** If your interviews feature regular attacks upon your organization's integrity—or your own—odds are that you are facing a public relations problem, rather than a series of personality quirks on the part of your interviewer. See the advice that appears later in this chapter on dealing with negative media storms or PR crises.)

WHAT IS—AND ISN'T—A STORY

"Why don't they give us the coverage? This is a major news event!" Maybe—and then again, maybe not. Editors have a way of asserting their independence and objectivity when it comes to alloting print space, and they may choose to ignore any appeal they deem either too boring or too biased for their readers. Here are three questions to ask about the way you're going about trying to win media attention and some suggestions on how to go about making them interesting to the people who matter—print and broadcast editors:

➤ *Is the story you're outlining easy to express in two or three* compelling *sentences of interest to the editor's audience?* Two or three sentences is about all the time a reporter will have to get the idea across to someone else in the organization. Compare these two press release openings:

> "DATAMASTER 14-J INCORPORATES THIRTY-FIVE PRODUCT IMPROVEMENTS OVER LAST YEAR'S RELEASE! The new DATAMASTER 14-J program from Widgetco has been completely redesigned for the age of the Internet and incorporates thirty-five separate improvements over the previous year's release. Among the improvements are increased compatibility with Widgetco's Lightningware products, shorter defragging time, and an enhanced communications module that features a full directory of *Fortune* 500 e-mail addresses that will be of interest to corporate researchers and job seekers. (The module includes full names and verified e-mail addresses of personnel directors and features a résumé template that allows users to pass along career highlights via e-mail.)"

> "NEW INTERNET TOOL ALLOWS JOB SEEKERS TO FIND JOBS OVER THE NET! A new software product known as DATAMASTER 14-J enables job seekers to send their résumés through cyberspace—directly to personnel directors at *Fortune* 500 companies."

Which press release would you be more likely to devote your time to—or try to explain to a superior?

➤ *Is the topic you're drawing attention to a good match for the publication or program you're contacting?* *Rolling Stone* and *Pet Care Monthly* appeal to very different audiences and focus on entirely different kinds of stories. Of course, it's *possible* that the story you're trying to promote could be picked up verbatim by both publications, but how *likely* is it? At the very least, customize your cover letter and/or your press release to the varying demands of the media outlets you are targeting.

➢ *Is there an "expert angle" you can exploit?* Media is an information-driven business, and it thrives on experts. Whatever the topic you are trying to promote, it will gain more interest from members of the news media if there is an individual with expert credentials available to discuss it at a moment's notice. Do some digging in your organization. Is there a person you can attach to your appeal whose research, background, or life experience renders him or her more likely to attract attention than the average person? If so, try to persuade that person to help you in your promotional efforts.

WHY CALLING FIRST IS BETTER THAN SENDING A "COLD" PRESS PACKET

Don't fall into the trap of preparing an elaborate, multi-layered, photo-included press kit before you talk to anyone at the media outlet you're targeting. Although there is some disagreement on the topic of when to call contacts among PR people, my research and promotional work leads me to believe that you should phone before you send anything along. (The one exception to this rule: A brief, intelligently composed fax version of your press release. See the next section for advice on putting this powerful promotional tool to use for your organization.) Here are the four most important reasons why you should call ahead first, no matter what you may hear or read anywhere else:

➢ *Editors and reporters admit, in private moments, that they'd rather develop new contacts, which represents doing work they enjoy, than wade through mountains of mail.* If they were to say this openly, they'd have voice mailboxes bulging with even more messages than what already come across the transom, but the fact of the matter is that most editors and reporters prefer the chance to have a *brief,* intelligent conversation about whether or not a story is right for them than to deal with another press kit that isn't. There's a catch to this approach, however: When your contact tells you that he or she is not interested in pursuing a story, you must respect that—and avoid applying the hard sell! There's always another story, right? Of such tactful withdrawals are long-term relationships built. Never mind what the receptionist says about "mailing any written materials you may have"—contact the reporter directly. When your contacts are not busy writing stories or recording shows, a healthy number of journalists are conducting their business over the phone. Far from intruding on their day, you are likely to help move it forward by making a *short* telephone query or leaving an inventive message on a company voice-message system.

➤ *Many, and perhaps most, reporters and editors don't even bother to read a single word of unsolicited press kits.* It's important to remember that these people are usually *inundated* with press releases and media kits. It is certainly true that many reporters are difficult to get hold of on the phone, but that's no reason not to try. Spending a few minutes doing so is probably a better use of your time (and the reporter's) than preparing and mailing a press kit no one at the organization is going to read.

➤ *It's cheaper to send along packages only to those who have expressed an interest in them.* The average media kit represents a dollar or two in materials, three dollars or so for postage, and perhaps five dollars or more in labor costs. Is that ten-dollar-a-piece mailing *really* worth sending to one hundred contacts when good phone work can identify the ten people who will respond well to the press kit at a fraction of the cost?

➤ *Calling first allows you to customize your approach.* You never know exactly *how* a reporter will be able to incorporate your materials until you talk to someone at the media outlet. If your contact is running an anything-goes morning radio show, you'll be able to point your materials in a different direction than you would if you were sending them along to a conservative public-affairs show.

HOW TO USE YOUR FAX MACHINE TO WIN MEDIA COVERAGE

The humble fax machine is a blessing to those in search of publicity. Intelligently employed, it can win you the coverage deserved—but used in an amateurish way, it can burn bridges you have yet to cross. Herewith the Ten Commandments of an intelligent fax-driven promotional campaign. If your fax message does not receive a passing grade on all ten points, go back to the drawing board.

➤ *The first commandment: Thou shalt not tie up the line.* Think in terms of brief, one-page updates, not twenty-page epistles. Monopolizing an active fax line at a busy news operation (or any other office, for that matter) is not the behavior of people who win allies.

➤ *The second commandment: Thou shalt never bore thy audience with long-winded appeals.* That audience is a dual one: the members of the media outlet and their readership and/or viewership. Send along fax messages that appeal to both constituencies. (Example: JOB SEARCH EXPERT TO HOLD FREE SEMINAR FOR LOCAL DOWNSIZING VICTIMS.)

➤ *The third commandment: Thou shalt not be rude or offensive.* An especially important point when directing a national campaign. Remember that the standards for acceptable content in Salt Lake City are likely to be different from those in New York City.

➤ *The fourth commandment: Thou shalt address thy fax to a specific human being, the spelling of whose name thou shalt double-check.* Misspelled names mean all your work is in vain. Call ahead and confirm the spelling of the first and last names, even if (especially if) both names seem simple and direct to you.

➤ *The fifth commandment: Thou shalt include all thy own contact information, the accuracy of which thou shalt enlist the aid of another to double-check.* You'll never understand the importance of this step until you've faxed (or mailed!) a piece with erroneous return contact information to fifty or sixty people. This information is a vital component of any message, faxed or otherwise, and it is frequently entered in haste erroneously—and duplicated, erroneously, on internal computer systems. Don't assume that you know how to type out your own contact information accurately. It is human nature to zoom through those procedures we are familiar with, and when we zoom, we err. Unless you want to run the risk of putting in a good deal of hard work for no particular reason—and of leaving a bad impression with the person whose interest you have aroused—enlist the aid of a colleague to double-check your return contact information.

➤ *The sixth commandment: Thou shalt summarize thy main point in a single sentence.* Offer as much supporting detail as you feel is appropriate in the remainder of the page, but condense your "hook" into one impossible-to-miss headline at the top of the document.

➤ *The seventh commandment: Thou shalt not send the same fax twice.* You say they didn't respond to the first message? There's certainly nothing wrong with trying again tomorrow, but if you repeat your message verbatim for two or more days in a row, you run the risk of alienating the journalists you want to attract. Find another way to make your appeal, and wait at least another day before sending the next fax.

➤ *The eighth commandment: Thou shalt not phone to confirm receipt.* Newsrooms and editorial offices are busy places. Call directly if you want (see the previous section for some guidelines), but don't tax your contact's memory and patience by demanding a status report on whether or not your fax has been read.

➤ *The ninth commandment: Thou shalt not overload thy page with text.* Less really is more, especially where fax messages are concerned. Remember that we live in a visually oriented society. This doesn't mean that you must incorporate an illustration of some kind (although that's probably a good idea to consider), but you should be willing to let the white space on the page work for you. The person who receives your fax will, at least initially, be scanning it, rather than reading it word for word.

➤ *The tenth commandment: Thou shalt not continue to send faxes after a request to cease and desist.* You're trying to win friends in the media, not earn a reputation as a pest. Some news organizations will react well to the daily-fax-appeal approach; others won't. Respect the wishes of the ones in the latter category.

FIVE TIPS FOR FIELDING UNEXPECTED PRESS INQUIRIES

Eureka! You've gotten an inquiry from a member of the press, and you didn't even have to beg for it. It's a blessing in disguise . . . or is it? Here are five guidelines to review before you or anyone else in your organization responds to any unexpected press inquiry:

➤ *Don't go off half cocked.* Before you agree to any interview, plead the tight-schedule blues and talk the matter over with your superior, your colleagues, or anyone else who may be able to enlighten you as to the best way to proceed. It's possible that others in your organization have been approached by the same reporter or that there have been events in the recent past that make press relations a matter of strategic concern. If a reporter calls you out of the blue, there's a chance you are being interviewed for a story that will paint you or your organization in an uncomplimentary light. Whether or not this is the case, you and your fellow team members will need to develop a message to emphasize, and return to when appropriate, during your interview.

➤ *Don't break new ground.* If, during the interview, you run up against an area about which you are unsure or for which you have developed no strategy, *don't improvise.* Explain that you aren't familiar with the topic under discussion and offer to follow up after you've had the chance to review the matter with the appropriate people within your organization.

➢ *Develop a story of your own, and take the opportunity to tell it during the interview.* This is not to say that you should attempt to take over the discussion, but that you should be prepared with a positive, upbeat message, one you can feel comfortable reinforcing even if the interview takes a turn you did not expect. (For more about staying "on message," review the later section in this chapter on dealing with negative attention from the media.)

➢ *Tailor your response.* Deadlines are deadlines, right? By offering appropriate, objectively positioned press releases early on in the process, you may be able to get more of your message across. Take as your assignment the task of composing a one-of-a-kind press kit that fits nearly exactly into the format of the newspaper, magazine, or broadcast outlet that will be interviewing you. Supply a list of potential questions as part of the press kit. (This is standard practice among public relations people and will not cause any problems—as long as you understand that the reporter is under no obligation to ask questions from your list!)

➢ *Never criticize the interviewer or demand that an interview be terminated mid-discussion.* Even if you're under attack, even if the interviewer has used questionable techniques, even if you feel flustered. When you take an antagonistic stance with a reporter, demand that an interviewer stop asking questions, or complain that you've been "set up," you guarantee *prominent, sustained* negative coverage where there may well have been only the possibility of *brief, passing* negative coverage. Focus on the message you have prepared, and don't dwell on negatives.

HOW TO DEAL WITH UNEXPECTED NEGATIVE MEDIA ATTENTION

It's every corporate PR person's nightmare: What happens if there's a sudden storm of negative press attention? How do you respond? What should you say? What *shouldn't* you say? Here are eight suggestions for handling press inquiries on sensitive or controversial topics. Review them closely—and practice your media technique with a friend or colleague—before you agree to be interviewed on a potentially troublesome or challenging subject.

➤ *Ask yourself: Was there, in fact, a serious oversight or misdeed?* If there was— and especially if there was a potentially catastrophic problem relating to such issues as product safety, legal liability, or consumer fraud—*do not deny the story that has arisen* until you have read the next section on dealing with a true public relations crisis. You should strongly consider acknowledging the dimensions of the problem once you discover them, rather than attempting to minimize the damage by downplaying or denying the story, and you should discuss the matter with legal counsel before you make any response to the press.

➤ *Stay "on message."* In other words, do what the politicians do when someone tosses them a tricky question: Briefly address the issue that's been raised, then find a way to make a transition to the positive, flattering message you've rehearsed. It may sound a little oily, but the truth of the matter is that when you're under attack, you very often cannot afford to follow the reporter or journalist in any direction he or she chooses to lead you. If you or your organization has been accused of specific wrongdoing or oversight, bear in mind that a direct yes-or-no answer to a question could carry serious legal consequences!

Here's an example of an exchange in which the interviewee manages to stay on message:

> *Reporter:* Ms. Banks, isn't it true that Bigcorp failed to report safety violations to appropriate state agencies in the three months preceding the accident? *(**Warning!** This is a direct question on a matter of potential legal liability to your company. You must find a way to address it indirectly and truthfully, but not specifically, and then move on to the message you want to get across.)*
>
> *Interviewee:* Chet, we're conducting an ongoing internal investigation right now to get more information about a wide variety of issues related to this incident, and our communications with state safety authorities is obviously going to be one of the things we'll be reviewing. *(Having touched on the issue the reporter raised, you should now find a way to broadcast a positive, accountable message that deals with the larger topic under discussion.)* At Bigcorp, we're deeply concerned about any and every on-the-job accident, and we're constantly looking for ways to make our workplace safer. Although the kind of incident that occurred yesterday was a tragedy for everyone concerned, we do pride ourselves on having one of the lowest accident rates in our industry, and I think the way we conduct the review of this event will bear out the fact that we put worker safety first and foremost in our operations.

The idea, of course, is to touch briefly on the specifics of the question, but not to let the interview become a debate on the specifics of the topic of the reporter's choice (in this case, Bigcorp's possible failure to observe required reporting procedures). Instead, use your rhetorical position as question-answerer to put the focus on the topic *you* want to get out on the issue in question (in this case, Bigcorp's exemplary long-term safety record and its ongoing commitment to improve working conditions).

➤ *Give 'em a hook you like before they decide on one you don't like.* Face it. The reporter has been assigned to the story; that means he or she is looking for drama, and drama means conflict. Instead of stonewalling (which is one story—you or your organization against the probing eye of the reporter), try to highlight an unusual but positive survival-oriented aspect of the situation (thereby providing another story, one of conflict raised and resolved). Is there a human-interest angle to which you can convincingly appeal? Are any employees of your company worth pointing the reporter toward? Think in terms of obstacles overcome, lives put back together after hardship, or fences mended. Any one of these approaches may help you to identify a workable lead for a story, which is usually all reporters are looking for. If you can find some way to put the accent on overcoming adversity, rather than identifying good guys and bad guys, you may be able to win the reporter over to your side. Make the reporter's job a little easier and you could just come out unscathed.

➤ *Don't get paranoid; remember that negative attention from the media is often a price for admission to the big leagues.* Have you ever noticed how potentially damaging information about social and political figures tends to emerge only after it's clear that these people have attained a certain degree of name recognition? There are two reasons for this. One is that knocking down people with low name recognition isn't news. Another is that reporters (good reporters, at any rate) see themselves as surrogates for the public, and they feel they have a duty to probe for deception, corruption, or incompetence among people and institutions who hold positions of high influence in society.

What does this boil down to? Well, let's pretend you're running for governor of your state. Before you win the nomination of your party, an innocent five-hundred-dollar error on the part of your accountant in preparing your tax return six years ago, and since corrected, is probably an innocuous bit of trivia that isn't the least bit newsworthy. After you've emerged as one of the two people in the state likely to have the final say over the life and death of people sentenced to the electric chair, that same error may become evidence of your character, judgment, and honesty, evidence that a powerful state news editor could reasonably conclude is worth sharing with voters. What's changed? Not the original event. Your status.

The same principle applies to virtually any person or institution in the news. It's worth noting, too, that knocking down people and organizations that set themselves up on pedestals makes good copy, and tracking down good copy is what reporters do for a living.

If you find yourself sucked into this spiral, don't assume that everyone in the media is out to get you. (Paranoia makes good copy, too.) Setting up the media as the enemy will only encourage an already skeptical group of reporters to believe that you have something to hide.

➤ *When dealing with television jounalists, remember that stillness counts, and that the camera isn't as important as the interviewer.* The best advice you can follow if you anticipate a potentially antagonistic interview on television is to *get coaching.* Working with a professional media consultant is best, of course, but if scheduling or financial constraints prevent you from following this course, then recruit a friend, set up a home video camera, and engage in some role-playing games. Among the many sobering lessons you will learn upon reviewing the tape are these two: (1) Stillness is strength, so don't fidget, and (2) You look more trustworthy when you're addressing your interviewer eye to eye than when you're trying to find a way to appeal directly to the camera. (Unless you've spent a good deal of time in and around broadcast television, you shouldn't attempt to play Follow the Bouncing Red Light.)

➤ *Don't restate a negative.* Restating a reporter's negative is a classic public-relations blunder that makes guilty people look more guilty and innocent people look guiltier than they ought to. The most famous example of this media management error is probably Richard Nixon's, whose unconvincing "I am not a crook" remark during a Watergate-era news conference led to one of history's most famous sound bites. Nixon, never a particularly smooth operator when it came to dealing with antagonistic reporters, forgot one of the most important rules of the modern media age: When responding to an attack, you must not defend it directly.

In other words, if a reporter asks you whether or not it's true that you slept with a pair of giraffes at high noon in the middle of Central Park and you indulge your (entirely understandable) urge to say, "I've never slept with a giraffe in my life," you run two risks. The first is that your denial will only serve to fuel the story further ("Manager Denies Sleeping with Giraffe"). The second risk is that you won't respond appropriately to all the treacherous qualifiers with which the reporter laced the question ("Manager Evades Question of Tryst with Giraffes at High Noon in Central Park—Denies Liaison with Single Animal, but Ducks Specifics on Threesome").

Sometimes reporters will try to throw you off balance by asking absurd questions or making outrageous implications. If you rise to the bait, you'll give them what they need: a quote from a flustered newsmaker under attack. Instead of dealing point by point with the reporter's negative, stay with your positives and don't be afraid to do so in a colorful, quotable fashion: "I'm a happily married man, and the only love of my life over the last twenty-five years has been my wife, Mildred. The closest I've ever come to a giraffe has been during visits to the zoo, when they were behind bars and I was chaperoned by my wife." (The entire exchange may sound more than a little absurd, but a few deft touches of quotable humor may well be your best line of defense when it comes to dealing with hostile members of the media.)

➤ *Concede valid points.* Nothing hardens a reporter's resolve more than someone who insists that nothing he or she has ever done was out of line. You'll gain credibility and stand a better chance of coming out of the onslaught with your internal organs intact by acknowledging one of the points of your detractors and vowing to work toward improving yourself in this area. Here's an example of what it might sound like.

> "Mark, I'm not sure the Senator would agree with your overall characterization of the budget resolution, but I think you do raise a valid issue. We should have worked harder to wrap this legislation up much, much earlier than we did. I think the Senator's constituents, and people across the country, have expressed some legitimate frustration with how long this process took to iron out, and we're going to try to find ways to keep these kinds of bottlenecks from occurring again on important budget legislation."

➤ *Focus on the road ahead.* If you follow the reporter's instinct, you'll spend all or most of your time talking about the specifics of an incident that's in the past, rather than your (or your organization's) goals for the future. If there has been a significant lapse or misdeed, you will definitely benefit by focusing not on the details of the event the reporter is fixating on, but by persuasively outlining goals for the future. The way you structure and deliver your outline of these goals should make it clear that you (or the organization you represent) have learned from what has happened, that you are not approaching matters in a rigid, inflexible manner, and that you have a commitment to fulfilling your future goals in a responsible, ethical, and enthusiastic manner.

MEDIA MAYHEM: HOW TO HANDLE A CRISIS

Product safety problems? Recalls? Ethical or legal problems? Personal scandal? In such scenarios, it's often not a question of *whether* you'll receive bursts of negative media attention, but how to manage the damage-control campaign during a prolonged assault on a number of fronts. Here are four suggestions on how to conduct yourself or your organization during a turbulent period of potentially disruptive media coverage:

➤ *Skip the cover up.* First, consult with your attorney. Then, while following his or her best counsel, strive mightily to pursue your damage-control campaign by means of following this simple principle: If there was a problem, say so. You should, if at all possible, outline exactly what went wrong, say what the organization should have done differently, detail what plans are being implemented to make sure that the oversight doesn't occur again, and explain how your people have been trained (or are being trained) in any new procedures that seem worth mentioning. The idea here is to avoid encouraging an "us-vs.-them" mentality in your interactions with the press, and to send the message to the public at large that your organization has gotten the message and is taking appropriate corrective steps. Some years back, Chrysler showed exactly how this technique can pay off. It headed off an emerging scandal at the pass by taking out a series of full-page advertisements acknowledging that there had been *some* instances where the odometers of automobiles that had recently come off the assembly line had been tampered with to conceal the true mileage the vehicles had been driven. By admitting *early* that the practice of altering the odometers of vehicles being sold as "new" was wrong, acknowledging that this had occurred in a very few situations, and outlining the steps the company was taking to make sure that it never happened again, Chrysler was able to take the lead role in the crisis—and get the right message out to its customers.

In such a situation, an instinct on the part of Chrysler executives to downplay or deny the initial reports would certainly have been understandable. But following those instincts would have made the damage-control job infinitely more perilous.

➤ *When dealing with television media, avoid sending visual signals that undercut or contradict your verbal message.* You may remember the devastatingly on-target Martin Short routine of some years back that parodied a *60 Minutes* interview. Short played a stonewalling corporate executive trying desperately to project a "we-have-nothing-to-hide" message for his company. But there were some problems: Sweat was streaming down his face; each of his curt, unconvincing responses was delivered between clenched teeth and followed by a taut (and apparently painful) nervous smile; and Short held between his fingers a burning cigarette with a huge unflicked ash. That final image—the unflicked cigarette—served as the perfect visual metaphor for the situation. Short's less-than-persuasive character was clearly a quarter of an inch or so away from an unflattering on-camera collapse.

File Short's memorable routine under "Don't Let This Happen to You." Make sure the visual symbols you send *support* the message you present to the visual media. If the spokesperson you have selected to deal with television reporters does not come across *onscreen* as confident, poised, prepared, and unhurried, find another spokesperson. In considering whether or not to make such a change, bear in mind that not everyone on earth is telegenic, and dealing with the media requires a certain visual appeal that some of your team members will have and others will not. Don't indulge someone's vanity at the expense of the organization. If you are dealing with a crisis, choose someone whose media-friendly persona will help you bring that crisis to a successful conclusion.

➤ *Return to your chosen message at the earliest opportunity in every exchange.* You are under no obligation to answer the details of every question a member of the media chooses to present. See the advice for "staying 'on message'" outlined earlier in this chapter.

➤ *Draw the line at personal issues.* After a long period of unfortunate excess, our culture appears to have entered, at long last, a phase in which the viewing and reading public supports the right of a public figure to tactfully deflect questions of an intimate nature, even if other issues relating to the public welfare are on the table during the same interview. You may or may not take some deserved heat in the press for ducking issues in the latter category, but you are unlikely to face prolonged public scrutiny if you refuse, from the get-go, to address inappropriate, personal questions. Granted, there's no law barring the media from asking questions relating to your personal life or that of others in your company, but there's also no law requiring you or any representative of the organization to answer such questions. Say so in no uncertain terms and return to your chosen message.

STARTING FROM SCRATCH: SIX STRATEGIES FOR BUILDING STRONG TIES WITH THE COMMUNITY IN WHICH YOUR ORGANIZATION OPERATES

If you are working on developing your organization's relationship with the surrounding community from the bottom up—that is to say, without the hindrance of past difficulty or conflict within that community—you enjoy an extraordinary opportunity. You are in an excellent position to develop strong relationships, make a positive impact on the others in the surrounding area where your organization operates, and forestall future problems with locals by developing a reputation for accountability *right now.* But you must take action now, rather than postpone things. The fact that there's "never been any problem" should not lull you into a sense of complacency. The time to undertake work in this area is *before* there is a serious breach with your neighbors, not afterwards.

The task of developing (and maintaining) solid community relations is, sadly, often one of the last items on an organization's to-do list. It shouldn't be! In one New England town, a chemical processing plant eased the potential concerns of nearby residents by making regular appearances at county fairs, holiday festivals, and the like, at which events it would hand out detailed summaries of the safety procedures it had implemented in the past and was contemplating in the future. The company also made a point of making contributions—both financial and logistical—to the town's volunteer recycling committee. Finally, it offered seminars on home fire safety, free of charge, to all the town's residents during a town-sponsored Fire Awareness Week. The safety seminars had no direct connection to the firm's operations in town, but the message to local residents was clear: The company was eager to pass on all that it possibly could to help people in the surrounding area. It was eager to become a contributing, responsible member of the community. The message got across.

Can *your* organization send the same message? Absolutely. Here are six strategies that will help you begin to build the right kinds of connections in your community:

➤ *Contact the town or city entity most likely to be responsible for overseeing or regulating your organization's work.* If you have no one, take the initiative to make contact first. Introduce yourself and your organization; discuss your firm's operations; discuss your willingness to work with municipal officials and your openness to new ideas on the best ways to operate in the best interests of the surrounding community. If there is *no* municipal entity with direct oversight responsibility over what your business does, consider approaching the mayor's office, perhaps with the scheduling aid of the local Chamber of Commerce, for a "get-acquainted" meeting. The idea, of course, is to become something more than a faceless, unknown operation among the various members of town government and to show that your organization is eager to get feedback on issues of interest to all in the area.

➤ *Try to get a high official at your organization to attend important community events.* Should your organization be attending the local town meetings, community festivals, or city fairs? There may not be an immediate "bottom-line" benefit to such a decision, but the presence of one of your company's "high and mighty ones" at such a gathering can be a major plus when it comes to developing goodwill in the community.

➤ *Review your files for past requests from members of the community.* Are there any you can reconsider? Does your organization's correspondence file feature requests for appearances, logistical support, supplies, or donations? You can't say yes to all such requests, of course, but you can review them all for potential budget-friendly areas of contact with the community. Perhaps the requests were denied at a time when establishing good relationships with community members wasn't a priority. Make it a priority!

➤ *Hold an open house or other community-friendly event.* Sponsor a community event of some kind that will allow local residents to take a look at your facilities close up or to meet with your organization's officials at a different locale if your own facilities are not suitable for the event as a result of insurance requirements. (A job fair, if it is appropriate to your circumstances, is one of the very best ways to get to know the residents of the surrounding community. Are there openings within your organization for which you could be interviewing local candidates?)

➤ *Designate someone in your organization as Coordinator of Community Relations.* No, you (probably) don't have to allocate a new budget line for this. The idea is to nominate someone in your group to be point man, or woman, when it comes to handling requests from the community, responding to local information queries about the organization's operations, and suggesting appropriate opportunities for your organization to participate in local activities. Designating someone as being responsible for work in these areas usually doesn't take much time, but doing so *does* clarify your group's overall intent when it comes to interacting with the surrounding community.

➤ *Hook up with the municipality's World Wide Web site (or sites).* More and more communities—or parts of communities—are setting up sites on the World Wide Web, the graphic component of the Internet. If your organization maintains a web site for marketing or promotional purposes—and something in excess of 25 percent of public and private organizations do these days—you should strongly consider taking steps to link up with local sites. This will allow Net-surfers in your community to click easily onto the same information about your operations that are available to others in cyberspace.

MENDING FENCES: SIX STRATEGIES FOR RESTORING YOUR ORGANIZATION'S IMAGE WHEN YOUR RELATIONSHIP WITH THE LOCALS IS IN CRISIS

There's been a problem. Because of a slipup on your organization's part, or perhaps to an overzealous series of news reports during sweeps week, the surrounding community now has doubts about your group's actions and intentions. Maybe things have even gotten a little ugly at times. What do you do?

Here are six steps your organization can take to regain the trust of its neighbors and resume (or establish) its position as a responsible member of the community. Note that these steps are *not* the same as those associated with handling hostile attention from the media, which is dealt with in detail earlier in this chapter. The focus here is on getting the message across to members of the community through channels your company controls or at least has a role in controlling. If you've been burned by members of the print and broadcast media, the decision to focus on alternate means of getting your message through to your neighbors probably won't be a difficult one to justify.

➤ *Hold a private meeting with community leaders to discuss the matter.* The higher the rank of the person in charge of conducting the meeting, the better. Obviously, for a meeting like this to work, a good deal of preparation will probably be necessary. But the work is worth doing because the opportunity to get your (unedited) message across to religious leaders, members of city or town government, or leaders of citizens' groups is one you should not pass by. The two alternatives to bringing in influential members of the community for an open discussion of problems and potential solutions—namely, calling an open press conference at which you can expect to be savaged once again by aggressive print or broadcast reporters or a "circle-the-wagons" approach that excludes *all* community input—will probably lead to further estrangement from your neighbors. *Do not assume that all community action groups or government entities represent implacable enemies to your organization's cause!* Although the print and broadcast media may have a vested interest in playing up areas of conflict in your situation (big fights make for good copy, after all), the "battle lines" may not be drawn with quite the finality that press reports lead people to believe.

➤ *If your organization has made a mistake, state this clearly and frankly and outline your plan to rectify the situation.* Be sure to check with qualified legal counsel before you make any admissions or pledges on this score, of course, but bear in mind that true success lies in accountability. The idea is not to concede points for the sake of conceding them but to make sure people understand you know what fair play means. Press reports often edit out an organization's desire to make amends with the community. Whatever forum you choose for getting your message through—and this could include meetings with community leaders just outlined, paid advertisements, or even a citizen-by-citizen telephone campaign—make sure the true nature of your organization's response to the situation is getting through to its intended audience.

➤ *If you're quite confident that your organization hasn't made a mistake, take steps to get that message across forcefully and immediately.* This is a case where prompt use of paid media—perhaps in the form of a forceful and concise full-page advertisement in a local newspaper—may be the best option. (It should go without saying that you must promptly share your account of the story with the media representatives in question, as well.) Don't tax people's attention spans; pick three or four points that vividly illustrate the exaggerations and distortions of the other side. The act of unhesitatingly standing your ground when this act is supported with persuasive evidence will usually go a long way toward repairing your organization's status in the community. Paid advertisements—particularly full-page advertisements—afford an ideal forum for getting the key points out without assaults from members of the press. Other means of communication in such situations include mail campaigns and op-ed pieces for the local newspaper (although beware of "editorial decisions" in the latter case that deprive you of space). If yours is a case where the facts of the situation simply do not support the allegations people have associated with your group, it is incumbent upon you to take dramatic, impossible-to-miss action to counteract the misimpression that has been left. The inability to take such action has been associated with the failure of any number of high-level political campaigns. Although your organization may not be running for office, it *is* dependent on the opinions and reactions of others. Assuming that irresponsible—but newsworthy—accusations will fade simply because of their inherent absurdity is a mistake your group does not have the luxury of committing.

➤ *Stay "on message."* This idea was discussed in the earlier section on strategizing your relations with the press during trying times. It is just as important to bear in mind when mending fences with members of the local community. Condense your response to the accusations against your group into a few memorable, but not arrogant, sentences. Be prepared to *elaborate* on those few sentences when circumstances permit you the opportunity to do so, and be willing to field questions from concerned members of the community without appearing to be doing so from rote memory. But you should nevertheless *return* to the main theme of the "big ideas" you are working to get across and do so tirelessly.

➤ *Pick someone who won't get overheated to handle the job of getting the message out.* The personality of the individual who is selected to help repair relations with the community can make all the difference. Relying entirely on a set of facts that seems to put your organization at an advantage will be pointless if the person making the case comes across as callous, insensitive, or inarticulate. Select a person who can be counted on to remain poised at all times, who has a firm sense of personal and organizational purpose, who can crack a smile in response to an attack, and who knows how to avoid responding in kind when irresponsible charges have been launched

➤ *Don't try to control the final outcome.* The odds are that you won't be able to do so, no matter what happens. Content yourself with knowing that you have acquitted your organization well by following core principles, reinforcing the messages that need to be reinforced, showing fairness and generosity during times of conflict, displaying a measure of calm even in the midst of turmoil, and summoning a certain inspired presence of mind when adapting to the demands and concerns of the community. If you follow these steps, you will be well positioned to re-establish your organization's role in the community over the long haul, even if temporary obstacles appear as you move toward that goal.

Dealing with Outside Vendors

The people who supply your organization with goods and services are critical players in any organizational battle plan, and they deserve to be treated as such. The development and maintenance of these alliances will have a great deal to do with your organization's success or failure. It is far easier to nurture and support an existing relationship with a dependable vendor than it is to build a new relationship from scratch. Unfortunately, when cost-cutting mania sweeps through the ranks of an organization's top decision makers, this fact is often neglected.

In this chapter, you'll learn about the most effective ways to interact with suppliers and service providers, and you'll find out about some of the best ways to turn your relationships with the best of these players into long-term partnerships that benefit both sides.

TEN TIPS FOR EFFECTIVE ONGOING INTERACTIONS WITH OUTSIDE VENDORS

1. *Ask yourself: Is this vendor someone with whom I can count on working in the long term?* Yes, you *can* watch the budget and work to develop a long-term relationship with a key supplier. Most of us live in an era of extreme on-the-job budget consciousness, of course, and that's not an entirely unhealthy development. But there are times when frugality can be expensive. It's not at all uncommon these days for vendors and service suppliers to be called upon to justify their existence on a quarterly (or even more frequent) basis. Vendors *should*, from time to time, be shaken up a bit and encouraged to deliver the best value for the

money by having to develop more competitive approaches to pricing, quality, and delivery. But there is a real danger inherent in "vendor-hopping," and it is a danger that too many managers are inclined to pass over in silence. How, for instance, is the organization quantifying the "expense" of the additional person-hours necessary to accommodate staff to a new vendor's way of doing things? How much is your organization paying when it comes to bringing a new vendor up to speed on initiatives with which an older vendor was quite familiar? There are certainly times when it makes sense to switch to a more economical, faster, or more responsive vendor, but there are also times to respect the partnership role that has been developed over a period of years with a vendor you have come to rely on and trust. With the right relationship in place—one based on regular meetings, shared discussion of goals, and a carefully cultivated mutual respect—little or no cajoling will be necessary when it's time to bring a vendor into line on a key issue. The short message: Pick the most important vendors on your list and take the time to find out what makes *their* organizations tick, and to develop face-to-face relationships with the most important people.

2. *When developing relationships with new vendors, ask to meet the representative of the highest possible rank.* Who knows? You may have an opportunity to meet with the president—and that may translate into lower defect levels, faster turnaround times, or better service. Your leverage for arranging such a meeting is much stronger at the beginning of the relationship than it is after you have assigned a purchase order.

3. *When considering new vendors, mount a fax attack.* In tracking down a new partner, you can use today's communications technology to your organization's advantage—and save yourself a good deal of time in the process. By faxing a series of bid requests and requesting completed faxes in return, you'll spend less time on hold trying to get in touch with the right person. You'll also get an idea of the potential new vendor's promptness in getting back to you. Include all necessary specifications and time requirements, and be sure the words "REQUEST FOR BID" (or some variation) appear prominently at the top of your fax.

4. *Before you decide to give business to a new vendor, talk to at least one current or previous customer—preferably two or three.* References turn out to be just

as important when selecting a new vendor as they are when deciding whether or not to hire a new employee. (Often, they're a good deal *more* important. That receptionist you're considering taking on may slip up, but not in a way that results in hundreds of irate customers.) An eye-popping quote that incorporates an impressive price and an unbeatable delivery time may not be as reliable as you thought. Take the time to find out who else the outfit has worked for. Pick up the phone and ask some questions. Ask the customer with experience: Are you still working with this firm? If you changed vendors, why did you decide to do so? Were there any unexpected fees or surcharges that undermined the original quote? Was the agreed-upon delivery time adhered to? Were there any serious quality-control problems?

5. *Beware of false savings.* If you're located in Virginia and a manufacturing vendor in Massachusetts offers you a quote that is a percentage point or two lower than a vendor in New Hampshire, your best bet is probably to opt for the closer vendor. The reason? Shipping costs to your facility will probably erase any savings from the more far-flung vendor. Similar false savings may accompany a service provider who does not provide the same training and follow-up procedures of a competing firm, or an equipment purchase program that incorporates a much more expensive repair contract option than another supplier's. Be sure to evaluate such issues carefully before you commit to any vendor.

6. *Always work from written quotes and estimates.* If you don't, you may regret it later on. Unexpected overruns, surcharges, and unauthorized deviations from agreed-upon specifications have a way of materializing in invoices. Keep a copy of the original quote or estimate and base your purchase order on it. Reference the quote by number and date in all communications with the vendor. That way, you'll be in a better position to contest any problems that may arise. The commitments embodied in verbal "quotes" have a way of evaporating when you're not looking.

7. *If yours is a twenty-four-hour-a-day business, ask if there is twenty-four-hour-a-day service availability.* Is it important to you to be able to get things up and running after an unexpected shutdown at two in the morning? If so, ask about any "on-call" options your vendor or service provider may be willing to make available to you. You're much better off asking for an option like this *before* you provide someone with a purchase order than *after.* Who needs to have a supply line shut down for an extra day?

8. *If there are quality-control or design problems, assume a partnership mindset in resolving them.* Even with superior vendors, there are occasional problems. Although you should focus with great intensity on the vendor's ability to deliver superior products and/or services *before* you make a purchase commitment, a more flexible approach is the order of the day once your "marriage" to the vendor has been finalized, even for a small job in a comparatively unimportant area. This transition can be difficult to manage, but it is nevertheless absolutely essential that it be consciously undertaken. You may be able to afford a "deliver it this way or hit the road" mindset when *evaluating* potential suppliers, but such an attitude can bring on a world of troubles if it is employed with a key *current* vendor.

The more catastrophic the implications of a lapse or flaw, the more vital it is that you address the matter from a cooperative, rather than a confrontational, point of view. Why? Your vendor or supplier is in possession of vast amounts of technical information and years of applied experience. You will need those assets in addressing the problem you face. If you assume the point of view that the agreement you signed or the purchase order you issued allows you the right to behave in a bullying manner toward a supplier who has come up short, you may feel at the end of your tirade as though you have accomplished something, but you will in fact have set the problem-resolution process back by several steps—and at the very time you can least afford to do so. By engaging in legalistic desk-pounding, you will have encouraged the people who have the knowledge you need—your vendor's team members—to stop passing along facts and focus on the task of defending themselves and proving that the problem is either less serious than you say it is or not as completely their fault as you say it is. *Those are not the topics you need them to be thinking about!* Instead, you should find some way to help them focus on the development of new alternatives—even alternatives that seem unworkable at first. By working as a team, you will minimize the amount of energy that is wasted in deciding who is or is not to blame for the situation you face.

Fix it first. Blame later. And while we're on the subject of blame . . .

9. *If you are facing a serious quality-control or product-flaw crisis, postpone talk of legal penalties or contractually permitted sanctions until after the situation has been resolved.* Even if the situation is so serious that legal action against the supplier may be in order, that does not change the situation you face now. Does it change your need for informed technical

advice? Does it change your need for an inspired approach on how best to resolve product flaws or misinformation that has already reached the public? Does it change your need for help in retooling or repairing existing stock or altering an existing system? Does it change the fact that you want people volunteering information about the problem you face, rather than attempting to cover it up? The fact of the matter is, you and your vendor must work together to address quality problems. If there are legal issues or contractual penalties to address, focus on them *after* the crisis passes.

This point, and the previous one, are of paramount importance when addressing problems with a vendor or supplier and are therefore highlighted here. For more information on addressing quality-control problems with a vendor, see the later section on this topic in this chapter.

10. *Don't wait for a crisis.* Meet regularly with the most important vendors even if things are currently going well, even if other matters require your attention, and even if you have no reason to believe there are problems on the horizon. These are people who are eager to share their most recent discoveries with you, and you should let them. Your key vendors should serve as an important source of new trends and information likely to affect your business, not simply as the fulfillers of tasks you assign to them.

HOW TO NEGOTIATE WITH VENDORS

Countless books have been written on the fine art of negotiating agreements; the space constraints here permit only a brief survey of a few of the important tactics at your disposal. (For more information, you may wish to consult Herb Cohen's fine book *You Can Negotiate Anything,* published by Lyle Stuart.) Here are six good ideas for getting the best deal you can from a vendor:

➢ *Avoid asking yes-or-no questions, especially those to which you do not know the answer.* Instead of asking something like "If we agree to this price, can you guarantee a thirty-day turnaround?" you should avoid boxing yourself in by asking a more hypothetical form of the question. It could sound like this: "If we were able to get approval for the price you've outlined, would you be willing to incorporate a written guarantee of a thirty-day turnaround?"

➤ *Make selected points conditional upon outside approval.* In other words, you may have to check everything over with your supervisor before making any commitments. This is an excellent way to get concessions; by staging "internal discussions" on issues you planned to yield to the vendor anyway, you may be able to win better terms.

➤ *Beware of habitual lowballing.* There's certainly nothing wrong with trying to win the best possible terms from your vendor, but making a habit of clinging to offers that only encourage hostility on the part of your negotiating partners may make it difficult for you to develop sound long-term relationships with them. If you can, point your offer toward a figure that represents a realistic opening gambit, given the prevailing standards of your industry.

➤ *If you must cling to a specific figure, make it a little odd.* In other words, if you have no alternative other than to stick to a budget-imposed amount, alter that figure slightly so that it is not an even number. Try it. You'll be surprised at the results. You will win more points for credibility by insisting that you can only pay seventy-nine and two-thirds cents per unit than you will by insisting you can only pay eighty cents. The former figure sounds as though it's the result of an all-night number-crunching session, perhaps one overseen and/or approved by the president of the organization. The latter number has the ring of arbitrariness—and that which is arbitrary is open for discussion.

If you've ever spent much time in a big city, you've probably been approached by a panhandler asking not simply for a dollar but for three dollars and forty-four cents, the precise amount needed to fill the gap between cash on hand and "the price of a ticket home." The same basic idea applies here; people are more willing to give in when there appears to be a specific demand or (implied) rationale behind a particular figure.

➤ *Bear in mind that payment* terms *often turn out to be of greater consequence than payment* rates. There's a business-school joke that goes something like this: "You can name the price if I can name the terms." If you are having difficulty getting a vendor to move down on a price that doesn't work for you, ask about the possibility of an extended payment plan. You may be able to find a plan that makes that previously inaccessible asking price a little easier to swallow.

➤ *Remember: Self-confidence counts.* You are not engaged in a logical, point-by-point analysis, but in a ritual contest of sorts in which the person who demonstrates the greatest willingness to walk away from the deal holds the upper hand. This dynamic pervades all negotiations, and it tends to give buyers an advantage over sellers. Since you are buying, you are (technically speaking, at least) probably the beneficiary of a superior negotiating position. Long-term relationships with vendors tend to even out the odds on this score somewhat, but the basic principle still applies: The person who shows the greatest sense of certainty about what he or she is after and who clearly knows what is and is not worth sacrificing in order to attain that objective is likely to hold the advantage.

HOW TO ESTABLISH A SCHEDULE THAT WILL WORK FOR EVERYONE

Irresistible force versus immovable object—or is it? You know *who* you want to work with, but you can't seem to get the organization to commit to the date you have in mind. Many a manager has gotten caught in the middle of this classic problem.

Here are four ideas for working with your vendor to find ways to improve the projected schedule. With luck, you'll be able to use them to make headway the next time you hear someone say, "We just can't make that date."

➤ *Offer a meaningful incentive.* If you can get clearance to do so, you may want to offer an accelerated payment schedule—or even a cash bonus—for delivery according to an aggressive schedule. Other incentives that may prove to be effective include advance purchase orders for future business, adherence to an inventory storage plan or other program that the vendor's company has been lobbying you to consider, or written endorsements for use in the vendor's marketing efforts.

➤ *Appeal, via fax and later telephone follow-up, to the head of the department or division.* Sometimes moving up through the chain can yield dramatically different scheduling estimates. It's entirely possible that the service representative with whom you have been dealing up to now simply lacks formal authority to make the change you need.

➤ *Appeal, via fax and later telephone follow-up, to the president of the organization.* Presidents and CEOs have a way of making supposedly impossible things happen when they see evidence that an important customer is in a tight spot. Try faxing after four o'clock—but not too much later, as you want the fax to arrive in time for the start of business the following day—and then following up by phone very early the next morning. *Alternate, quick-start approach:* Call the president with *no* fax preceding, but place the call late at night or before eight in the morning (the better to catch the workaholic at the desk) and explain your case from the bottom up. With a little preliminary research, you may be able to reach the president directly. (They often answer their own lines during off hours.) If you reach the top person's assistant or secretary, make every effort to turn this person into an ally. These "gatekeepers," often thoughtlessly dismissed or treated as unthinking roadblocks, are very often among the most important people in the entire organization. If you can get the president's secretary to plead your case, consider that a step forward. *Whoever you reach in the Inner Sanctum, respect that person's time!* Don't make a long-drawn-out appeal; get right to the point. You'll be likelier to get results from the top if you do.

➤ *If all else fails, inform the vendor that you need a schedule revision that meets your demands within forty-eight hours, or you will be forced to find another supplier.* Obviously, this is not an option you should pursue unless you are facing a serious, impossible-to-overcome time crunch, one that is worth disrupting the relationship. (If you are dealing with a vendor with whom you have developed a deep, long-term alliance, you probably should not push this button unless the fate of the company hangs in the balance!)

In the rare event that you do decide to inform your vendor of this decision, you must follow through as promised. You will be in the best bargaining position if you can supply the name of a competing vendor who is in fact capable of meeting your time requirements. (You may be forced to pay a substantial premium to work with this vendor, but there's no need to go into that with the organization you're trying to talk into committing to a better schedule.)

HOW TO DEAL WITH PRODUCT OR SERVICE PROBLEMS

As outlined earlier in this chapter, it is in your best interests to leave any thoughts of punishment, retribution, or blame on the back burner while dealing with the immediate effects of a quality or design problem with a vendor. If the problem is not one with far-reaching implications, you will want to confirm the dimensions of the lapse in quality, determine how much of your business it affects, and use your vendor's expertise in your troubleshooting efforts. If the problem is one that could cause your organization serious problems with clients, customers, or the media, you *must* put thoughts of "getting even" on the back burner. If you don't, you will run the risk of:

- Polarizing the situation instantly.

- Encouraging a coverup within the vendor's organization that will keep you from getting the facts you need about how widely the problem has spread.

- Short-circuiting any meaningful attempts to implement repairs or corrections.

- Distributing inaccurate information to customers or the media—information that could make the problem much worse.

Whether or not you like it, you and the vendor are facing the situation together until it is resolved. Only at that point should you address questions of compensation or of whether or not to terminate the relationship.

A family counselor in Massachusetts, while discussing a patient's impending decision regarding a potential separation, once argued that divorce—at least as the term is applied to a husband and wife who have had a child together and are not interested in total abandonment—is really an impossibility. His argument: Once you and someone else have decided to bring another human being into the world, a human being you and your partner each wish to see every now and then, you are in fact married, in some sense, for the rest of your life. No matter what the courts may choose to say about the arrangement, you and your former partner are joined in the task of being parents to that person. Marriage *means* being joined. The person who holds the position of fellow-parent is going to be a part of your life, no matter what, for years to come, and at least for as long as the child requires care, attention, and supervision from adults. The only question is whether or not the two of you are going to make each other's life miserable in the process.

Much the same point can be made about a vendor who delivers products or services to your company. Whether or not you are happy with the relationship, the truth is that it now exists. The two of you share stewardship over a "child" of sorts. While that child still requires attention, you are best advised to make the best of things, rather than indulge in recrimination that will only make the situation worse.

That's the big message. Here are three additional points to bear in mind as you work with your vendor to address a product or service problem:

➤ *Avoid overstatement, generalization, and buck-passing.* You have to deal with this problem, and you have to do so in such a way that your vendor's technical expertise comes into play effectively. Accordingly, you must give your vendor the most accurate, reliable information possible. Avoid responding to requests for data with answers like:

> "Just assume the virus is on every system we use." (The vendor, like you, is dealing with limited resources. If you ask them to put on a full-court press, without bothering to identify where the problem truly lies, you will waste valuable time.)

> "Maybe half the products you shipped had the flaw." (Inaccurate estimates of the problem area, based on anecdotal evidence from your end, will make it more difficult for the vendor to identify what production processes have gone awry. Stick with what you know. If you've spotted problems with half the items in a single box, say that.)

> "That's production's department. You guys are the ones who fouled up. You go track them down." (Buying out of the problem when it's time to supply critical internal information should be an option. Whether you like it or not, the vendor has the technical information and you have the ability to move things along quickly on your end—or, at any rate, more quickly than the vendor would. If you disclaim any responsibility for tracking down the internal data or oversight your vendor needs, you will needlessly prolong the process of fixing the problem.)

➤ *Make it clear that you understand that the problem represents a temporary lapse, not an ongoing problem.* Even if you *are* looking at a chronic quality-control problem, is there any advantage in focusing on that right now? *This* problem exists, and it's the one that must be resolved in the short term.

What we think people think about us matters. By at least assuming a rhetorical position that allows the vendor to proceed from a common assumption that the current situation represents an exception, not the rule, you will allow the other side to focus on the important issues, rather than on how mad you are or are likely to become.

➤ *Understand that any long-term relationship has its good and bad moments.* If you have undertaken to develop long-term relationships with key vendors—and you should—then you are, by definition, exposing yourself to the possibility of error. Humans are fallible, and so are the organizations and institutions they set up. If you have made a strategic decision to build a long-term partnership with a particular vendor, do not attempt to make the relationship contingent upon the notion that the vendor will never, under any circumstances, allow error to slip into the process. A successful long-term alliance with a vendor is more than a little like a marriage—and how many of those don't feature mistakes and oversights? Yes, serious quality problems must be addressed and resolved. All the same, you should view the occasional problem in the proper context. If you've been working with a specific manufacturer for ten years and have enjoyed aggressive pricing schedules for most of that period as a result of your alliance, don't view the first deviation from a manufacturing tolerance as a personal betrayal.

HOW TO WIN CREDIT OR EXTENDED PAYMENT TERMS FOR LATE DELIVERIES OR PAST QUALITY-RELATED PROBLEMS

The crisis has passed. You've shown an exemplary team-first spirit in working with the vendor to resolve whatever quality problems arose. Now it's time to talk about compensation.

These negotiations can be long-lived, but a strong alliance with the vendor will usually result in an outcome both parties can live with. Here are five ideas to consider when discussing what should happen next as a result of a vendor's past lapse in quality or failure to deliver on time:

➤ *Quantify, quantify, quantify.* How much time, effort, and energy did you and your people spend in addressing this problem? You should think not only in terms of wages paid, but also in terms of what people *could* have been doing. The aim is to develop a healthy estimate of the dollars paid out—and the opportunities lost—because of the efforts you extended in dealing with the vendor's lapse in quality. (In the case of a late delivery, focus on the lost sales or lost productivity associated with the date slippage.) Invest the research time up front and then . . .

➤ *Get it all down in black and white.* Develop a concise (preferably, one-page) summary of all the costs, both direct and indirect, your vendor exposed you to as a result of the problem. (Remember, the shorter the memo, the more likely it is to be read in the first place—and you want this one read.) If you must combine a thick sheaf of spreadsheets to support a particularly complex claim, be absolutely certain that the covering document gets right to the point and is easy for technician and nontechnician alike to understand. Then . . .

➤ *Pass your summary along to the vendor and ask what he or she thinks should happen next.* You may want to present the cost summary as a document that both you *and* the vendor must somehow deal with, then let the vendor know that your superior is interested in the outcome of your discussions with the vendor. (Most of us can identify with the dilemma of having been commanded by Someone in Charge to deliver results in a certain area. If this situation isn't one that justifies appealing to such a maneuver, no situation is.)

➤ *Make it clear that you are interested in continuing to do business with the vendor, but that you need to resolve the issue of compensation for the quality or service lapse first.* Focus on the positive; keep the lines of communication open; emphasize the role your organization played in helping to detect and/or resolve the problem. (Even if the other party made such a hash of things that key people in your organization have sworn at all costs to avoid a repeat performance, you should hold out, if at all possible, the potential that you personally will agree to review future requests for business, which is true enough.)

If the vendor still hedges on cash refunds for the job that went awry or seems uneasy about discussing your valid request for price reductions on future jobs, then . . .

➤ *Ask for more attractive payment terms on the job in question.* Assuming you have authorization to do so, you may decide that it makes sense to agree to take out "compensation" for the job that featured the quality or service lapse in the form of an extended payment plan. Although this is unlikely to be a particularly popular option with your vendor, it may represent the best possible compromise for the situation you face.

HOW TO RESPOND TO AGGRESSIVE OR ANTAGONISTIC VENDOR REPRESENTATIVES

They're out there: vendor representatives who haven't been able to incorporate a customer-first focus in their day-to-day interactions with you. If the fates have assigned you an antagonistic service representative who doesn't seem likely to change his or her ways as a result of discussions with you, you have three options, (besides, of course, changing vendors):

➤ *Appeal, tactfully, to the head of the department—or to the salesperson with whom you initially met at the vendor's organization.* Without rancor or antagonism, explain the problems you've been having with the rep in question; cite the specific instances of oversight, abuse, or neglect that have made interactions with this person difficult. Make it clear that you are not out to get the person fired, only to encourage the rep to take a different approach to interactions with you. In the vast majority of cases, a quiet appeal along these lines will do the trick, and the problematic behavior will disapper. If it doesn't . . .

➤ *Ask directly for a new representative.* If two weeks or more go by without your having seen any improvement in the service rep's behavior, you are perfectly within your rights to ask that the organization assign someone else to your account. In the extremely unlikely event that this request is denied, you should . . .

➤ *Simply contact someone else in the organization to resolve problems for you.* This boils down to making the reassignment yourself. Good candidates for the "promotion" you have in mind include the head of the department in question (if you have a good relationship with that person) and/or the salesperson who met with you initially about the account. If you have gone to the trouble of establishing, on your own, a new contact within the organization to resolve questions and disputes, you will have made a very clear statement of where you stand on the issue of dealing with the rep with whom you can't seem to get along. Any further static from the vendor, or any attempt to make you deal with someone who is clearly not willing to accord you and your organization the respect you deserve, should be considered grounds for an appeal to the president of the organization—or, if you are not comfortable with that option, for finding some other vendor.

MORE IDEAS FOR BUILDING LASTING RELATIONSHIPS WITH YOUR VENDORS

Building partnerships with the right people is, in the end, what this is all about. If you've got the right relationship with a superior vendor, any of the problem areas we've discussed in the chapter can be ironed out. If you don't, there are likely to be headaches. Often, it is through the resolution of the very trial-by-fire episodes that we are discussing that the seeds of long-term partnerships come to fruition. And that brings us to the issue of what *you* are willing to do for *your vendor* to help ensure a success in the relationship over the long haul.

When a vendor has repeatedly shown a willingness to go above and beyond the call of duty for you and when people at many levels of the vendor's organization have demonstrated a commitment to delivering the very best value, service, and delivery schedules possible to your organization, you should take an active role in agitating on that organization's behalf within your firm. You are, in all likelihood, dealing with the kind of vendor who should be incorporated into your long-term planning process. Here are ten steps to solidify your relationships with vendors who represent the cream of the crop. If you follow them, you'll encourage these allies to help you win victories over the long haul.

➤ *Express your appreciation in writing.* It's relatively easy to put things down in black and white when we're less than thrilled with the way a job came out. How often do we take the time to do so when things went swimmingly?

Supplying written endorsements and formal praise for a vendor who has done a superb job for you is a tiny investment of time that can help your supplier attract new business. It can, as a result, pay off in unexpected ways for *you* for years to come.

Here's what your letter might look like:

Dear Greg:

I just wanted to let you know how happy everyone on this end was with Tanco's superior workmanship and on-time delivery of our new line of children's wear. We got the merchandise—which was in full accordance with the specs we agreed on—in time for shipment during the holiday ordering season. As you know, this two-month period represents 67 percent of our company's yearly revenue.

Everyone on this end was thrilled with the way you came through on what was, after all, an extremely demanding and complex series of designs. Thanks again for helping to make it happen.

We look foward to working with you on many jobs in the future.

Sincerely,

Brenda Fairleigh
Senior Designer

➤ *Introduce the vendor's representatives to the team members you work with day in and day out.* Make it clear that you consider members of the vendor's organization to be something akin to co-workers, not simply suppliers.

➤ *Invite the vendor's representatives to company gatherings and celebrations.* Send the message that you aim to find ways to celebrate victories *and* overcome obstacles.

➤ *Ask for input on where the vendor's representatives believe the industries within which you work are headed.* Request advice from key salespeople and managers on short-term issues (for instance, impending increases in the price of raw materials) as well as long-term issues (what kinds of competitors the vendor thinks you'll be likely to have to do battle with over the next two to three years). Offer your own assessments of issues of common interest, as well.

➤ *Ask for suggestions on new products or services you should be offering.* Representatives of the vendor's organization may have a unique perspective on some approaches you should be considering. Learn what they are!

➤ *Visit the plant or office.* Taking the time and trouble to arrange a visit to the vendor's manufacturing facility will help you solidify your relationship with the key contacts at that organization.

➤ *Admit areas where you or your organization can improve and help the vendor do a better job.* One of the big differences between a short-term relationship and a long-term alliance is improved communication—and the ability of *both* parties to recognize areas for improvement. If you can identify ways to give the vendor's representatives what they need more quickly or remove some internal obstacles your own organization presents, say so and then take steps to make things run more smoothly.

➤ *Share your company's goal or vision statement with key people at the vendor's organization.* If this information is important enough to share with a recently hired receptionist who will be working with you on a part-time basis, it's important enough to share with the people who will be supplying you with key materials, products, and services over the next few years.

➤ *When offering suggestions for improvement, cite previous success stories for which the vendor's organization was responsible—stories that bear out your point about what needs to happen next.* The idea is to use the programs that worked to illustrate what needs changing in the programs that don't. Even if you have to stretch a bit to make your point, the basic idea— things have worked in the past and can work in the future—is worth reinforcing. What you say could sound like this:

"What we're trying to track down is a four-color printing process that offers the same crispness and definition on internal pages that our two-color jobs with you have had. You remember how sharp the *Productive Play* series looked? We're hoping to identify some process that's not too much more expensive than that, but that will deliver that same sharp edge."

➤ *Arrange a meeting with a representative of the vendor's organization and the highest official you can track down in your own.* Make your case to the president or CEO if you have to. If necessary, document in hard numbers the specific instances of heroic service that have inspired you to sing the vendor's praises.

Why bother to arrange such a meeting? Because a vendor with whom you develop an enduring relationship is much, much more than a source of products and services. This top-tier-category vendor is a source of knowledge that represents a *strategic advantage,* an advantage of the kind that should be made available to the highest people in your organization. Obviously, you won't go to the trouble of setting up high-level meetings with the top people in your organization for a vendor who did a top-notch job just once in coordinating a seminar for you or supplying some short-term printing work. If you find yourself wondering whether you should take up an hour of a top decision maker's time with a meeting with such suppliers, you're right. You shouldn't.

But what about the firm that's allowed your company to save hundreds of thousands of dollars over a period of three or four years by outsourcing all your sales-training work—and gotten far better results from your sales staff than the old way of doing things did? Or what about the outside creative team that's helped you develop graphic design in printed materials that have launched five of the seven biggest new accounts on the board over the past eighteen months? Those aren't just suppliers. They're *top-tier suppliers*—people who are adding significant value to your company's operations—and everyone will benefit from their connecting with the organization's top decision makers, including you.

Managing Conflict

"Absolutely not."

"What, are you kidding?"

"Gee, I don't know about that."

"Let's try a different approach."

"Have you thought about . . .?"

Although they are phrased differently, all the above statements mark the onset of a conflict situation. In each case, the speaker is expressing—with varying degrees of directness—some discomfort with a planned course of action. The recipient of the message may choose to challenge that discomfort, to work with the person who has voiced it in developing new options that neither person has yet considered, or to yield to the other person's challenge. Whatever he or she does, though, it will be in response to a situation in which two outlooks are in opposition.

The ability to deal well with situations marked by conflict is among the most important survival skills in the business world. Some of the conflicts we encounter are overt, some are understated, and some are stretched out over a period of months or years. But they must all be addressed in some way.

In this chapter, you'll learn about some of the most effective techniques for handling workplace conflicts effectively and in a way that encourages positive outcomes and keeps exchanges from descending into energy-wasting cycles that seem only to keep people "going around in circles."

TEN TIPS FOR EFFECTIVE DAY-TO-DAY CONFLICT MANAGEMENT

1. *Avoid "win-lose" outcomes.* Effective managers know that the most creative solutions arise not from attempts to prove who's right and who's wrong, but from more creative approaches to situations when people and ideas are set in opposition. Your conversational partner will be more likely to see new options and try new ideas if his or her intelligence and self-esteem are not at issue. That means focusing not on the person ("You told me the Johnson numbers would be higher than this") but on the event ("How do you think we can get the Johnson numbers to come in closer to the budget figures we passed along?").

2. *Respect your conversational partner's personal space.* There is very little you can do that has more likelihood of polarizing an interaction with another person than positioning yourself inside his or her "bubble." This zone of personal comfort and space extends for at least eighteen inches around the person's body, and, yes, the rule applies even if you are the person's superior. No matter how important the topic under discussion is, you will elicit both resentment and impossible-to-ignore chemical reactions (based on the "fight-or-flight" response inherent to our species) if you violate the eighteen-inch rule. Curb your instinct to "lean in" or to stalk behind the person's desk in order to thrust an ominous piece of written evidence into reading position or to insert yourself into the middle of a conversation by means of "space invasion." Such techniques will prompt only defensive reactions and not clear thinking on the part of the people with whom you are trying to contact. (Personal-space issues are among the most common and commonly overlooked motivating factors behind workplace relationships marked by long-term antagonism.)

3. *Watch your eye contact.* Maintaining continuous eye contact during a dispute is a challenge signal that can be just as potent as invading the other person's physical space. If you are used to holding another person's gaze during conversations, it's quite possible that you are sending messages you don't intend to and needlessly polarizing exchanges. Let the other person "breathe" now and then by looking away from time to time. If you encounter another person who seems intent on staring you down, you can help to minimize the possibility of later conflict by raising your eyebrows briefly, smiling in a nonthreatening way, and looking away. This sends the message, "I know what you're doing,

but I don't feel like engaging in a staring contest right now. Let's find another way to talk about this."

4. *Don't mistake ego issues for content issues.* For many people (especially superiors), ego and control are all-consuming passions. Conflicts with such people tend to focus on such issues as who gets credit, who has authority, who has to consult with whom, or other disputes that have nothing to do with the specifics of an initiative. If you find yourself dealing with a person to whom ego and control are primary issues, ask yourself these questions: Does it really matter who has control of this process? Can I allow this person to take the lead role he or she is so eager to have—and still guide the initiative toward a successful outcome? Finally, can I find some way to satisfy this person's need for control of the situation *and* resolve the problem successfully by asking for guidance and comment, rather than by demanding the final say in the matter? In many situations, the simple act of ceding *formal* control of the process to your conversational partner will yield *informal* (and, in many cases, effective) control of the process to you!

5. *Recognize "ritual opposition" for what it is.* In her book *Talking from 9 to 5*, Deborah Tannen points out that many of the "disputes" that can seem initially imposing to some team members are in fact ritualized efforts to probe the advantages and disadvantages of a particular idea under discussion. This technique of ritual opposition, which Tannen points out is generally more familiar as an analytical tool for men than it is for women, requires the person who is proposing or supporting an idea to defend it from all angles. This can feel a little like an inquisition. If you are unfamiliar with the process or leery of any interaction that shares a structural similarity with a personal attack, being questioned in this manner can be an imposing experience. It's important to understand, though, that the process of ritual opposition is widely accepted, even though it has the unfortunate effect of discouraging many women from suggesting or defending their ideas. At some companies, ritual opposition represents the primary method of planning and evaluating options! If you work for such an organization, you will probably have to learn to distinguish the act of defending an idea from the act of defending yourself—even though the two may look quite similar at times when you're on the receiving end of the questioning. Responding in an antagonistic or hostile way to ritual opposition is not the best way to further your career.

6. *Don't get hung up on whether or not people were telling you the truth.* At least, not unless there's a truly important issue at stake. Most human beings expect the truth from those with whom they must deal, but they occasionally shade the truth themselves. Fixating on whether or not your conversational partner was misleading you will shut down lines of communication, cast needless aspersions on the other person's fundamental integrity, and waste energy that could be going in more productive directions.

    This principle is especially important to bear in mind if the answer you are holding the other person responsible for giving you is one you dragged out after a protracted struggle! If you make the mistake of browbeating people until they give you the answer you want, don't turn around and accuse them of falsifying things. Sometimes the force of our own personalities elicits responses people wouldn't normally give. In most cases, that's more our problem than it is theirs.

7. *Wherever possible, emphasize the commonalities of your mindset groups—or, for even better results, assume the mindset of the person with whom you are dealing when posing issues and questions.* If you are a Lone Ranger engaged in a disagreement with a Cheerleader, there is a potential common approach for you to exploit: Both of you are likely to exhibit a strong deadline orientation, and both are likely to exhibit a powerful attraction to the idea of focusing on big time-sensitive issues first and so-called "marginal details" later. Make the most of these commonalities as you assess where you and your conversational partner should go from here: Focus on a deadline you must both address, or assume your conversational partner's deadline as your own. You may also want to try phrasing questions and suggestions from the mindset you believe the other person to be operating from—that is, asking the Sharpshooter what potential problems he or she sees in the approach to a certain problem. Often, the simple act of raising a question in a way that will allow your conversational partner to indulge his or her primary mindset will help you to minimize the potential negative effects of a conflict.

8. *Pay more attention to body language than you do to verbal content.* Many an unproductive communication cycle has been initiated by one partner's failure to adapt an approach to clear physical signals. Don't get sidetracked by the words; if the person you're talking to is sending physical signals that clearly indicate that the approach you're taking isn't working out, back off and try another way of dealing with the question at hand.

9. *Don't get trapped in paranoid cycles.* When we establish enemies and assume the worst about people, we usually shut down communication and make meaningful progress toward mutually acceptable goals much more difficult. Your mental attitude toward the person with whom you are dealing really does count. Make sure that the way you are thinking about the person with whom you're dealing isn't undercutting your efforts to find solutions that will work for both of you.

10. *Avoid comparing your conversational partner with someone else who understands what you're getting at more completely, carries out ideas more effectively, or operates more efficiently.* Each of us is unique; when we receive a veiled (or straightforward) message that we don't quite measure up to the standards set by another person, we are likely to tune out the rest of what the other person is saying. Even an innocent message remarking on the varying approaches people take to different problems runs the risk of being misinterpreted and initiating a tussle that need not take place. If you want to minimize antagonism, reduce the likelihood that your conversational partner will perceive what you're saying as a personal attack, and encourage individual initiative, address the person your talking to on his or her own merits.

RESOLVING PROBLEMS BEFORE THEY GET OUT OF HAND: THE SHARED-DILEMMA APPROACH

One of the best ways to address an emerging conflict situation is to move quickly to define the issue as a shared challenge—rather than a battle of wills. Here are five ways to do an end-run around unproductive exchanges by emphasizing some aspects of the situation you and the person with whom you are speaking both face:

➤ *Move past personality issues and focus on the facts you both face.* It's going to be difficult to get your conversational partner to alter his or her personality, so don't try. Instead of getting hung up on "what you do that irritates me"—an issue that can probably never be resolved satisfactorily—consider placing the emphasis on the following points.

➤ *When trying to focus on a common problem you share with a Lone Ranger, emphasize a common deadline you both must meet.* Point out that you are as eager as the Lone Ranger to resolve the current problem so that both of you can get back to work. (Being able to get back to work counts for a great deal in the Lone Ranger's universe.)

➤ *When trying to focus on a common problem you share with a Sharpshooter, emphasize how much depends on the two of you working together to identify potentially serious errors.* Volunteer to conduct an informal critique of whatever issue is under dispute—and to submit the results to the Sharpshooter for final analysis. As pointed out repeatedly, one of the best ways to resolve problems with Sharpshooters is to give them something to correct.

➤ *When trying to focus on a common problem you share with a Professor, emphasize your willingness to work with the Professor to follow established procedures.* Point out that you and the Professor share an interest in promoting a harmonious work environment, one in where people will keep each other informed, follow the rules, and check for approval before launching untested initiatives.

➤ *When trying to focus on a common problem you share with a Cheerleader, emphasize the importance of an imminent deadline, and make it clear that you intend to follow the Cheerleader's lead in attaining the goal associated with it. Or identify some other shared challenge that seems likely to help you put things in the proper perspective.* Take the lead by offering to develop new alternatives. Working from a "we" perspective, rather than an "I" and "you" perspective, is your best bet.

> "Well, whatever went wrong, we need to find some way to get Mr. Robertson those samples by Tuesday. I can think of a couple of ways we could go on that: I could call up Alice in Production and ask if there's any way she could assemble a couple for us from scratch. She owes me one from a favor I did for her last week. We could also take a few people off the Birdland design project and ask them to take an hour or two to construct something for us. Can you think of any other ideas, or does one of those seem likely to work for you?"

RESOLVING PROBLEMS BEFORE THEY GET OUT OF HAND: THE THIRD-PARTY APPROACH

Another good way to go when you find yourself stuck in an unproductive situation that doesn't seem likely to resolve itself without special effort is to suggest an appeal to an objective party. By incorporating the input of another colleague (not a superior), you may be able to break the logjam. Here are four ideas for convincing the person you're talking to of the advantage of this approach:

➤ *When trying to convince a Lone Ranger of the advantages of letting a third party review the situation and make a recommendation,* point out that while the matter is under review you will both be able to focus on tasks you have fallen behind on.

➤ *When trying to convince a Sharpshooter of the advantages of letting a third party review the situation and make a recommendation,* point out that this person may flag errors that you and the Sharpshooter may have overlooked.

➤ *When trying to convince a Professor of the advantages of letting a third party review the situation and make a recommendation,* emphasize any experience in dealing with similar situations that the third party may possess. (Professors tend to react well to options that allow them to minimize the possibility of entering uncharted territory.)

➤ *When trying to convince a Cheerleader of the advantages of letting a third party review the situation and make a recommendation,* emphasize the objectivity of the person to whom you're appealing and make it clear that the Cheerleader will have the opportunity to outline his or her priorities on a face-to-face basis. (You may need to let the Cheerleader exercise a couple of vetos before you arrive on a satisfactory third party.)

RESOLVING PROBLEMS BEFORE THEY GET OUT OF HAND: THE DISENGAGE, THEN, FOLLOW-UP-LATER APPROACH

This one's pretty simple. Sometimes you will be presented with a situation in which your conversational partner is exhibiting much more emotion than the situation warrants. In such a case, there's a good chance that something else is bothering the person you're talking to or that high stress levels are keeping the issue from being viewed in an objective way. Sometimes you'll be able to ask questions that point the person in other, more constructive, directions. Sometimes you won't. When facing one of the latter situations, consider the following options:

➤ *Disengage.* Don't worry about who's right or who's wrong; don't worry about what's true and what's not. These issues are not going to help you move the discussion toward a more civil tone. Simply remove yourself from the situation tactfully. Do this without indulging any temptation you may feel to get the last word in or making any type of editorial comment about the attitude your conversational partner is displaying.

Remember, disengaging *now* is not the same thing as dropping the issue *permanently*. Your aim is to follow up at an appropriate time later, once you see evidence that a better frame of mind has emerged. It won't hurt your cause to begin that follow-up exchange by citing something that you found, after some thought, to be correct in the person's argument last time. This is a variation on the repeating-the-message-to-prove-that-you-really-heard-it technique discussed earlier, which is worth bearing in mind when dealing with any conflict situation.

➤ *When returning to an area of potential conflict with a Lone Ranger,* make it clear that you don't need much time. Quickly and politely outline at least three options you see for resolving the problem you both face, then ask if there are approaches you haven't considered that should be discussed. *Do not make any reference to the past occasion when this person showed less than complete emotional control.*

➤ *When returning to an area of potential conflict with a Sharpshooter,* identify a flaw in your own approach to the problem last time around. If you possibly can, say the words "I made a mistake," or some obvious variation on them. This will win you attention and interest from the Sharpshooter. Move quickly to outline what you want to do, then ask if there are approaches you haven't considered that should be discussed. *Do not make any reference to the past occasion when this person showed less than complete emotional control.*

➤ *When returning to an area of potential conflict with a Professor,* cite a parallel situation from the past that supports your point of view. Make it clear that what you are proposing strongly resembles another case that turned out well. Then outline what you have in mind and ask if the Professor has suggestions on alternate ways to proceed. *Do not make any reference to the past occasion when this person showed less than complete emotional control.*

➤ *When returning to an area of potential conflict with a Cheerleader,* try to find a way to let the Cheerleader do most of the talking. (Usually, this won't be difficult.) You may wish to offer a suggestion, but make it clear that you have deep reservations about one particular aspect of the problem you both face. This is not an appeal for technical expertise but an opportunity to allow the Cheerleader to do what he or she does best: Get people pointed in a particular direction. You may be able to resolve the conflict once the Cheerleader has had the chance to take an objective look at the situation, and once he or she has been allowed the opportunity to take the lead role in refining your approach. *Do not make any reference to the past occasion when this person showed less than complete emotional control.*

MANAGING CONFLICTS WITH SUPERIORS

Specific approaches to handling difficult moments with the Lone Rangers, Sharpshooters, Professors, and Cheerleaders you may report to were discussed in Chapter 5, which you may wish to review. Here are five additional suggestions for handling conflicts with your boss that may be helpful.

➤ *Address the person's emotional state first and the "facts of the matter" second.* Don't overlook the power of statements such as, "You're absolutely right; it shouldn't have happened. I can understand your frustration." By addressing the immediate emotional issues, you'll probably pave the way toward a more reasoned, productive discussion.

➤ *Don't restate what your boss already knows.* Some encounters with superiors can be pretty intimidating, but there's no reason to keep repeating the same facts over and over again, as though they were a part of a mantra that might get you out of the situation. (The same point goes double for defenses.) Try to outline new options for review; if you can't think of any or if every option you come up with seems to make the conflict worse, silence is a better option than saying the same thing repeatedly.

➤ *Beware of "can't."* There are any number of reasons not to focus during everyday exchanges with your superior on that which is, in your opinion, impossible. When you and your boss have found your way into a conflict situation, dismissing his or her ideas as unworkable will serve only as an invitation to further unpleasant polarization. Instead of telling your boss that something can't be done, you may, in a difficult situation, decide to express your opinion about the possibility for success, then commit to giving your best effort and following up afterward with a status report.

➤ *Restate your boss's message before proceeding to make your own points.* This basic communication tool is worth remembering in virtually any conflict situation, but it is particularly important to bear in mind when you find yourself in an argument with a superior.

➤ *Break through "either-or" roadblocks even if your superior doesn't ask you to.* Sometimes your boss will focus with great intensity on determining which is the best of two unpleasant options. In such situations, you may be able to help bring the situation to a better outcome by volunteering—not waiting until you are asked to supply—a third or fourth option. It's human nature to focus on black-and-white outcomes; consider it part of your job to point these out when you see them, even if your superior doesn't seem to be in a "new idea" mode. If you identify the *right* way to resolve the dilemma you face—or ask for time to do so—you may be able to resolve the conflict in short order.

DEALING WITH SUBORDINATES AND PEERS WHO *CONSTANTLY* DRAW YOU INTO CONFLICTS

Some people simply like to start fights. You're not always in a position to get rid of such people and you may not be able to avoid them all the time, but you can minimize the possibility that they'll *always* make your life miserable, and you can make an effort to set the guidelines for proper behavior. Here are some ideas on the best ways to deal with people who seem to live for conflict:

➤ *Show understanding for the person's outlook, position, frustration and/or predicament.* Aggressive behavior is sometimes nothing more than a plea for attention. Even faking your way through an empathetic assessment of the hurdles your conversational partner faces may put you in a position to resolve the conflict successfully.

➤ *Encourage the person to talk, and ask questions that help to clarify his or her points.* Many hostile exchanges escalate unnecessarily because one partner tries to keep the other from talking. Restatement of key points can be extremely effective in lowering the volume level of the exchange, as can the act of posing sensitive, noncombative questions (e.g., "How did you first find out about this problem?"). The more energy your conversational partner spends on making his or her points, the less energy will remain for attacking you.

➤ *Don't stand eye-to-eye.* Body positioning is extremely important when you're attempting to defuse an escalating conflict. Stand at least three feet away from the person who is talking to you. Stand at an angle, rather than facing each other down.

➢ *If you're dealing with a chronic interrupter, stop talking* immediately. Let the resulting awkward transition in the conversation serve as a signal that you are unwilling to pretend that the interruption didn't happen.

➢ *Project unflappability.* Confident, poised body language and a clear, non-threatening gaze will help you much more than anything you may decide to say in this situation. The words you select are important, of course, but the visual signals you send will do a much better job of letting the other person know that you are not about to be intimidated by any theatrics.

➢ *Set intelligent limits.* Do things seem to be getting out of hand? You don't have to talk to a colleague or subordinate who uses foul language, insults you, or shows signs of acting in a violent manner. Say so calmly and coolly—and then back your words up by disengaging if the person you are talking to insists on repeating the inappropriate behavior.

Winning the Results You Need from Groups

In this chapter, we'll take a look at some of the best ways to incorporate the various techniques you've been reading about to your interactions with groups. We'll also examine a number of ways you can fine-tune your ideas to maximize attention and interest when making a presentation to more than one person.

If you are taking a lead role in the group and will have an important say in which aspects of the group task will be assigned to particular team members, review the later sections of this chapter for ideas on the best ways to take advantage of the strengths of each member.

If you are not taking a lead role in the group and will be performing tasks that are delegated to you without offering strategic input, consider these ten ideas for performing harmoniously with others on a day-to-day basis.

TEN TIPS ON MAKING GROUP DYNAMICS WORK FOR YOU

1. *Find some way to praise the instinct behind every question someone directs to you.* The idea is to project a willingness to address even tough issues and make it clear to the other members of the group that you're accountable for what you do. This is not to say that you should embrace a frontal attack, find something praiseworthy—if only the desire to obtain all the information possible—in the question that has been posed. By sending the message that you are not the type of person to duck issues, you will enhance your standing within the group.

2. *Put out fires quickly.* When a dispute or misunderstanding seems likely to sidetrack the group, don't be afraid to play peacemaker. If two or more of your colleagues are engaging in a protracted, pointless cycle of one-upmanship, you will help increase group cohesion and productivity if you politely suggest that they take up the matter in private and allow the group to focus on more important issues.

3. *Praise the efforts of colleagues publicly when there is reason to do so.* Group reinforcement is a powerful motivator. If you spot a situation where someone's contribution merits recognition but has not yet received it, you will increase cooperation, build bridges, and enhance your own standing by calling attention to the person's accomplishment at an appropriate moment.

4. *Help to shift the group out of a blame focus when difficulties arise.* If publicly offered praise can work wonders for a team member's self-esteem, publicly offered criticism can bring on the kind of downward productivity spirals of which career plateaus are made. Even a well-intentioned "what-can-we-learn-from-this-situation" lecture, in which no names are mentioned, can have a debilitating effect on the self-confidence of the person whose work is being indirectly criticized. (Bear in mind that some of the more sarcastic team members in your group may take the opportunity to use these stories as opportunities to settle personal grudges without appearing to launch a direct attack.) If you notice your colleagues in your work group focusing on a particular team member's lapse in a prolonged, unproductive way, take the initiative and try to steer the conversation toward something positive about the team member's performance.

5. *Tactfully decline "do my work" invitations from a colleague during a group meeting.* Group meetings are often seen as opportunities to foist one's work off on someone else. The idea seems to be that if you're a real team player, you won't shatter group morale by refusing to take on a job that a fellow team member should, by rights, be performing. Handle this situation in exactly the same way you would if it happened in a one-on-one setting: Be polite but firm about your own personal limits and don't let silence mean yes. You might do this by saying something like, "Shelly, I'd like to be able to help you out on the Vericapt project, but the fact of the matter is my own plate is a little too full right now to be able to give that job the attention it deserves. I'm afraid you're going to have to find some other way to handle this."

6. *Don't get on a high horse.* It doesn't matter how much education you have, how many degrees you've earned, or how many years you've put in. If you're part of a team-oriented work group in either the short or the long term, you owe it to your colleagues to show appropriate professional respect and goodwill at all times. Today's business environment rewards people who are capable of working flexibly and harmoniously with others—and that means accepting (and acknowledging) good ideas, no matter who they come from.

7. *Contribute appropriately to the verbal give and take.* That means making a point of neither monopolizing the floor nor sitting in the silence befitting a Zen master in a far corner of the room. If you talk too much, you will run the risk of sending the message that you want to commandeer the meeting. If you talk too little, you may give the impression that you aren't pulling your fair share of the weight.

8. *Ask about estimated running times* before *the meeting starts, then mention the projected closing time only as you approach the final minutes of the meeting.* As the meeting is beginning, it is entirely appropriate to ask (or confirm) how long it is expected to last. If you make this query the *leitmotif* of all your verbal contributions to the session, however, you may incur the resentment of the Professors and Sharpshooters in your midst. These team members, you may recall, are loath to call off any effort to track down problems or refine systems and procedures. Unless the meeting really should be drawing to a close, don't ask these team members to put their quality-control campaigns into a "wrap-it-all-up" mode. Unless you are placed in formal control of a meeting, avoid telling a colleague that the group does not have time to address a particular quality-control issue.

9. *Respect a colleague's need to leave the meeting at the appointed ending time.* Unless you have been placed in formal control of the discussion, do not try, independently, to extend a meeting past its alloted running time. The Lone Rangers and Cheerleaders in your group, you may remember, are given to a certain pragmatic tunnel vision when it comes to focusing on important projects. For them, long-running discussions of what *might* go wrong, what *could* go wrong, what *didn't* go wrong, and what *should have* gone wrong but somehow didn't are very likely anathema. These team members live and die by present-tense challenges, and there are, more than likely, quite a few waiting for them on a desk somewhere right now. Acknowledge their commit-

ment to the process, and try to respect their wishes when the agreed-upon time to close the meeting comes around. If necessary, schedule appropriate meetings of smaller subgroups to review important matters after the main meeting has concluded.

10. *Stick to the agenda—and encourage others to do so as well.* Now is not the time to engage in lengthy monologues or pursue matters only tangentially related to the meeting's stated topic. If a colleague in the group starts to go off on a tangent, make a brief, tactful suggestion that the group return to the matter for which you have all convened.

HOW TO ADAPT THE IDEAS IN THIS BOOK TO TEAM-ORIENTED WORK GROUPS

Today's organizations are placing an increasing emphasis on autonomous, cooperative, results-oriented work groups. If you are part of such a group or are taking a leading role in structuring one, how can you make the best use of the ideas in this book? Part of the answer lies in knowing which tasks are likely to be performed best by members of the four mindset groups: Lone Rangers, Sharpshooters, Professors, and Cheerleaders.

The concise version of what follows can perhaps best be expressed in the following way:

> *The perfect initiative is one that the Lone Ranger develops from scratch, the Sharpshooter troubleshoots and redirects, the Professor plans internally and checks for problems in execution, and the Cheerleader inspires everyone to complete on time.*

For the Lone Ranger in Your Work Group . . .

➤ *Assign projects that this team member can work on more or less independently.* Allow him or her to report the results of the work to you, and to the group, at appropriate intervals, but try to find some way to allow this team member to operate without constant review and oversight.

➤ *Emphasize your projected deadline.* There is no guarantee that the Lone Ranger will always *hit* the time line you outline, but these team members, as a general rule, tend to take tasks more seriously—and get their best work done—when they must focus with full attention on a project that is due by a certain time.

➤ *Remember that the Lone Ranger may perform best in the following work categories:* Development of original written or graphic materials; development of initial or preliminary concepts and plans; instruction or training of other team members (as long as everyone understands ahead of time who is to be the center of attention); overhaul of a project that has gone awry (as long as everyone understands who is in charge); "big idea" generation; independent long-term research and problem solving; telephone work; trend spotting; sales and marketing activities.

For the Sharpshooter in Your Work Group . . .

➤ *Assign projects that this team member can work on more or less independently.* Allow him or her to report the results of the work to you, and to the group, at appropriate intervals, but try to find some way to allow this team member to operate without constant review and oversight.

➤ *Emphasize the mistakes you hope the person can track down.* There is no guarantee that the Sharpshooter will identify every problem in the material you pass along, but he or she is more likely than other team members to consider the responsibility for the quality-control task you assign as a personal challenge.

➤ *Remember that the Sharpshooter may perform best in the following work categories:* Review of written materials and agreements for errors or deviation from established or accepted form; review of products and service plans for deviation from quality standards; fact-checking; troubleshooting; supplemental or confirming research; exposure of flaws in logic or inconsistencies; development of strategies of attack against a competitor's or rival's weak spots; engineering or related activities; legal or regulatory activities.

For the Professor in Your Work Group . . .

➤ *Assign projects that this team member can work on in concert with other people.* Allow him or her to develop findings or summarize materials independently if that is necessary, but try to find some way to allow this team member to operate for most of the workday in a way that allows for the free exchange of ideas with others.

➤ *Emphasize the mistakes you hope the person can track down and/or the new approaches you hope this team member can develop for other people in the organization.* There is no guarantee that the Professor will identify every problem in the material you pass along or will be able to implement all the solutions others need, but he or she is more likely than other team members to develop new and effective ways of working based on past group experience.

➤ *Remember that the Professor may perform best in the following work categories:* Implementation of policies and procedures; development of written or verbal instructions; development of contingency and emergency plans; introduction of other team members to potentially imposing new technologies; evaluation of new ideas and initiatives; administrative and support areas; troubleshooting activities (especially those requiring experience with previous and alternate systems; efficiency-improvement initiatives; ombudsman and conflict-resolution areas.

For the Cheerleader in Your Work Group . . .

➤ *Assign projects that this team member can work on in concert with other people.* Allow him or her to develop findings or summarize materials independently if that is necessary, but try to find some way to allow this team member to operate for most of the workday in a way that allows for the free exchange of ideas with others. If you can, put the Cheerleader in charge of summarizing the results of a group of two or more team members.

➤ *Emphasize your projected deadline.* There is no guarantee that the Cheerleader will always *hit* the time line you outline, but these team members, as a general rule, tend to take tasks more seriously—and get their best work done—when they must focus with full attention (and encourage others to focus with full attention) on a project that is due by a certain time. They also tend to respond well to tasks that involve instructing others, coordinating the efforts of other team members, or conducting interviews or meetings.

➤ *Remember that the Cheerleader may perform best in the following work categories:* Project management and coordination of group efforts; execution of clearly defined group initiatives; motivational and personal improvement campaigns; public speaking; public relations and promotional work; teaching and related activities; seminar-related work; social activism and/or agitation; business activities involving networking; business activities focusing on improved internal morale and group cohesion.

FOUR MORE IDEAS THAT WILL HELP YOU DEVELOP A PLAN THAT WILL DEVELOP BROAD SUPPORT

Customizing your approach to take into account the needs and predispositions of the Lone Ranger, Sharpshooter, Professor, and Cheerleader in your work group is one way to better the odds that the members of your team will take on the plan with gusto. Here are four more:

➤ *Remember the power of opening up the floor.* Once you've outlined the broad goals of your plan, see what happens when you keep the *means* of attaining those goals relatively flexible. Ask for your team's input on the best ways to get from point *A* to point *B*—and write down every idea that comes your way on a flipchart or chalkboard that everyone can see. The task of being part of coming up with "the next idea"—a cycle that can be reinforced with visual stimuli such as flipcharts, as we've discussed elsewhere in this book—will help your team feel more involved in the task at hand.

Don't try to dictate the entire plan. Consider opening up the floor and asking your team about the best ways to make the big goals happen.

➤ *Acknowledge important corrections gratefully.* Is there a point in your plan— or in a previous one—where the input of a team member helped you avoid making a catastrophic mistake? Many managers hurry over such situations, pretending either that the person's input was routine when it wasn't or that the incident never took place at all. Instead of trying to cover up a problem that existed, glorify it! Make it clear to that person and to all the rest of the people on your team that without the correction you would have made a serious misstep. This leaves the way open for others in the group to offer similarly constructive criticisms and input, and input is what buy-in is all about. You might *think* that people would abuse the privilege of passing along their suggestions about how to make something work better, but the truth is that they very rarely do.

➤ *Leave time for unstructured brainstorming.* So often we tend to expect good results and personal investment in a project to arise from one of two situations: We're either talking *at* someone (or a group of someones) or they're talking back *at* us, one at a time. Why not set aside a ten- or fifteen-minute period for something other than enforced quiet while waiting for one's turn to speak? Allow the group some time away from your guiding hand—time during which they can interrupt each other, finish each other's sentences, or sit placidly until a good idea comes along if they choose. (By the way, the dynamic will probably work most in your favor if *you* leave the room, rather than asking everyone to march out and march back in again at a predetermined time. The idea is to leave a sense of the absence of structure for a time, and it's hard to do that when the session begins and ends with orders about departing and arriving.)

➤ *Let 'em sleep on it.* Who says you need the final word today? By allowing your people the chance to review the dimensions of an important problem, then take it home and think about it and report back the next day with their thoughts, you'll help them to become more fully involved in the task at hand. There's nothing wrong with a "results-first" culture that rewards swift action and cut-to-the-chase reasoning, but every once in a while the members of your team will react more positively to the chance to put a whole day's worth of thought and reflection into the details of the plan you want them to embrace.

HOW TO GET EVERYONE TO COMMIT TO PRODUCTIVITY— EVEN WHEN YOU'RE NOT AROUND

Can you lead your workplace out of a time of disorder and confusion and into a time of personal productivity that needs little or no oversight? This is a long-term process, of course, and one that demands constant effort, but there are a number of steps you can take in this direction. Here are four of them:

➤ *Open up the working environment.* People are more likely to commit to team goals and offer constant support for group initiatives if the workplace itself takes their status as *team members,* rather than as isolated players. Could your team benefit from a more open physical layout? Consider one in which people aren't pointed toward private corner cubicles but are instead allowed to interact with each other more easily, perhaps by starting from a circular structure in which each team member's personal space is set apart, yet accessible to (and visible to) everyone else in the group. It's amazing how much more work gets done when people know that the rest of the team is watching.

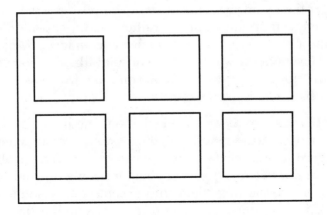

Instead of cubicles that make for six closed areas . . .

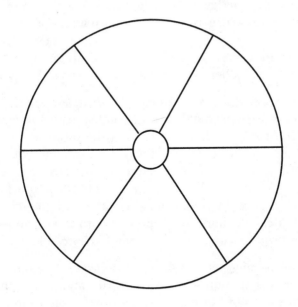

. . . consider a more dynamic work area that allows everyone to feel as though he or she is part of a whole.

Whatever floor plan you settle on, try to emphasize a system that allows group interaction and stimulus, rather than a closeted feeling. The more the people in a work group are encouraged, by means of the physical layout of the workplace to consult with one another, appeal to each other for help, and pitch in on common problems, the more productive the group is likely to be.

➤ *Get public commitments.* We've talked about the power of public *praise* from a manager to a subordinate; the power of a group's public *promise* with regard to a particular outcome can be quite remarkable, as well. No, we're not talking about humiliating people in front of their colleagues or browbeating them into accepting a deadline under the force of peer pressure. The idea is to use group meetings as a forum for group review of key commitments and to formalize the objective by discussing it in a nonthreatening way during group meetings. If an undertaking needs to be reviewed—or stopped in its tracks—proper input and discussion at the group level will help you to put things in perspective and win devotion to the task at hand. (Remember that people tend to focus with greater attention on work for which they are personally responsible than on "committee assignments." If you have not yet designated a single individual to head up an effort, you may want to do so and then elicit the public promise from that person.)

➤ *Put more-experienced staffers in charge of helping less-experienced staffers.* You can often resolve a productivity problem by turning one group member into a mentor for another. By allowing the more senior person to discourse at length about the "right way" to do things, you may be able to get the more-experienced person to reinforce positive work habits in his or her own routine. Of course, if there is a hardcore performance problem on the part of the senior person, this technique may well backfire. But in other cases, where you hope simply to sustain an already existing pattern of productivity, the mentor maneuver can be just the thing.

➤ *Make a habit of going out on a limb for your team.* As noted earlier, manager's willingness to fight—not necessarily always win, but fight—the good fight for his or her team members can have an incredible impact on the team's productivity. When it comes to questions of resources, recognition, scheduling, pay scales, or training, you owe it to your team to make the best possible effort to help them win what they deserve. Most of the members of the work group will be looking for signs that the person in charge at least makes an *effort* to resolve organizational roadblocks. Show them those signs. If you don't make the effort, you can't deliver (occasional) results, and if you don't deliver results, you can't become a hero. There is an advantage to being seen as a hero. People tend to try to return the favor.

PREPARING TO DELIVER A PRESENTATION TO A GROUP

Regardless of whether the group is made up of colleagues, superiors, or people who report to you, review the following five ideas for making successful in-person appeals to your audience. They'll help you focus and hone your message, win commitment to important goals from your listeners, and keep the audience listening attentively for the full running time of your talk.

> ➤ *If you can, boil down what you have to say to three main points, then reference those three points briefly at the beginning of your talk.* The number three has a certain magic about it; it's big enough to represent a pattern that must be taken seriously but small enough to make remembering each individual point a realistic possibility. You can go into as much detail as you want regarding each *individual* point (but see the note that follows) and you can also add subpoints as the topic demands. But structuring your speech or presentation around three primary ideas is a proven formula for success. (This may be because it gives your audience an impossible-to-misunderstand roadmap of your talk—and allows them to make realistic estimates of how far along you are in your presentation throughout your talk.)

> ➤ *Remember that your audience has a 1990s-era attention span.* For better or for worse, we live in an era in which television has profoundly affected the amount of information a speaker can realistically expect an audience to take in during a single sitting. The television programs on which most of us were raised doled out information in twelve- to fifteen-minute hunks (and then took a commercial break). Not surprisingly, today's audiences get restless when asked to take in information that is presented in formats that extend for longer than twelve to fifteen minutes.

> If you can't condense your message into a total length of no more than fifteen minutes (and you should try), then arrange for short breaks—or incorporate brief, catchy, attention-getting "commercials" that don't tax your audience's minds too much—at appropriate points in your talk.

➤ *Make it visual.* We live in a visually oriented society, so don't overwhelm your audience with an undiluted stream of facts, figures, citations, and cross-references. Wherever possible, incorporate compelling, attractive graphs and charts that will help your audience make sense of the technical data you're presenting. If you can, use color to highlight your points.

➤ *Deflect, but don't reject, inappropriate questions.* If you do decide to take questions on specific topics within the main body of your presentation, prepare yourself for the possibility that someone will raise a question having nothing whatsoever to do with the subject under discussion. In such cases, you may want to inform the questioner that you'll be happy to address his or her issue informally, on a one-on-one basis, after the talk has been completed.

➤ *Let them know when you're almost done.* No matter how fascinating your topic may be, audiences have a vested interest in knowing when the presentation is about to conclude. They'll respond more enthusiastically if they know when they can expect things to wrap up, so tell them. And don't make the classic mistake of uttering those (usually welcome) words "in conclusion" unless you *really are* entering the last minute or two of your speech. If you send signals indicating you're nearly complete and then move on to another major point, your audience will disconnect and your points won't get through.

Nurturing Yourself— and Mastering Long-Term Leadership Skills

You've just learned many techniques that can help you get results from the people you interact with regularly. Knowing when to apply these ideas is less a matter of following a rulebook than of honing sound instincts over time and constantly refining your approach. If you commit to improving, over time, the ways you interact with people on a professional level—and if you acknowledge that mastering this art is a lifelong direction rather than an end result—you will find that people will begin looking to you more often for advice, inspiration, and new initiatives. In other words, by making a commitment to constantly improving the ways you work with others, you will be developing yourself as a leader.

YOUR LONG-TERM INVESTMENT IN THE ART AND SKILL OF DEALING WITH PEOPLE

Working effectively with others means paying attention to them on their own terms and working together to achieve a mutually satisfactory result. The seemingly simple act of intelligently committing one's full attention to another may seem like a basic communication skill, and it is. But applied consistently, in as many settings as possible, and with a genuine interest on your part to improve the *level and specificity* of the attention, the technique will not only resolve the difficulties you face in the situation in question, but also hasten your emergence as a real leader within the organization.

You've learned about the four initial mindsets that will help you focus your appeals to others within your organization, and you've learned about some specific techniques for making those appeals pay off in particular situations. As you begin to apply the concepts you've learned, remember that every interaction with another person ought to begin with full, appropriate attention. It is, of course, easier to accept this idea in theory than it is to execute it in practice, but the fact remains that learning *how* to execute it in practice is a habit that successful leaders tend to cultivate.

Full attention is the "trick" that will help you get the best out of others, put new information at your fingertips, and help you make correct adjustments to the new situations you face. Full attention—true listening—is the preliminary to virtually every idea you've reviewed in *The Art and Skill of Dealing with People*

Legendary basketball coach Pat Riley, in his book *The Winner Within,* put it this way: "Sometimes, when you need to inspire people, all you have to do is pay attention. They will inspire you with the insight of how to inspire them." Mastering this knack for tuning in to others in a way that benefits you both isn't an overnight matter. But it is something you can commit yourself to learning over time.

FOUR STEPS TO TAKE TO IMPROVE YOUR PERSONAL PERFORMANCE *AND* YOUR LEADERSHIP CAPACITY

Paying proper attention to others is part of the equation. Paying proper attention to *yourself* is another part.

Here are four simple-sounding ideas—ideas that may look modest from a distance and are all fairly easy to incorporate into your daily routine, but they can have an immense impact on your long-term potential for balance and improvement in virtually any area.

These four ideas for daily personal effectiveness will, I believe, help you to get a handle on the art of caring for, getting the best from, and nurturing *yourself.* I hope you agree that attending to your own daily efficiency (and overall well-being), as outlined below, is a necessary prerequisite for getting the best out of those with whom you work.

> ➤ *Take ten minutes at the very beginning or very end of each day to evaluate the efforts of the day that just passed.* Take the time—or make the time—to review the events of the day closely. (I like to do this in the early-morning hours, in order to gain a better perspective on the previous day's events, but some people find that late-afternoon reviews make the most sense for them.) What worked? What didn't? What priorities have shifted since you last set up your to-do list? What lessons can you draw from

the positive experiences of the day? What new approaches can you take the next time a situation that resembles one that didn't turn out well materializes?

➤ *Identify the negative cycles you find yourself indulging in regularly to recognize and/or compensate for them when they materialize the next time.* We're talking about *recognizing* the cycles here, not ripping them out by the roots. (That often proves difficult, anyway.) Each of us has emotional cycles that emerge during the course of a day—cycles that affect the way we perceive the world around us. What kind of unproductive habits arise as a result of these cycles? For my part, I've found that I have to take account of a certain predictable cynicism that tends to creep into my viewpoint between the hours of four and six in the late afternoon. For me, this is a time when things may look more difficult or complicated than they actually are. It's also a time, I've learned, when my own snap judgments are not the most inspired. Accordingly, I try to avoid making important decisions during this period, and I also try to avoid meetings with others at this time. (If a meeting in the late afternoon is unavoidable, I make a conscious effort to keep generalizations and instant judgments on my part to the bare minimum.)

That's my pattern. What's yours? Sometimes our most costly errors can be avoided and our most inspiring opportunities can be maximized if we only take the time to learn about our most common patterns . . . and act intelligently when we notice them beginning to exert their influence.

➤ *Keep a personal notebook handy at all times.* By making plenty of notes about *your* insights, you deepen your sense of confidence, your experience, your level of observation, and your ability to make mature judgments—in other words, your capacity for success when it comes time to "call 'em as you see 'em." (Talk about a leadership skill!) Make a habit of writing down all your "light-bulb" insights relevant to your field of expertise—or learn to use a dictation system. You don't have to *implement* every idea that makes it into your notes, but you should certainly get into the habit of *recording* every idea.

➤ *Know when you've passed your peak—and when it's time to rest up until the next day's efforts.* Sure, deadlines are deadlines, but it's important to realize when you're no longer working at your optimum level. There is a time to be content with what one has achieved. If you pay close attention to your work (and your interactions with others), you'll learn the warning signs that will alert you to the time to try to stop forcing things. Proceeding past this point can result in work that is less than your best—and, not infrequently, unnecessary conflict in your dealings with others.

CHECKING IN ON YOUR GOALS

Most of these ideas can be applied to immediate, pressing problems—the problems that have a tendency to occupy our attention most dramatically when we show up for work in the morning. Bear in mind, however, that the leader must also learn to think about issues that require attention over time.

You can refashion a short-term crisis-resolution mindset into a long-term leadership mindset by monitoring regularly your own progress toward key goals through periodic self-assessment, asking yourself important questions during those times of personal evaluation and answering the questions honestly.

Commit right now to a plan for long-term goal assessment. Although you may end up feeling comfortable with another schedule, once every two months is a good timetable to start with. Among the queries you should be posing for your own benefit are these:

➤ *Am I a better listener now than I was sixty days ago?* If not, perhaps you should make a point of altering your routine during your interactions with others. You may decide, after reviewing the ideas laid out in Chapter 2, to institute a private rule, one that requires you to ask three or four appropriate questions before suggesting any course of action.

➤ *Have I built more and deeper alliances with other people inside the organization over the past sixty days?* If you haven't, you may want to take the time to read over some of the sections most appropriate to your situation in Chapters 3, 4, 5, and 9.

➤ *Have I improved my relationships with people outside the organization over the past sixty days?* Do I feel more comfortable in the task of eliciting support and action from these people? Are my interactions with clients and customers on a sounder footing than they were two months ago— and is this reflected in the level of business coming the organization's way? If the answers to these questions are no, you may want to take another look at the ideas in Chapters 6, 7, and 8.

➤ *Have I made progress toward my own key goals during this period?* Such goals might include the successful completion of specific projects, attainment of sales and revenue targets, or steps toward personal, spiritual, or career growth. If a particular goal you considered to be important has not been addressed at all over the past sixty days, review your day-to-day priorities!

THE ONE WHO "GETS THINGS DONE"

Earning a reputation as someone who "gets things done" and demonstrating that you can achieve results without coming across as manipulative or exploitative are great ways to improve your career prospects. It's my hope that the ideas you've learned through this book will be of help to you in winning such a reputation.

If your interactions with others make them feel better about themselves and the organization for which they work than they did before you took a look at a particular situation, if your presence is a calming rather than a polarizing element during tough times, if your advice on managing relationships with others in the organization is frequently sought and freely given, if you add something of value to the day of each person with whom you come in contact—if these signposts of success flash past as you make your way through the varied demands of your job—then your long-term commitment to mastering the art and skill of dealing with people is paying off, both for you and for those with whom you work.

Real artists vow never to stop growing. Keep moving in the direction you're heading, the direction of continuous improvement and change. When you commit to developing, over time, to master the art and skill of dealing with people, you join the ranks of a group that may just include the most important artists of all: the ones who know that the greatest masterpiece is always yet to be undertaken.

Bibliography

Brinkman, Dr. Rick, and Dr. Rick Kirschner. *Dealing with People You Can't Stand: How to Bring Out the Best in People at Their Worst.* McGraw-Hill, New York, NY, 1994.

Booher, Diana. *Communicate with Confidence: How to Say It Right the First Time and Every Time.* McGraw-Hill, New York, NY, 1994.

Maslow, Abraham. *Motivation and Personality.* Harper, New York NY, 1954.

Nirenberg, Jesse. *Getting Through to People.* Prentice-Hall, Inc., Englewood Cliffs, NJ, 1963.

Parinello, Anthony. *Selling to VITO (The Very Important Top Officer).* Adams Publishing, New York, NY, 1994.

Riley, Pat. *The Winner Within.* Putnam, New York, NY, 1993.

Schiffman, Stephan. *Asking Questions, Winning Sales.* Workshops on Tape, New York, NY, 1996.

Tannen, Deborah. *You Just Don't Understand: Women and Men in Conversation.* William Morrow, New York, NY, 1990.

Tannen, Deborah. *Talking from 9 to 5.* Avon Books, New York, NY, 1995.

Toropov, Brandon. *303 Off-the-wall Ways to Get a Job.* Career Press, Franklin Lakes, NJ, 1996.

Weaver, Richard L., III. *Understanding Interpersonal Communication.* Scott, Foresman, Dallas, TX, 1978.

Index

E